Beginning Rails 3

Cloves Carneiro Jr.
Rida Al Barazi

Apress®

Beginning Rails 3

ISBN-13 (pbk): 978-1-4302-2433-4

ISBN-13 (electronic): 978-1-4302-2434-1

Printed and bound in the United States of America 9 8 7 6 5 4 3 2 1

President and Publisher: Paul Manning
Lead Editor: Ben Renow-Clarke, Jim Markham
Technical Reviewer: Eldon Almeda
Editorial Board: Clay Andres, Steve Anglin, Mark Beckner, Ewan Buckingham, Gary Cornell, Jonathan Gennick, Jonathan Hassell, Michelle Lowman, Matthew Moodie, Duncan Parkes, Jeffrey Pepper, Frank Pohlmann, Douglas Pundick, Ben Renow-Clarke, Dominic Shakeshaft, Matt Wade, Tom Welsh
Coordinating Editor: Jim Markham
Copy Editor: Tiffany Taylor
Compositor: Bytheway Publishing Services
Indexer: BIM Indexing & Proofreading Services
Artist: April Milne
Cover Designer: Anna Ishchenko

Distributed to the book trade worldwide by Springer Science+Business Media, LLC., 233 Spring Street, 6th Floor, New York, NY 10013. Phone 1-800-SPRINGER, fax (201) 348-4505, e-mail orders-ny@springer-sbm.com, or visit www.springeronline.com.

For information on translations, please e-mail rights@apress.com, or visit www.apress.com.

Apress and friends of ED books may be purchased in bulk for academic, corporate, or promotional use. eBook versions and licenses are also available for most titles. For more information, reference our Special Bulk Sales–eBook Licensing web page at www.apress.com/info/bulksales.

The source code for this book is available to readers at www.apress.com. You will need to answer questions pertaining to this book in order to successfully download the code.

For my family, Jane and Noah.

—Cloves

For my parents, Mezyan Al Barazi and Lina Jano.

I wouldn't be here without your support.

—Rida

Contents at a Glance

Contents

About the Authors

 **Cloves Carneiro Jr.** is a software engineer and web application developer with over 12 years of experience creating web applications for companies in many fields, including startups and telecommunication and financial companies. He has been using Ruby on Rails since its early days and has been a full-time Rails developer for four years. He currently works for Unspace Interactive in Toronto. Born in Brazil and having lived in many parts of the world, Cloves now lives in Toronto, Canada, with his wife, Jane. He also maintains a personal web site at www.ccjr.name.

 **Rida Al Barazi** is a passionate web developer who is experienced in building smart web applications for startups. He has been designing and building for the Web since 2002. He started working with Rails in 2005 and has spoken at various web and Rails conferences in Europe and the Middle East. Rida was raised in Kuwait, grew up in Syria, started his career in Dubai, and currently lives in Toronto. In his free time, he enjoys music, concerts, movies, traveling, and meeting new people. Rida's contact information can be found on his website, www.rida.me.

About the Technical Reviewer

■ Originally hailing from Northern California, **Eldon Alameda** is currently trapped in the harsh climates of Kansas City and is a web developer with over 8 years of experience building web applications and over 15 years in I.T. He is the author of an intermediate level Rails book named Practical Rails Projects and is currently working for a startup looking to revolutionize the digital coupon industry.

Eldon discovered Ruby and Rails in September of 2005 after a period of questioning whether he had made the wrong career choice as a web developer, and quickly found his passion for development reignited.

He has been fortunate enough to have been working professionally with Ruby ever since. Eldon is also an active member of his local Ruby Users Group and strives to give presentations on a semi-regular basis. When not coding, Eldon can be found blogging at his personal blog www.simplifi.es and as a contributor to RubyInside.com and RailsInside.com, spending time with his daughter, or planning their next Disneyworld vacation.

Acknowledgments

You read this at the beginning of most books, and now we're painfully aware of how true it is: writing a book is an enormous amount of work. Although their names don't appear on the cover, without the help, support, and encouragement of several people, this book would never have been completed.

We would like to thank all the folks at Apress who made this book a reality. Thanks to Ben Renow-Clarke and James Markham, who worked tirelessly to keep us on schedule despite an ever-moving Rails 3 release; to our technical reviewer, Eldon Alameda, for having the patience to find bugs and suggesting improvements all over this book; and to our copy editor, Tiffany Taylor, for her countless suggestions and valuable advice.

Any book on an open source project owes a debt of gratitude to the community that produced it. Thanks to David Heinemeier Hansson, the Rails core team, and the hundreds of contributors worldwide, for developing, supporting, and continually improving such a beautiful framework.

We would like to thank our families and friends for their patience in tolerating our long nights and mysterious absences while writing this book. We're sincerely looking forward to being able to spend more time with you again.

Cloves would especially like to thank his wife, Jane, for putting up with him while writing this book, which consumed way more time than expected. Cloves also would like to thank Pete Forde at Unspace, for allowing him the time to work on this project. This book would also never have been possible without the support and encouragement of friends and peers.

Rida would like to thank his parents, Mezyan and Lina, for believing in him and giving him the support he always needed, and most of all for being great parents who planted the seed of curiosity and self-confidence in him. Rida also wants to thank Cloves Carneiro Jr. for giving him the opportunity to work on this book with him and for being a great inspiration, not only as a colleague and a business associate, but also as a best friend. Finally, Rida would like to thank John Kremer for his great help in reviewing the book and the great feedback he offered throughout the writing process.

Introduction

A number of books have been written about getting started with Ruby on Rails. We've read a lot of them and found a few to be quite helpful. But what we've found to be lacking is a resource that, although tailored to the complete beginner, still imparts enough of the Rails culture and philosophy to be a useful building block. Rails is a large topic, and too many books are spread sufficiently thin that they're rendered ineffective at conveying the core functionality of Rails. This book is different.

This book is particularly well suited to those with little or no experience with web application development, or who have some experience but are new to Rails 3. We assume that you're familiar with the technologies that make up the Web, including HTML, and that you're comfortable installing software. But you don't need to know how to program, how to use web servers, how state is maintained on the Web, or how to create and connect to a database. This book will teach you the basics of how web applications work and how Rails 3 makes their construction easier.

Everyone starts as a beginner. We certainly did. And when we began writing this book, we thought about the information we would have found most useful when we were first starting out with Rails. What do we wish we had known? What would have made things easier? We set out to write a book that would make sense of the complexities of web development and get beginners started on the right foot.

If you're seeking a book full of advanced techniques for experienced Rails programmers, you're going to be disappointed. This book does not delve into every arcane detail of Ruby or Rails. You won't find a discussion of Rails' support for self-referential polymorphic joins or advanced caching techniques. Instead, we focus on the pieces of the framework that will get you the most mileage. Rather than bury you with a lot of details, we want you to be comfortable in the Rails environment as soon as possible. That's why we've designed each chapter in this book around a specific component of the framework and focused on the most useful features of each piece.

If you've never programmed before, you should start by reading the introduction to Ruby in Appendix A. If you're new to data-driven applications, you should read the introduction to relational databases in Appendix B. When you're ready, Chapter 1 introduces you to "the Rails way," and Chapter 2 walks you through installing Ruby and Rails on your machine. The rest of the book takes you on a tour through the components of the Rails framework as you incrementally build a working application.

This book spends more time on the features you'll use the most and less time on those that you'll use less often. Most everything you do in Rails is related to your models, so you need to understand Active Record, the library that Rails uses to communicate with your database. Active Record is easily the largest component of the Rails framework, so it makes sense that you'll spend a lot of your time working with it and that we spent a lot of time writing about it (Chapters 4 and 5). If you know how to model your domain and how to effectively work with database objects, you'll be in good shape when it comes to building the rest of your application. By the time we delve into Action Pack (Chapter 6 and 7), the web component of Rails, you'll have built your entire model and taken it for a test run. In Chapter 6 and 7, you learn how to build controllers and views that expose your model objects via the Web. Chapter 8 explains how to use Ajax and other techniques to improve the user interface. Chapter 9 shows you how your applications can send and receive mail using Action Mailer. The remaining chapters teach you the most important things you need to know about testing your application and creating applications with internationalization support; installing, using, and creating plug-ins; and, finally, deploying your application and making it available to the world.

In addition to providing conceptual explanations about the Rails framework, this book tries to use tools that senior developers recommend, such as version control—you can learn about git in Appendix D–and testing. With every code listing, you'll find a link to a Gist, which is a snippet of code that represents the changes in the book; this may help you avoid typing too many lines of code.

Rails 3 is a big step forward and a fast-moving target. During the creation of this book, several features have been added, refined, deprecated, and removed, and we've struggled to keep the text up to date and relevant. This book covers up to Rails 3, and we've included notes and tips about what to expect in future versions where applicable. If you're using a newer version of Rails, you may notice that a few things have changed; but for the most part, you shouldn't have any trouble.

To be sure, Rails is a big framework, and it's capable of much more than any one book can cover. However, despite its size and capabilities, Rails is conceptually easy to grasp—and therein lies its strength. With this book, you'll learn everything you need to know to get started building web applications with Rails 3.

The Beginning Rails Website

Be sure to check out this book's website at http://beginningrails.com. In addition to the most up-to-date version of the source code used in the book, you'll find errata, notes, tips, and other important updates. You can connect with the authors, ask technical questions, and receive help when you need it. If you have questions you think the authors can help you with, feel free to join the discussion on the book's mailing list at http://groups.google.com/group/beginning-rails.

## CHAPTER 1

Introducing the Rails Framework

Rails is a web application framework for the Ruby programming language. Rails is well thought out and practical: it will help you build powerful web sites quickly, with code that's clean and easy to maintain.

The goal of this book is to give you a thorough and complete understanding of how to build dynamic web applications with Rails. This means more than just showing you how to use the specific features and facilities of the framework, and more than just giving you a working knowledge of the Ruby language. Rails is quite a bit more than just another tool: it represents a way of thinking. To completely understand Rails, it's essential that you know about its underpinnings, its culture and aesthetics, and its philosophy of web development.

If you haven't heard it already, you're sure to notice the phrase "the Rails way" cropping up every now and again. It echoes a familiar phrase that has been floating around the Ruby community for a number of years: "the Ruby way." The Rails way is usually the easiest way—the path of least resistance, if you will. This isn't to say that you can't do things your way, nor is it meant to suggest that the framework is constraining. It simply means that if you choose to go off the beaten path, you shouldn't expect Rails to make it easy for you. If you've been around the UNIX circle for any length of time, you may think this idea bears a resemblance to the UNIX mantra: "Do the simplest thing that could possibly work." You're right. This chapter's aim is to introduce to you the Rails way.

The Rise and Rise of the Web Application

Web applications are increasingly gaining in importance. As the world becomes more connected, more of what we do is on the Web. We check our e-mail on the Web, and we do our banking on the Web. We take courses, share photos, upload videos, manage projects, and connect with people all over the world from the comfort of our browsers. As connections get faster, and as broadband adoption grows, web-based software, and similarly networked client/server applications, are poised to displace software distributed by more traditional (read, outdated) means.

For consumers, web-based software affords greater convenience, allowing people to do more from more places. Web-based software works on every platform that supports a web browser (which is to say, all of them), and there's nothing to install or download. And if Google's stock value is any indication, web applications are really taking off. In fact, the change in the Web has been so dramatic in recent years that its current incarnation has been dubbed Web 2.0. All over the world, people are waking up to the new Web and the beauty of being web-based. From e-mail and calendars, photos and videos, to bookmarking, banking, and bidding, we're living increasingly inside the browser.

Due to the ease of distribution, the pace of change in the web-based software market is fast. Unlike traditional software, which must be installed on each individual computer, changes in web applications can be delivered quickly, and features can be added incrementally. There's no need to spend months or years perfecting the final version or getting in all the features before the launch date. Instead of spending months on research and development, you can go into production early and refine in the wild, even without all the features in place.

Can you imagine having a million CDs pressed and shipped, only to find a bug in your software as the FedEx truck is disappearing into the sunset? That would be an expensive mistake! Software distributed this way takes notoriously long to get out the door because before a company ships a product, it needs to be sure the software is bug-free. Of course, there's no such thing as bug-free software, and web applications aren't immune to these unintended features. But with a web application, bug fixes are easy to deploy.

When a fix is pushed to the server hosting the web application, all users get the benefit of the update at the same time, usually without any interruption in service. That's a level of quality assurance you can't offer with store-bought software. There are no service packs to tirelessly distribute and no critical updates to install. A fix is often only a browser refresh away. And as a side benefit, instead of spending large amounts of money and resources on packaging and distribution, software developers are free to spend more time on quality and innovation.

Web-based software has the following advantages:

- Easier to distribute

- Easier to deploy

- Easier to maintain

- Platform-independent

- Accessible from anywhere

The Web Isn't Perfect

As great a platform as the Web is, it's also fraught with constraints. One of the biggest problems is the browser itself. When it comes to browsers, there are several contenders, each of which has a slightly different take on how to display the contents of a web page. Although there is a movement toward unification, and the state of standards compliance among browsers is steadily improving, a lot is left to be desired. Even today, it's nearly impossible to achieve 100% cross-browser compatibility. Something that works in Internet Explorer doesn't necessarily work in Firefox, and vice versa. This lack of uniformity makes it difficult for developers to create truly cross-platform applications, as well as harder for users to work in their browser of choice.

Browser issues aside, perhaps the biggest constraint facing web development is its inherent complexity. A typical web application has dozens of moving parts: protocols and ports, the HTML and CSS, the database and the server, the designer and the developer, and a multitude of other players, all conspiring toward complexity.

But despite these problems, the new focus on the Web as a platform means the field of web development is evolving rapidly and quickly overcoming obstacles. As it continues to mature, the tools and processes that have long been commonplace in traditional, client-side software development are beginning to make their way into the world of web development.

The Good Web Framework

Among the tools making their way into the world of web development is the framework. A *framework* is a collection of libraries and tools intended to facilitate development. Designed with productivity in mind, a good framework provides you with a basic but complete infrastructure on top of which to build an application.

Having a good framework is a lot like having a chunk of your application already written for you. Instead of having to start from scratch, you begin with the foundation in place. If a community of developers uses the same framework, you have a community of support when you need it. You also have greater assurance that the foundation you're building on is less prone to pesky bugs and vulnerabilities, which can slow the development process.

A good web framework can be described as follows:

- *Full stack:* Everything you need for building complete applications should be included in the box. Having to install various libraries or configure multiple components is a drag. The different layers should fit together seamlessly.

- *Open source:* A framework should be open source, preferably licensed under a liberal, free-as-in-free license like BSD or MIT.

- *Cross-platform:* A good framework is platform-independent. The platform on which you decide to work is a personal choice. Your framework should remain as neutral as possible.

A good web framework provides you with the following:

- *A place for everything:* Structure and convention drive a good framework. In other words, unless a framework offers a good structure and a practical set of conventions, it's not a very good framework. Everything should have a proper place within the system; this eliminates guesswork and increases productivity.

- *A database abstraction layer:* You shouldn't have to deal with the low-level details of database access, nor should you be constrained to a particular database engine. A good framework takes care of most of the database grunt work for you, and it works with almost any database.

- *A culture and aesthetic to help inform programming decisions:* Rather than seeing the structure imposed by a framework as constraining, see it as liberating. A good framework encodes its opinions, gently guiding you. Often, difficult decisions are made for you by virtue of convention. The culture of the framework helps you make fewer menial decisions and helps you to focus on what matters most.

Enter Rails

Rails is a best-of-breed framework for building web applications. It's complete, open source, and cross-platform. It provides a powerful database abstraction layer called Active Record, which works with all popular database systems. It ships with a sensible set of defaults and provides a well-proven, multilayer system for organizing program files and concerns.

Above all, Rails is opinionated software. It has a philosophy of the art of web development that it takes very seriously. Fortunately, this philosophy is centered around beauty and productivity. You'll find that as you learn Rails, it actually makes writing web applications pleasurable.

Originally created by David Heinemeier Hansson, Rails first took shape in the form of a wiki application called Instiki. The first version, released in July 2004, of what is now the Rails framework was extracted from a real-world, working application: Basecamp, by 37signals. The Rails creators took away all the Basecamp-specific parts, and what remained was Rails.

Because it was extracted from a real application and not built as an ivory tower exercise, Rails is practical and free of needless features. Its goal as a framework is to solve 80% of the problems that occur in web development, assuming that the remaining 20% are problems that are unique to the application's domain. It may be surprising that as much as 80% of the code in an application is infrastructure, but it's not as far-fetched as it sounds. Consider all the work involved in application construction, from directory structure and naming conventions, to the database abstraction layer and the maintenance of state.

Rails has specific ideas about directory structure, file naming, data structures, method arguments, and, well, nearly everything. When you write a Rails application, you're expected to follow the conventions that have been laid out for you. Instead of focusing on the details of knitting the application together, you get to focus on the 20% that really matters.

As Rails became increasingly popular, it also started to become bigger. This motivated a group of smart developers to create Merb, a fast and modular alternative Ruby web framework. After Merb 1.0 was launched, the Rails and Merb development teams agreed to join forces and merge both projects into what is now known as Rails 3, bringing all the great features of Merb under the Rails umbrella.

Rails Is Ruby

There are a lot of programming languages out there. You've probably heard of many of them. C, C#, Lisp, Java, Smalltalk, PHP, and Python are popular choices. And then there are others you've probably never heard of: Haskel, IO, and maybe even Ruby. Like the others, Ruby is a programming language. You use it to write computer programs, including, but certainly not limited to, web applications.

Before Rails came along, not many people were writing web applications with Ruby. Other languages like PHP and ASP were the dominant players in the field, and a large part of the Web is powered by them. The fact that Rails uses Ruby is significant because Ruby is considerably more powerful than either PHP or ASP in terms of its abilities as a programming language. This is largely another symptom of the Web's maturity. Now that it's attracting a larger audience, more powerful languages and tools are falling into the fold.

Ruby is a key part of the success of Rails. Rails uses Ruby to create what's called a *domain-specific language* (DSL). Here, the domain is that of web development; when you're working in Rails, it's almost as though you're writing in a language that was specifically designed to construct web applications—a language with its own set of rules and grammar. Rails does this so well that it's sometimes easy to forget that you're writing Ruby code. This is a testimony to Ruby's power, and Rails takes full advantage of Ruby's expressiveness to create a truly beautiful environment.

For many developers, Rails is their introduction to Ruby—a language whose following before Rails was admittedly small at best, at least in the west. Although Ruby had been steadily coming to the attention of programmers outside Japan, the Rails framework brought Ruby to the mainstream.

Invented by Yukihiro Matsumoto in 1994, it's a wonder Ruby remained shrouded in obscurity as long as it did. As far as programming languages go, Ruby is among the most beautiful. Interpreted and object-oriented, elegant and expressive, Ruby is truly a joy to work with. A large part of Rails' grace owes to Ruby and to the culture and aesthetics that permeate the Ruby community. As you begin to work with the framework, you'll quickly learn that Ruby, like Rails, is rich with idioms and conventions, all of which make for an enjoyable, productive programming environment.

In summary, Ruby can be described as follows:

- An interpreted, object-oriented scripting language

- Elegant, concise syntax

- Powerful metaprogramming features

- Well suited as a host language for creating DSLs

Appendix A of this book includes a complete Ruby primer. If you want to get a feel for what Ruby looks like now, skip to that appendix and take a look. Don't worry if Ruby seems a little unconventional at first. You'll find it quite readable, even if you're not a programmer. It's safe to follow along in this book learning it as you go, and referencing the appendix when you need clarification. If you're looking for a more in-depth guide, Peter Cooper has written a fabulous book titled *Beginning Ruby: From Novice to Professional*, Second Edition (Apress, 2009). You'll also find the Ruby community more than helpful in your pursuit of the language. Be sure to visit `http://ruby-lang.org` for a wealth of Ruby-related resources.

Rails Encourages Agility

Web applications aren't traditionally known for agility. They have a reputation of being difficult to work with and a nightmare to maintain. It's perhaps in response to this diagnosis that Rails came on to the scene, helping to usher in a movement toward agile programming methodologies in web development. Rails advocates and assists in the achievement of the following basic principles of software development:

- Individuals and interactions over processes and tools

- Working software over comprehensive documentation

- Customer collaboration over contract negotiation

- Responding to change over following a plan

So reads the Agile Manifesto,[1] which was the result of a discussion among 17 prominent figures (including Dave Thomas, Andy Hunt, and Martin Fowler) in the field of what was then called "lightweight methodologies" for software development. Today, the Agile Manifesto is widely regarded as the canonical definition of agile development.

Rails was designed with agility in mind, and it takes each of the agile principles to heart almost obsessively. With Rails, you can respond to the needs of customers quickly and easily, and Rails works well during collaborative development. Rails accomplishes this by adhering to its own set of principles, all of which help make agile development possible.

Dave Thomas's and Andy Hunt's seminal work on the craft of programming, *The Pragmatic Programmer* (Addison-Wesley, 1999), reads almost like a roadmap for Rails. Rails follows the *don't repeat yourself* (DRY) principle, the concepts of rapid prototyping, and the *you ain't gonna need it* (YAGNI) philosophy. Keeping important data in plain text, using convention over configuration, bridging the gap between customer and programmer, and above all, postponing decisions in anticipation of change are institutionalized in Rails. These are some of the reasons that Rails is such an apt tool for agile development, and it's no wonder that one of the earliest supporters of Rails was Dave Thomas himself.

The sections that follow take you on a tour through some of Rails mantras and, in doing so, demonstrate how well suited Rails is for agile development. Although we want to avoid getting too philosophical, some of these points are essential to grasping what makes Rails so important.

Less Software

One of the central tenets of Rails' philosophy is the notion of *less software*. What does less software mean? It means using convention over configuration, writing less code, and doing away with things that

---

[1] `http://agilemanifesto.org`

needlessly add to the complexity of a system. In short, less software means less code, less complexity, and fewer bugs.

Convention Over Configuration

Convention over configuration means that you need to define only configuration that is unconventional.

Programming is all about making decisions. If you were to write a system from scratch, without the aid of Rails, you'd have to make a lot of decisions: how to organize your files, what naming conventions to adopt, and how to handle database access are only a few. If you decided to use a database abstraction layer, you would need to sit down and write it, or find an open source implementation that suited your needs. You'd need to do all this before you even got down to the business of modeling your domain.

Rails lets you start right away by encompassing a set of intelligent decisions about how your program should work and alleviating the amount of low-level decision-making you need to do up front. As a result, you can focus on the problems you're trying to solve and get the job done more quickly.

Rails ships with almost no configuration files. If you're used to other frameworks, this fact may surprise you. If you've never used a framework before, you should be surprised. In some cases, configuring a framework is nearly half the work.

Instead of configuration, Rails relies on common structures and naming conventions, all of which employ the often-cited *principle of least surprise* (POLS). Things behave in a predictable, easy-to-decipher way. There are intelligent defaults for nearly every aspect of the framework, relieving you from having to explicitly tell the framework how to behave. This isn't to say that you can't tell Rails how to behave: most behaviors can be customized to your liking and to suit your particular needs. But you'll get the most mileage and productivity out of the defaults, and Rails is all too willing to encourage you to accept the defaults and move on to solving more interesting problems.

Although you can manipulate most things in the Rails setup and environment, the more you accept the defaults, the faster you can develop applications and predict how they will work. The speed with which you can develop without having to do any explicit configuration is one of the key reasons why Rails works so well. If you put your files in the right place and name them according to the right conventions, things *just work*. If you're willing to agree to the defaults, you generally have less code to write.

The reason Rails does this comes back to the idea of less software. Less software means making fewer low-level decisions, which makes your life as a web developer a lot easier. And easier is a good thing.

Don't Repeat Yourself

Rails is big on the DRY (don't repeat yourself) principle, which states that information in a system should be expressed in only one place.

For example, consider database configuration parameters. When you connect to a database, you generally need credentials, such as a username, a password, and the name of the database you want to work with. It may seem acceptable to include this connection information with each database query, and that approach holds up fine if you're making only one or two connections. But as soon as you need to make more than a few connections, you end up with a lot of instances of that username and password littered throughout your code. Then, if your username and password for the database change, you have to do a lot of finding and replacing. It's a much better idea to keep the connection information in a single file, referencing it as necessary. That way, if the credentials change, you need to modify only a single file. That's what the DRY principle is all about.

The more duplication exists in a system, the more room bugs have to hide. The more places the same information resides, the more must be modified when a change is required, and the harder it becomes to track these changes.

Rails is organized such that it remains as DRY as possible. You generally specify information in a single place and move on to better things.

Rails Is Opinionated Software

Frameworks encode opinions. It should come as no surprise then that Rails has strong opinions about how your application should be constructed. When you're working on a Rails application, those opinions are imposed on you, whether you're aware of it or not. One of the ways that Rails makes its voice heard is by gently (sometimes, forcefully) nudging you in the right direction. We mentioned this form of encouragement when we talked about convention over configuration. You're invited to do the right thing by virtue of the fact that doing the wrong thing is often more difficult.

Ruby is known for making certain programmatic constructs look more natural by way of what's called *syntactic sugar*. Syntactic sugar means the syntax for something is altered to make it appear more natural, even though it behaves the same way. Things that are syntactically correct but otherwise look awkward when typed are often treated to syntactic sugar.

Rails has popularized the term *syntactic vinegar*. Syntactic vinegar is the exact opposite of syntactic sugar: awkward programmatic constructs are discouraged by making their syntax look sour. When you write a snippet of code that looks bad, chances are it *is* bad. Rails is good at making the right thing obvious by virtue of its beauty and the wrong thing equally obvious by virtue of ugliness.

You can see Rails' opinion in the things it does automatically, the ways it encourages you to do the right thing, and the conventions it asks you to accept. You'll find that Rails has an opinion about nearly everything related to web application construction: how you should name your database tables, how you should name your fields, which database and server software to use, how to scale your application, what you need, and what is a vestige of web development's past. If you subscribe to its world view, you'll get along with Rails quite well.

Like a programming language, a framework needs to be something you're comfortable with—something that reflects your personal style and mode of working. It's often said in the Rails community that if you're getting pushback from Rails, it's probably because you haven't experienced enough pain from doing web development the old-school way. This isn't meant to deter developers; rather, it means that in order to truly appreciate Rails, you may need a history lesson in the technologies from whose ashes Rails has risen. Sometimes, until you've experienced the hurt, you can't appreciate the cure.

Rails Is Open Source

The Rails culture is steeped in open source tradition. The Rails source code is, of course, open. And it's significant that Rails is licensed under the MIT license, arguably one of the most "free" software licenses in existence.

Rails also advocates the use of open source tools and encourages the collaborative spirit of open source. The code that makes up Rails is 100% free and can be downloaded, modified, and redistributed by anyone at any time. Moreover, anyone is free to submit patches for bugs or features, and hundreds of people from all over the world have contributed to the project over the past two years.

You'll probably notice that a lot of Rails developers use Macs. The Mac is clearly the preferred platform of many core Rails team developers, and most Rails developers are using UNIX variants (of which Mac OS X is one). The UNIX operating system is hailed by hackers and used almost exclusively among the hacker elite. There are several reasons for this, not least of which is the fact that UNIX is a well-tested and proven operating system, forged in an open source ecosystem, with contributions from some of the smartest programmers on the planet. Having been born in the 1970s, the UNIX operating system has evolved into a lean and powerful example of open source craftsmanship. UNIX's beauty, simplicity, and singularity of purpose isn't lost on the creators of Rails.

Although there is a marked bias toward UNIX variants when it comes to Rails developers, make no mistake, Rails is truly cross-platform. With a growing number of developers using Rails in a Windows environment, Rails has become easy to work with in all environments. It doesn't matter which operating system you choose: you'll be able to use Rails on it. Rails doesn't require any special editor or IDE to write code. Any text editor is fine, as long as it can save files in plain text. The Rails package even includes a built-in, stand-alone web server called WEBrick, so you don't need to worry about installing and configuring a web server for your platform. When you want to run your Rails application in development mode, simply start up the built-in server and open your web browser. Why should it be more difficult than that?

The next chapter takes you step by step through the relatively painless procedure of installing Rails and getting it running on your system. But before you go there, and before you start writing your first application, let's talk about how the Rails framework is architected. This is important because, as you see in a minute, it has a lot to do with how you organize your files and where you put them. Rails is a subset of a category of frameworks named for the way in which they divide the concerns of program design: the Model-View-Controller (MVC) pattern. Not surprisingly, the MVC pattern is the topic of our next section.

The MVC Pattern

Rails employs a time-honored and well-established architectural pattern that advocates dividing application logic and labor into three distinct categories: the model, view, and controller. In the MVC pattern, the model represents the data, the view represents the user interface, and the controller directs all the action. The real power lies in the combination of the MVC layers, which Rails handles for you. Place your code in the right place and follow the naming conventions, and everything should fall into place.

Each part of the MVC—the model, view, and controller—is a separate entity, capable of being engineered and tested in isolation. A change to a model need not affect the views; likewise, a change to a view should have no effect on the model. This means changes in an MVC application tend to be localized and low impact, easing the pain of maintenance considerably while increasing the level of reusability among components.

Contrast this to the situation that occurs in a highly coupled application that mixes data access, business logic, and presentation code (PHP, we're looking at you). Some folks call this *spaghetti code* because of its striking resemblance to a tangled mess. In such systems, duplication is common, and even small changes can produce large ripple effects. MVC was designed to help solve this problem.

MVC isn't the only design pattern for web applications, but it's the one Rails has chosen to implement. And it turns out that it works great for web development. By separating concerns into different layers, changes to one don't have an impact on the others, resulting in faster development cycles and easier maintenance.

The MVC Cycle

Although MVC comes in different flavors, control flow generally works as follows (see Figure 1-1):

- The user interacts with the interface and triggers an event (for example, submits a registration form).

- The controller receives the input from the interface (for example, the submitted form data).

- The controller accesses the model, often updating it in some way (for example, by creating a new user with the form data).

- The controller invokes a view that renders an updated interface (for example, a welcome screen).

- The interface waits for further interaction from the user, and the cycle repeats.

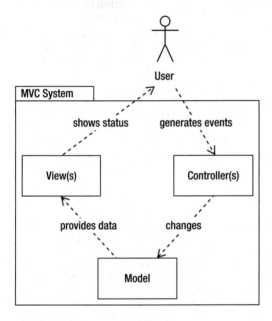

Figure 1-1. *The MVC cycle*

If the MVC concept sounds a little involved at first, don't worry. Although entire books could be written on this pattern, and people will argue over its purest implementation for all time, it's easy to grasp—especially the way Rails does MVC.

Next, you take a quick tour through each letter in the MVC and then learn how Rails handles it.

The Layers of MVC

The three layers of the MVC pattern work together as follows:

- *Model:* The information the application works with

- *View:* The visual representation of the user interface

- *Controller:* The director of interaction between the model and the view

Models

In Rails, the model layer represents the database. Although we call the entire layer the model, Rails applications are usually made up of several individual models, each of which (usually) maps to a database table. For example, a model called User may map to a table called users. The User model assumes responsibility for all access to the users table in the database, including creating, reading, updating, and deleting rows. So, if you want to work with the table and, say, search for someone by name, you do so through the model, like this:

```
User.find_by_name('Linus')
```

This snippet, although very basic, searches the users table for the first row with the value Linus in the name column and returns the results. To achieve this, Rails uses its built-in database abstraction layer, Active Record. Active Record is a powerful library; needless to say, this is only a small portion of what you can do with it.

Chapters 4 and 5 give you an in-depth understanding of Active Record and what you can expect from it. For the time being, the important thing to remember is that models represent data. All rules for data access, associations, validations, calculations, and routines that should be executed before and after save, update, or destroy operations are neatly encapsulated in the model. Your application's world is populated with Active Record objects: single ones, lists of them, new ones, and old ones. And Active Record lets you use Ruby language constructs to manipulate all of them, meaning you get to stick to one language for your entire application.

Controllers

Let's rearrange the MVC acronym and put the *C* before the *V*. As you see in a minute, in Rails, controllers are responsible for rendering views, so it makes sense to introduce them first.

Controllers are the conductors of an MVC application. In Rails, controllers accept requests from the outside world, perform the necessary processing, and then pass control to the view layer to display the results. It's the controller's job to field web requests, like processing server variables and form data, asking the model for information, and sending information back to the model to be saved in the database. It may be a gross oversimplification, but controllers generally perform a request from the user to create, read, update, or delete a model object. You see these words a lot in the context of Rails, most often abbreviated as CRUD. In response to a request, the controller typically performs a CRUD operation on the model, sets up variables to be used in the view, and then proceeds to render or redirect to another action after processing is complete.

Controllers typically manage a single area of an application. For example, in a recipe application, you probably have a controller just for managing recipes. Inside the recipes controller, you can define what are called *actions*. Actions describe what a controller can do. If you want to be able to create, read, update, and delete recipes, you create appropriately named actions in the recipes controller. A simple recipes controller may look something like this:

```
class RecipesController < ApplicationController
  def index
    # logic to list all recipes
  end

  def show
    # logic to show a particular recipe
  end
```

```
def create
  # logic to create a new recipe
end

def update
  # logic to update a particular recipe
end

def destroy
  # logic to delete a particular recipe
end
end
```

Of course, if you want this controller to do anything, you need to put some instructions inside each action. When a request comes into your controller, it uses a URL parameter to identify the action to execute; and when it's done, it sends a response to the browser. The response is what you look at next.

Views

The view layer in the MVC forms the visible part of the application. In Rails, views are the templates that (most of the time) contain HTML markup to be rendered in a browser. It's important to note that views are meant to be free of all but the simplest programming logic. Any direct interaction with the model layer should be delegated to the controller layer, to keep the view clean and decoupled from the application's business logic.

Generally, views have the responsibility of formatting and presenting model objects for output on the screen, as well as providing the forms and input boxes that accept model data, such as a login box with a username and password, or a registration form. Rails also provides the convenience of a comprehensive set of helpers that make connecting models and views easier, such as being able to prepopulate a form with information from the database, or the ability to display error messages if a record fails any validation rules, such as required fields.

You're sure to hear this eventually if you hang out in Rails circles: a lot of folks consider the interface to *be* the software. We agree with them. Because the interface is all the user sees, it's the most important part. Whatever the software is doing behind the scenes, the only parts that an end user can relate to are the parts they see and interact with. The MVC pattern helps by keeping programming logic out of the view. With this strategy in place, programmers get to deal with code, and designers get to deal with HTML. Having a clean environment in which to design the HTML means better interfaces and better software.

The Libraries That Make Up Rails

Rails is a collection of libraries, each with a specialized task. Assembled together, these individual libraries make up the Rails framework. Of the several libraries that compose Rails, three map directly to the MVC pattern:

- *Active Record:* A library that handles database abstraction and interaction

- *Action View:* A templating system that generates the HTML documents the visitor gets back as the result of a request to a Rails application

- *Action Controller:* A library for manipulating both application flow and the data coming from the database on its way to being displayed in a view

These libraries can be used independently of Rails and of each other. Together, they form the Rails Model-View-Controller development stack. Because Rails is a full-stack framework, all the components are integrated, so you don't need to set up bridges between them manually.

Rails Is Modular

One of the great features of Rails 3 is that it was built with modularity in mind from the ground up. Although many developers appreciate the fact that they get a full stack, you may have your own preferences in libraries, either for database access, template manipulation, or JavaScript libraries. As we describe Rails 3 features, we mention alternatives to the default libraries that you may want to pursue as you become more familiar with Rails' inner workings.

Rails Is No Silver Bullet

There is no question that Rails offers web developers a lot of benefits. After using Rails, it's hard to imagine going back to web development without it. Fortunately, it looks like Rails will be around for a long time, so there's no need to worry. But it brings us to an important point.

As much as we've touted the benefits of Rails, it's important for you to realize that there are no silver bullets in software design. No matter how good Rails gets, it will never be all things to all people, and it will never solve all problems. Most important, Rails will never replace the role of the developer. Its purpose is to assist developers in getting their job done. Impressive as it is, Rails is merely a tool, which when used well can yield amazing results. It's our hope that as you continue to read this book and learn how to use Rails, you'll be able to leverage its strength to deliver creative and high-quality web-based software.

Summary

This chapter provided an introductory overview of the Rails landscape, from the growing importance of web applications to the history, philosophy, evolution, and architecture of the framework. You learned about the features of Rails that make it ideally suited for agile development, including the concepts of less software, convention over configuration, and DRY. Finally, you learned the basics of the MVC pattern and received a primer on how Rails does MVC.

With all this information under your belt, it's safe to say you're ready to get up and running with Rails. The next chapter walks you through the Rails installation so you can try it for yourself and see what all the fuss is about. You'll be up and running with Rails in no time.

CHAPTER 2

■ ■ ■

Getting Started

For various reasons, Rails has gained an undeserved reputation of being difficult to install. This chapter dispels this myth. The truth is that installing Rails is relatively easy and straightforward, provided you have all the right ingredients. The chapter begins with an overview of what you need to get Rails up and running and then provides step-by-step instructions for the installation. Finally, you start your first Rails application.

An Overview of Rails Installation

The main ingredient you need for Rails is, of course, Ruby. If you're lucky, Ruby may already be installed on your system, in which case you're halfway there. Most likely, however, it's not. You therefore need to install it. After you have Ruby installed, you can install a *package manager* (a program designed to help you install and maintain software on your system) called RubyGems. You use that to install Rails.

If you're a Ruby hacker and already have Ruby and RubyGems installed on your computer, Rails is ridiculously easy to get up and running. Because it's packaged as a gem, you can install it with a single command:

```
$ gem install rails
```

That's all it comes down to—installing Rails is a mere one-liner. The key is in having a working installation of Ruby and RubyGems. Before you get there, though, you need one other ingredient to use Rails: a database server.

As you're well aware by now, Rails is specifically meant for building web applications. Well, it's a rare web application that isn't backed by a database. Rails is so sure you're using a database for your application that it's downright stubborn about working nicely without one. Although Rails works with nearly every database out there, in this chapter you use one called SQLite. SQLite is open source, easy to install, and incredibly well supported for web development. Perhaps that's why it's the default database among Rails developers.

You start by installing Ruby and RubyGems, and you use the magical one-liner to install Rails. Then, you install SQLite and make sure it's working properly. Here are the steps in order:

1. Install Ruby 1.9.

2. Install Rails.

3. Install SQLite.

Before you begin, note that the "many ways to skin a cat" adage applies to Rails installation. Just as the Rails stack runs on many platforms, there are as many ways to install it. This chapter describes what

13

we feel is the easiest and most reliable way to install Rails for your platform. You go about the process differently for OS X, Linux, and Windows, but they all amount to the same thing.

No matter which platform you're using, you need to get familiar with the command line. This likely isn't a problem for the Linux crowd, but it's possible that some OS X users and certainly many Windows users don't have much experience with it. If you're using OS X, you can find a terminal emulator in /Applications/Utilities/Terminal.app. If you're on Windows, you can open a command prompt by choosing Start → Run, typing cmd, and clicking OK. Note that you'll use the command line extensively in your travels with Rails. A growing number of IDEs make developing applications with Rails even simpler, and they completely abstract the use of a command-line tool; but stick to the command line to make sure you grasp all the concepts behind many commands. If you later decide to use an IDE such as Aptana's RadRails, JetBrains' RubyMine, or Sun's NetBeans, you'll have a great understanding of Rails and will understand even better where the IDE is speeding up your work.

Also, a quick note for OS X users: if you're using a Mac and would prefer to use a package manager such as Fink or MacPorts, the Linux instructions will prove useful.

Go ahead and flip to the section that describes your platform (OS X, Windows, or Linux), and let's begin.

■ **NOTE** At the time of the writing of this book, Ruby 1.9.1 was the most recent stable Ruby version, so we recommend it when appropriate. Rails 3 is known to have some internal issues with Ruby 1.9.1, so install Ruby 1.9.2 if the final version has been released when you are preparing your setup. You can check if Ruby 1.9.2 is out at http://ruby-lang.org.

Installing on Mac OS X 10.6 Snow Leopard

You'd think that given the prevalence of OS X among Rails developers (the entire core team uses OS X), installing Rails on OS X would be easy. And you'd be correct. Mac OS X 10.5 and above comes with Ruby, Rails, and SQLite preinstalled, which is what we recommend using.

If you've never touched your Ruby/Rails environment, it's very likely that you need to update both RubyGems and the Rails gems; you can do so with a couple of quick commands, as you'll see shortly.

■ **NOTE** For an in-depth description of building Ruby, RubyGems, and Rails from source on Mac OS X, see Dan Benjamin's popular how-to article: http://hivelogic.com/articles/compiling-ruby-rubygems-and-rails-on-snow-leopard.

Installing the Apple Developer Tools (Xcode)

You need the Apple Developer Tools installed to be able to compile some of the Ruby gems you may need in the future. Before you can compile source code on your Mac, you need to install a compiler. Apple's Developer Tools package, Xcode Tools, includes a compiler and provides the easiest way to set up a development environment on your Mac. Xcode comes on your OS X installation DVD; if you can't

find your installation media, you can always download it from Apple at
http://developer.apple.com/technology/xcode.html.

■ **NOTE** Before proceeding, be aware that Xcode is a large download. Weighing in at over 1GB, it's not the sort of thing you want to be downloading over a slow Internet connection. Before you begin downloading, you may want to try to find it on your installation DVD.

Xcode is packaged as a regular Apple installer (look for it on the installation DVD), so all you need to do is double-click its icon and answer a few basic questions, and you should be on your way.

Updating RubyGems and Installing Rails

Updating RubyGems and Rails is straightforward. Enter the following commands in a Terminal window, and you're good to go:

```
$ sudo gem update --system
$ sudo gem sources -a http://gemcutter.org
$ sudo gem update rails
```

In these commands, you may need to enter you system password—don't be surprised by that. You can test to see if Ruby is installed correctly by asking Ruby for its version number:

```
$ ruby --version
```

```
ruby 1.8.7 (2008-08-11 patchlevel 72) [universal-darwin10.0]
```

Next, you can do the same with Rails:

```
$ rails -v
```

```
Rails 3.0
```

Although SQLite comes bundled with Mac OS X, you still have to install its Ruby *binding*—a Ruby library that allows you to talk with SQLite. To install the SQLite3 Ruby binding, issue the following gem command from the Terminal

```
$ sudo gem install sqlite3-ruby
```

Great! Ruby and Rails are installed and working correctly.

■ **NOTE** We want you to stick with Ruby 1.8.7 due to the ease of setup. However, you can install the latest Ruby version—1.9.1—by either compiling it from source or using the Ruby Version Manager (RVM) gem. For more details on RVM, check out `http://rvm.beginrescueend.com`.

Installing on Windows

Installation on Windows is easy thanks to installer packages. Although this is the norm for Windows, few installation procedures are without their gotchas, so be sure to check out the latest information on the Rails wiki (`http://wiki.rubyonrails.org/`) for help with specific problems. You start by installing Ruby 1.9.1.

Installing Ruby

Installing Ruby on Windows is marvelously easy thanks largely to the one-click installer for Ruby. You can read more and download the installer from its web site:

`http://rubyinstaller.org/`

The latest version of the installer at the time of this writing is 1.9.1-p378 for Ruby 1.9.1, which you can download using this URL:

`http://rubyforge.org/frs/download.php/69035/rubyinstaller-1.9.1-p378-rc2.exe`

After you've downloaded the installer, start the installation by double-clicking its icon. What follows is standard installer fare, and the defaults are sufficient for your purposes. When you select the location where you want to put Ruby (usually `C:\Ruby19`), as shown in Figure 2-1, select the Add Ruby Executables to Your PATH check box; the installer takes care of the rest. You have a fully functioning Ruby installation in minutes.

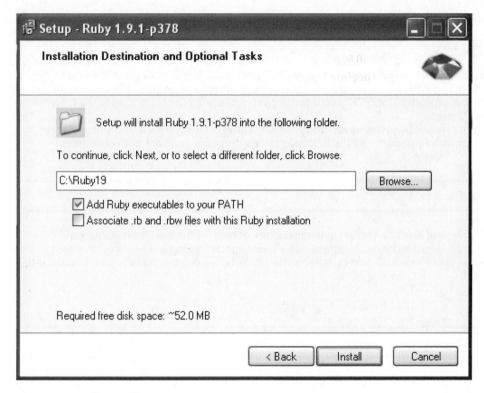

Figure 2-1. *Ruby installer*

When the installer is finished, you can test to see if Ruby is working and that your environment is correctly configured by opening your command prompt and asking Ruby its version number:

```
> ruby --version
```

```
ruby 1.9.1p378 (2010-01-10 revision 26273) [i386-mingw32]
```

Installing Rails

You'll be pleased to know that Ruby 1.9 comes bundled with RubyGems, a package-management system for Ruby (http://rubygems.org), which makes installing Ruby libraries, utilities, and programs a breeze. This includes Rails installation.

First, let's update RubyGems and its sources list. Open your command prompt, and issue the following gem commands:

```
> gem update --system
> gem sources -a http://gemcutter.org
```

17

Now, to install Rails, issue the following gem command in your command prompt:

```
> gem install rails
```

Be forewarned that the gem command can take some time. Don't be discouraged if it seems to be sitting there doing nothing for a few minutes; it's probably updating its index file. RubyGems searches for gems in its remote repository (http://gemcutter.org), so you need to be connected to the Internet for this command to work.

After spitting out some text to the screen and generally chugging away for a few minutes, the gem program should exit with something like the following before dumping you back at the command prompt:

```
Successfully installed rails-3.0
```

That's all there is to it! The one-click installer takes care of most of the work by installing and configuring Ruby; and because Rails is distributed as a RubyGem, installing it is a simple one-liner.

You can double-check that Rails was installed successfully by issuing the `rails --v` command at the command prompt:

```
> rails --v
```

```
Rails 3.0
```

Installing SQLite

To install SQLite on Windows, download the following files from the SQLite web site (www.sqlite.org/download.html):

```
sqlite-3_6_23_1.zip - http://www.sqlite.org/sqlite-3_6_23_1.zip
sqlitedll-3_6_23_1.zip - http://www.sqlite.org/sqlitedll-3_6_23_1.zip
```

Note that the version number may be different by the time you read this. Unzip both files, and move their contents to the Ruby bin directory C:\Ruby19\bin. When you're done, you can test that you correctly installed SQLite by issuing the following command from the command prompt:

```
> sqlite3 --version
```

```
3.6.23.1
```

Now that you've installed SQLite, let's install its Ruby binding—a Ruby library that allows you to talk with SQLite. To install the SQLite3 Ruby binding, issue the following gem command from the command prompt:

```
> gem install sqlite3-ruby
```

With Ruby, Rails, and SQLite happily installed, it's time to take them for a test drive. Unless you feel like reading the installation instructions for Linux, you're free to skip ahead to the "Creating Your First Rails Application" section.

Installing on Linux

Linux (and UNIX-based systems in general) comes in a variety of different flavors, but they share a lot in common. These instructions use a Debian-based variant called Ubuntu Linux (specifically, 9.10 the Karmic Koala), but they should apply to most UNIX systems with varying mileage.

■ **NOTE** Ubuntu Linux is a top-notch distribution that's rapidly gaining mindshare in the Linux community. At the time of this writing, it's poised to become the most popular Linux distribution for general use and is largely responsible for the increased viability of Linux as a desktop platform. It's freely available from `http://unbuntu.org` and highly recommended. Keir Thomas wrote an excellent book titled *Beginning Ubuntu Linux* (Apress, 2009). If you're new to Ubuntu (or to Linux in general), you may want to check it out.

Just about all Linux distributions (including Ubuntu) ship with a package manager. Whether you're installing programs or code libraries, they usually have dependencies; a single program may depend on dozens of other programs in order to run properly, which can be a struggle to deal with yourself. A package manager takes care of these tasks for you, so you can focus on better things.

Ubuntu Linux includes the Debian package manager apt, which is what the examples use. If you're using a different distribution, you likely have a different package manager, but the steps should be reasonably similar.

Before you begin installing Ruby, Rails, and SQLite, update the package library using `apt-get update`:

```
$ sudo apt-get update
```

The apt-get program keeps a cached index of all the programs and their versions in the repository for faster searching. Running the update command ensures that this list is up to date, so you get the most recent versions of the software you need.

Installing Ruby

Before you install Ruby, you need to install a few libraries required by the components you're installing. Enter the following command:

```
$ sudo apt-get install build-essential libssl-dev libreadline5
  libreadline5-dev zlib1g zlib1g-dev
```

You install Ruby 1.9 from source; use the following commands to download and install Ruby and its friends:

```
$ mkdir ~/src && cd ~/src
$ wget ftp://ftp.ruby-lang.org/pub/ruby/1.9/ruby-1.9.1-p376.tar.gz
$ tar -zxvf ruby-1.9.1-p376.tar.gz
$ cd ruby-1.9.1-p376
$ ./configure && make && sudo make install
```

This instructs the computer to get the latest version of Ruby 1.9 from the Internet, extract the contents of that file to the disk, and compile and install it to the disk. You can test that this is working by asking Ruby for its version number:

```
$ ruby --version
```

```
ruby 1.9.1p376 (2009-12-07 revision 26041) [i686-linux]
```

Next, make sure the instance of Ruby that the shell is finding is the one you expect, which should bein /usr/local/bin/ruby:

```
$ which ruby
```

```
/usr/local/bin/ruby
```

Updating RubyGems

Ruby uses a package-management system called RubyGems (http://rubyforge.org/project/rubygems) to manage the installation and maintenance of Ruby programs and libraries. Updating RubyGems is straightforward. Enter the following commands in a Terminal window, and you're good to go:

```
$ sudo gem update --system
$ sudo gem sources -a http://gemcutter.org
```

Installing Rails

Now that RubyGems is up to date, you can use it to install the Rails framework. Enter this command:

```
$ sudo gem install rails
```

After spitting out some text to the screen and generally chugging away for a little while, the gem program should exit with a message like the following:

```
Successfully installed rails-3.0
```

You can verify this claim by asking Rails for its version number:

```
$ rails --version
```

```
Rails 3.0
```

```
$ which rails
```

```
/usr/local/bin/rails
```

With Ruby and Rails happily installed, you're ready to move on to the next step: installing SQLite.

Installing SQLite

To install SQLite with apt-get, issue the following command:

```
$ sudo apt-get install sqlite3 libsqlite3-dev
```

If all goes according to plan, you can test your SQLite3 installation by invoking the sqlite3 program and asking for its version number:

```
$ sqlite3 --version
```

```
3.6.16
```

Now that you've installed SQLite, let's install its Ruby binding—a Ruby library that allows you to talk with SQLite. To install the SQLite3 Ruby binding, issue the following gem command from the command prompt:

```
$ sudo gem install sqlite3-ruby
```

With Ruby, Rails, and SQLite happily installed, it's time to take them for a test drive.

Creating Your First Rails Application

You'll start by using the rails command to create a new Rails project. Go to the directory where you want your Rails application to be placed; the rails command takes the name of the project you want to create as an argument and creates a Rails skeleton in a new directory by the same name. The newly created directory contains a set of files that Rails generates for you to bootstrap your application. To demonstrate, create a new project called (what else?) hello:

```
$ rails new hello
```

```
      create
      create  README
      create  Rakefile
      create  config.ru
      create  .gitignore
      create  Gemfile
      create  app
      create  app/controllers/application_controller.rb
      create  app/helpers/application_helper.rb
      create  app/views/layouts/application.html.erb
      create  app/mailers
...
      create  vendor/plugins
      create  vendor/plugins/.gitkeep
```

If you look closely at the output, you see that the subdirectories of app/ are named after the MVC pattern introduced in Chapter 1. You also see a name mentioned briefly in Chapter 1: *helpers*. Helpers help bridge the gap between controllers and views; Chapter 6 talks about them.

Rails generated a new directory called hello. If you look at the folder structure, you see the following:

Gemfile	app	db	log	test
README	config	doc	public	tmp
Rakefile	config.ru	lib	script	vendor

Starting the Built-In Web Server

Next, let's start up a local web server so you can test your new project in the browser. True, you haven't written any code yet, but Rails has a nice welcome screen that you can use to test whether the project is set up correctly. It even gives you some information about your Ruby environment.

Rails ships with a built-in, zero-configuration, pure Ruby web server that makes running your application in development mode incredibly easy. You start up the built-in web server using the rails server command. To start the server now, make sure you're inside the directory of your Rails application, and then enter the following commands:

```
$ bundle install
```

```
Fetching source index from http://rubygems.org/

Using rake (0.8.7) from system gems

…

Your bundle is complete! Use `bundle show [gemname]` to see where a

bundled gem is installed.
```

```
$ rails server
```

```
=> Booting WEBrick

=> Rails 3.0.0 application starting in development on http://0.0.0.0:3000

=> Call with -d to detach

=> Ctrl-C to shutdown server

[2010-04-22 14:26:54] INFO  WEBrick 1.3.1

[2010-04-22 14:26:54] INFO  ruby 1.9.1 (2010-01-10) [i386-darwin10.2.0]

[2010-04-22 14:26:54] INFO  WEBrick::HTTPServer#start: pid=5181 port=3000
```

The message from the rails server command tells you that a web server is running at the IP address 0.0.0.0 on port 3000. Don't be alarmed by this all-zeros address—it simply means that the server is running locally on your machine. The hostname localhost also resolves to your local machine and is thus interchangeable with the IP address. We prefer to use the hostname variant.

With the server running, if you open http://localhost:3000/ in your browser, you see the Rails welcome page, as shown in Figure 2-2. Congratulations! You've put Ruby on Rails.

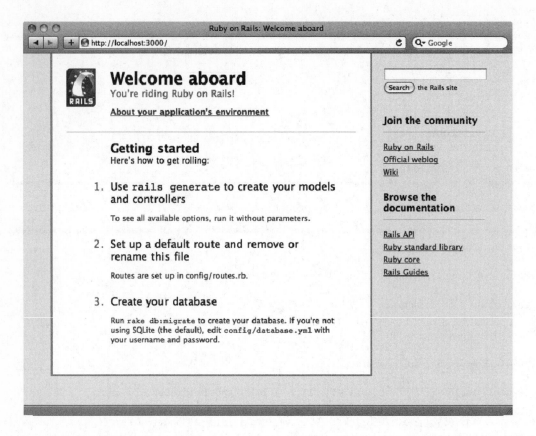

Figure 2-2. Rails welcome page

The welcome page is nice, but it doesn't teach you much. It's just an HTML page located in public/index.html. The first step in learning how Rails works is to generate something dynamic. You're about to learn why you called this project "hello"!

We're sure it would be in violation of the law of programming books if we didn't start with the ubiquitous "Hello World" example. And who are we to disobey? In the next few steps, you make your Rails application say hello; and in doing so, you learn a few new concepts. Your goal is to have a request with the URL http://localhost:3000/salutation/hello respond with a friendly "Hello World!" message.

First things first: stop the web server by pressing Ctrl+C in the command prompt window. That should bring you back to your prompt.

> ■ **NOTE** Notice how easy it is to start and stop a local server? That's the whole point of the built-in server in a nutshell. You shouldn't need to be a system administrator in order to develop a Rails application.

Generating a Controller

You use the rails command's generate option to create certain files within your project. Because you're dealing with the request and response cycle (you request a URL, and the browser receives a response), you generate a controller that is responsible for handling salutations:

```
$ rails generate controller salutation
```

```
      create   app/controllers/salutation_controller.rb

      invoke   erb

      create      app/views/salutation

      invoke   test_unit

      create      test/functional/salutation_controller_test.rb

      invoke   helper

      create      app/helpers/salutation_helper.rb

      invoke      test_unit

      create         test/unit/helpers/salutation_helper_test.rb
```

Not unlike the rails command you used to generate your application, the rails generate controller command creates a bunch of new files. These are mostly empty, containing only skeletal code (often called *stubs*). You could easily create these files on your own. The generator merely saves you time and the effort of needing to remember which files to create and where to put them.

The salutation controller was created in the app/controllers directory and is sensibly named salutation_controller.rb. If you open it with a text editor, you see that there's not much to it, as shown in Listing 2-1.

Listing 2-1. The app/controllers/salutation_controller.rb File

```
class SalutationController < ApplicationController
end
```

Creating an Action

If you want SalutationController to respond to a request for hello, you need to make an action for it. Open salutation_controller.rb in your text editor, and add the hello action, as shown in Listing 2-2.

Listing 2-2. The Updated app/controllers/salutation_controller.rb File:

http://gist.github.com/319866

```
class SalutationController < ApplicationController
  def hello
    @message = 'Hello World!'
  end
end
```

Actions are implemented as Ruby methods. You can always tell a method definition because of the def keyword. Inside the action, you set a Ruby instance variable called @message, the value of which you output to the browser.

Creating a Template

With your action successfully defined, your next move is to add some HTML into the mix. Rails makes it easy by separating the files that contain HTML into their own directory as per the MVC pattern. In case you haven't guessed, HTML is the responsibility of the view.

If you look in the app/views directory, you see another product of the controller generator: a directory called salutation. It's linked to the salutation controller, and it's where you put template files that correspond to your salutation actions.

■ **NOTE** Because Rails allows you to embed Ruby code in your HTML by using the ERb Templating library, you use the .html.erb (HTML + ERb) extension for your templates.

The default way to render a template in response to a request for an action is remarkably simple: name it the same as the action; this is another case of using a predefined Rails convention. Because you want to show a response to the hello action, name your file hello.html.erb, and Rails renders it automatically. This is easy to grasp in practice. Look at Figure 2-3 for a visual cue as to how controllers and templates correspond.

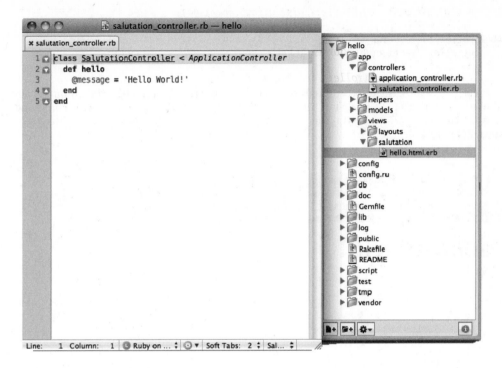

Figure 2-3. *Controllers correspond to a directory in app/views.*

Start by creating a new, blank file in app/views/salutation/. Name it hello.html.erb, and add the code shown in Listing 2-3. Notice the <%= %> syntax that surrounds the @message variable: these are known as Embedded Ruby (ERb) output tags. Chapter 6 talks more about ERb. For now, it's only important to know that whenever you see <%= %> in a template, whatever is between the tags is evaluated as Ruby, and the result is printed out.

Listing 2-3. The app/views/salutation/hello.html.erb File: http://gist.github.com/319910

```
<html>
  <body>
    <h1><%= @message %></h1>
  </body>
</html>
```

You now have to tell your Rails application how to respond to a URL. You do that by updating the config/routes.rb file. You don't need to worry about the details of how the routes file work for now, Chapter 7 covers that. Replace the contents of your config/routes.rb file, and make sure it looks like Listing 2-4.

Listing 2-4. The config/routes.rb file: http://gist.github.com/319933

```
Hello::Application.routes.draw do
  match ':controller(/:action(/:id(.:format)))'
end
```

It looks like you're all set. The salutation controller fields the request for hello and automatically renders the hello.html.erb template. Start up the web server again using the rails server command, and request the URL http://localhost:3000/salutation/hello in your browser. You should see the result shown in Figure 2-4.

Figure 2-4. The "Hello World" application

Sure enough, there's your greeting! The hello template reads the @message variable that you set in the controller and, with a little help from ERb, printed it out to the screen.

In case you didn't notice, the URL http://localhost:3000/salutation/hello maps directly to the controller and action you created because of the change you made to your config/routes.rb file. This is achieved by the following URL pattern:

```
:controller(/:action(/:id(.:format)))
```

For now, it's enough that you can make the mental connection between URL segments and the code in your application. When you read the URL `http://localhost:3000/salutation/hello`, you can translate it into a request for the `hello` action on the `salutation` controller.

Summary

This chapter covered a lot, so you should be proud of yourself. You went from not having Rails installed to getting a basic Rails application up and running. You learned how to install Ruby and how to manage packages with RubyGems (which you used to install Rails). You also learned how to create a new Rails project using the `rails` command and how to use the generator to create a new controller. And you learned how controller actions correspond to templates. The stage is now set for the next chapter, where you begin building a more full-featured project.

■ ■ ■

## CHAPTER 3

Getting Something Running

The best way to learn a programming language or a web framework is to dig in and write some code. After reading the first two chapters, you should have a good understanding of the Rails landscape. This chapter builds on that foundation by walking you through the construction of a basic application. You learn how to create a database and how to connect it to Rails, as well as how to use a web interface to get data in and out of the application.

You receive a lot of information in this chapter, but it shouldn't be more than you can absorb. The goal is to demonstrate, not to overwhelm. Rails makes it incredibly easy to get started, and that's a feature this chapter highlights. There are a few places where Rails really shines, and getting something running is one of them. By the end of this chapter, you'll have a working web application to play with, explore, and learn from. You'll build on this application throughout the rest of the book, adding features and refining functionality.

An Overview of the Project

In this chapter, you build a simple blog application that lets you create and publish articles, like WordPress or Blogger. The first iteration focuses on the basics: creating and editing articles.

Before you start coding, let's sketch a brief summary of the goals and flow of the application at a very high level. The idea isn't to focus on the nitty-gritty, but instead to concentrate on the general case.

Your application will have two kinds of users: those who post and publish articles and those who wish to comment on existing articles. In some cases, people will play both roles. Not all users will need to create an account by registering on the site. It will also be nice if people can notify their friends about interesting articles using a feature that sends a friendly e-mail notification to interested parties.

You add some of the features in later chapters. Other application requirements will likely come up as you continue, but these are enough to get started. In the real world, specifications are seldom correct the first time around, so it's best not to dwell on them. Rails doesn't penalize you for making changes to an application that's under construction, so you can engage in an iterative style of development, adding and incrementing functionality as you go.

You start with what matters most: articles. You may wonder why you don't begin with users. After all, without users, who will post the articles? If you think about it, without articles, what could users do? Articles are the epicenter of the application, so it makes the most sense to start there and work out the details as you go. Ready? Let's get started!

Creating the Blog Application

As you saw in Chapter 2, the first step is to create a new Rails application. You could come up with a fancy Web 2.0 name, but let's keep it simple and call the application blog. It's not going to win any awards for creativity, but it works.

To begin, from the command line, go the directory where you want to place your new application; then, issue the `rails` command to generate the application skeleton and base files:

```
$ rails new blog
```

```
create  README

create Rakefile

create config.ru

create  .gitignore

create  Gemfile

...
```

As you recall from the example in Chapter 2, the `rails` command takes as an argument the name of the project you want to create and generates a directory of the same name that contains all the support files. In this case, it creates a subdirectory called `blog` in the current working directory. Change into the blog directory, and get oriented. Figure 3-1 shows the directory structure.

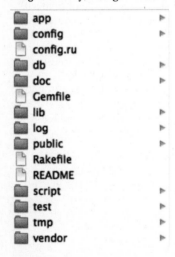

Figure 3-1. The Rails directory structure

You'll quickly get used to the Rails' directory structure, because all Rails applications follow this standard. This is another benefit of conventions: you always know where to locate files if have to work on a Rails project developed by someone else. Table 3-1 briefly explains the directory structure.

Table 3-1. Rails Directory Structure

Folder	Description
app	All components of your application.
config	Configuration files for all components of your application.
db	Files related to the database you're using, and a folder for migrations.
doc	Documentation for your application. May also contain documentation generated for your code and any files that may be helpful to other developers.
lib	Libraries that may be used in your application.
log	Log files that your application may require.
public	Static assets served by your application, such as images, JavaScript, and CSS files.
script	The always-important rails script.
test	Unit, functional, and integration tests.
tmp	A temporary folder used by your application.
vendor	External libraries, such as gems and plug-ins that your application bundles.

Your first stop is the config directory. Of the little configuration there is to do in a Rails application, most of it takes place in this aptly named location. To get an idea of what Rails expects as far as databases go, open the config/database.yml file in your editor and take a peek. You should see something like the file shown in Listing 3-1 (comments are omitted here).

Listing 3-1. The config/database.yml File

```
development:
  adapter: sqlite3
  database: db/development.sqlite3
  pool: 5
  timeout: 5000

test:
  adapter: sqlite3
```

```
    database: db/test.sqlite3
    pool: 5
    timeout: 5000

production:
    adapter: sqlite3
    database: db/production.sqlite3
    pool: 5
    timeout: 5000
```

The first thing you should notice is the different sections: development, test, and production. Rails understands the concept of *environments* and assumes you're using a different database for each environment. Therefore, each has its own database connection settings, and different connection parameters are used automatically. Rails applications run in *development* modes by default, so you really only need to worry about the development section at this point. Still, other than the database names (db/*.sqlite3), there should be little difference between the connection parameters for each environment.

This example uses the default SQLite database because of the advantages mentioned in the previous chapter. However, you can use the database-management system of your choice by passing the -d or --database= option to the rails command with one of the following options as per your preference: mysql, oracle, postgresql, sqlite2, sqlite3, frontbase, or ibm_db.

If you select a database other than SQLite, the rails command may prefill the database parameter based on the database server and project name: blog in this case. If you give your application a different name (say, a snazzy Web 2.0 name like blog.ilicio.us *beta) and a database server such as MySQL, you'll see something different here. It doesn't matter what you name your databases, as long as database.yml references the correct one for each environment. Let's stick with the convention and create the databases using the default names.

WHAT IS YAML?

The .yml extension refers to a YAML file. YAML (a recursive acronym that stands for YAML Ain't Markup Language) is a special language for expressing objects in plain text. Rails can work with YAML natively and can turn what looks like plain text into Ruby objects that it can understand.

YAML is whitespace-active: it uses spaces (not tabs) to convey structure and meaning. Make sure your editor knows the difference between tabs and spaces, and be sure that when you're editing YAML files, you use only spaces.

Creating the Project Databases

You may think that to create a new database, you'll use your favorite database-administration tool. However, because you already told Rails the database connection details, you can now run a Rake task that talks to the database and issues all the necessary commands to set up the databases. Jump to the command prompt and type

```
$ rake db:create
```

When using SQLite, you aren't forced to create the database, because a new database file is automatically created if one doesn't exist; but it will come handy when you try a different database engine. You also may see some message(s) like "db/development.sqlite3 already exists." Don't be afraid—this is an indication that a SQLite file was found. If you see that message, rest assured that your existing database was left untouched, and no database file has been harmed.

■ **NOTE** Rake is a build language for Ruby. Rails uses Rake to automate several tasks, such as running database migrations, running tests, and updating Rails support files. You can think of Rake tasks as little utility programs. For a list of all available Rake tasks, run `rake -T` from your Rails project directory. For more information about Rake, including complete documentation, see `http://rake.rubyforge.org/`.

Regardless of the database-management system you select, you should notice that the databases you want to use are created. This is another case in which Rails removes some complexity from your mind and helps you focus on your application.

■ **NOTE** Depending on how your environment is set up, you may not need to specify the username, password, and other options in your `config/databases.yml` file to create the database.

Although you're only concerned with the development environment at this time, it doesn't hurt to create the other databases while you're at it. Go ahead and create two more databases, one each for the test and production environments:

```
$ rake db:create:all
```

You can confirm the creation of the database by using the `rails dbconsole` program to look at the databases currently on your system:

```
$ rails dbconsole
```

```
SQLite version 3.6.17

Enter ".help" for instructions

Enter SQL statements terminated with a ";"

sqlite> .exit
```

At this point, you can issue any number of SQL statements and look at the tables and records that eventually will be in your application. (If you aren't familiar with SQL, you can learn more about it in

Appendix B.) When you're finished with the SQLite console, type the .exit command to go back to your regular prompt. You can test to see if your connection is working by running the following command:

```
$ rake db:migrate
```

If nothing exceptional is returned, congratulations! Rails can connect to your database. However, if you're using a database engine other than SQLite, and you may see something like this

```
rake aborted!

Access denied for user 'root'@'localhost' (using password: NO)
```

then you need to adjust your connection settings. If you're having problems, make sure the database exists and that you've entered the correct username and password in the config/database.yml configuration file.

Creating the Article Model

Now that you can connect to the database, in this section you create a model. Remember that models in Rails correspond to database table names. Because you want to model articles, let's create a model named Article. By convention, model names are singular and correspond to plural table names. So, an Article model expects a table named articles; a Person model expects a table named people.

■ **NOTE** Rails is smart enough to use the correct plural name for most common words; it doesn't try to create a persons table.

Like most things in Rails, models have their own generator script that makes it easier to get started. The generator automatically creates a new model file in the app/models directory and creates a bunch of other files to boot. Among these are a unit test (for testing your model's functionality, as discussed in Chapter 10) and a database migration. A *database migration* contains instructions for building the database table and the fields to create. Whenever you generate a new model, a migration is created along with it.

■ **NOTE** If you want to skip generation of the migration when generating a new model, you can pass the --skip-migration argument to the generator. This may be useful if you're creating a model for an existing database/table.

To see the generator's usage information, run it without arguments:

```
$ rails generate model
```

Usage:

```
  rails generate model NAME [field:type field:type] [options]
```

...

As you can see from the usage banner, the generator takes a model name as its argument and an optional list of fields. The model name may be given in *CamelCase* or *under_score* format, and options can be provided if you want to automatically populate the resulting migration with column information.

Let's run the generator now to create the first model, Article:

```
$ rails generate model Article
```

```
      invoke    active_record
      create    db/migrate/20100223220648_create_articles.rb
      create    app/models/article.rb
      invoke    test_unit
      create    test/unit/article_test.rb
      create    test/fixtures/articles.yml
```

If you look at the lines that start with create, you see that the generator has created an article model, an article test, an articles fixture (which is a textual representation of table data that you can use for testing), and a migration named 20100223220648_create_articles.rb. With that, your model is generated.

■ **NOTE** The first part of the migration file name is the timestamp when the file was generated. So, the file on your computer will have a slightly different name.

Creating a Database Table

You need to create a table in the database. You could do this with a database-administration tool or even manually using SQL, but Rails provides a much more efficient facility for table creation and maintenance called a *migration*. It's called a migration because it allows you to evolve, or migrate, your schema over time. (If you're not familiar with databases, tables, and SQL, consult Appendix B for the basics.)

■ **NOTE** *Schema* is the term given to the properties that make up a table: the table's name, its columns, and its column types, as well as any default values a column is to have.

What's the best part about migrations? You get to define your schema in pure Ruby. This is all part of the Rails philosophy that you should stick to one language when developing. It helps eliminate context switching and results in higher productivity.

As you can see from the output of the model generator, it created a new file in db/migrate called 20100223220648_create_articles.rb. As mentioned before, migrations are named with a numeric prefix, which is a number that represents the exact moment when the migration file was created. Because multiple developers can create migrations in a development team, this number helps uniquely identify this specific migration in a project.

Let's open this file and take a peek. It's shown in Listing 3-2.

Listing 3-2. The db/migrate/20100223220648_create_articles.rb File

```
class CreateArticles < ActiveRecord::Migration
  def self.up
    create_table :articles do |t|

      t.timestamps
    end
  end

  def self.down
    drop_table :articles
  end
end
```

In its initial generated form, the migration is a blank canvas. But before you go any further, let's note a few important items. First, notice the class methods: up and down. For each migration, you define instructions for updating in the up method, and you use the down method to roll back any changes. If you were to, say, create a new table in the up method, you would drop the table in the down method, thereby reversing your changes. That's exactly what the generator did for you already: the articles table is created on up and dropped on down. Pretty slick, isn't it?

■ **NOTE** You can easily spot the difference between class and instance method definitions in a Ruby class by looking for the self prefix. For more about Ruby classes, see Appendix A.

Listing 3-3 has the details filled out for you. Without having seen a migration before, you should be able to tell exactly what's going on.

Listing 3-3. Completed db/migrate/20100223220648_create_articles.rb File:
http://gist.github.com/312798

```
class CreateArticles < ActiveRecord::Migration
  def self.up
    create_table :articles do |t|
      t.string :title
      t.text :body
      t.datetime :published_at

      t.timestamps
    end
  end

  def self.down
    drop_table :articles
  end
end
```

Let's step through the code. First, you use the create_table method, giving it the name of the table you want to create. Inside the code block, the string, text, and datetime methods each create a column of the said type named after the parameter; for example, t.string :title creates a field named title with the type string. The timestamps method, in the t.timestamps call, is used to create a couple of fields called created_at and updated_at, which Rails sets to the date when the record is created and updated respectively. (For a full description of the available method types you can create in your migrations, see http://api.rubyonrails.org/classes/ActiveRecord/Migration.html.)

On its own, this migration does nothing. Really, it's just a plain-old Ruby class. If you want it to do some work and create a table in the database for you, you need to run it. To run a migration, you use the built-in db:migrate Rake task that Rails provides.

From the command line, type the following to run the migration and create the articles table. This is the same command you used to test the database connection. You sort of hijack it for this test, knowing that it will attempt to connect to the database and thus prove whether the connection works. Because there were no existing migrations when you first ran it, it didn't do anything. Now that you have your first migration, running it results in a table being created:

```
$ rake db:migrate
```

```
== CreateArticles: migrating ====================================================

-- create_table(:articles)

   -> 0.0019s

== CreateArticles: migrated (0.0023s) ===========================================
```

Just as the output says, the migration created the `articles` table. If you try to run the migration again (go ahead, try it), nothing happens. That's because Rails keeps track of all the migrations it runs in a database table, and in this case there's nothing leftto do.

Generating a Controller

You've created a model and its supporting database table, so the next step is to work on the controller and view side of the application. Let's create a controller named (wait for it) `articles` to control the operation of the application's articles functionality. Just as with models, Rails provides a generator that you can use to create controllers:

```
$ rails generate controller articles
```

```
      create    app/controllers/articles_controller.rb

      invoke    erb

      create    app/views/articles

      invoke    test_unit

      create    test/functional/articles_controller_test.rb

      invoke    helper

      create    app/helpers/articles_helper.rb

      invoke    test_unit

      create    test/unit/helpers/articles_helper_test.rb
```

The controller generator creates four files:

- `app/controllers/articles_controller.rb`: The controller that is responsible for handling requests and responses for anything to do with articles.

- `test/functional/articles_controller_test.rb`: The class that contains all functional tests for the `articles` controller (Chapter 10 covers testing applications).

- `app/helpers/articles_helper.rb`: The `helper` class in which you can add utility methods that can be used in your views (Chapters 6 and 7 cover helpers).

- `test/unit/helpers/articles_helper_test.rb`: The class that contains all helper tests for your helper class.

The controller generator also creates an empty directory in `app/views` called `articles`. This is where you place the templates for the `articles` controller.

Up and Running with Scaffolding

One of the most talked-about features that has given a lot of exposure to Rails is its scaffolding capabilities. *Scaffolding* allows you to create a boilerplate-style set of actions and templates that makes it easy to manipulate data for a specific model. You generate scaffolding using the scaffold generator. You're probably getting used to generators by now. Rails makes heavy use of them because they help automate repetitive tasks and generally remove the chances for errors when creating new files. Unlike you, the generator won't ever forget how to name a file; nor will it make a typo when creating a class. Let's use the scaffold generator now and solve the mystery of how this works:

```
$ rails generate scaffold Article title:string body:text published_at:datetime
--skip-migration
```

Because you've already generated a few of these files, Rails prompts you before it tries to overwrite any that already exist. Specifically, it warns about the articles controller, the articles functional test, and the articles fixture file. Because your articles controller was empty, it's safe to overwrite it. The same goes for the test and fixture, so go ahead and answer Y when you're asked. You used the --skip-migration option when calling the generator, because a migration creating the articles table already existed, and Rails would complain if you tried to create the same table twice.

The scaffold provides methods and pages that allow you to insert, update, and delete records in your database. That's all you need to generate a working scaffold of the Article model. Let's fire up the web server and test it. Start your local web server from the command line (rails server), and browse to the articles controller in your browser:

```
http://localhost:3000/articles
```

You should see the results displayed in your browser, as shown in Figure 3-2.

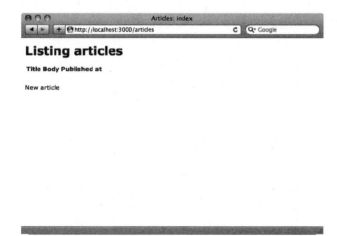

Figure 3-2. *Articles scaffolding*

Click the "New article" link, and you're taken to a screen where you can enter articles. Notice that the URL is http://localhost:3000/articles/new, which means you're invoking the new action on the articles controller. Go ahead and add a few articles and generally play with the application. Figure 3-3 shows an example of an article entered on this screen.

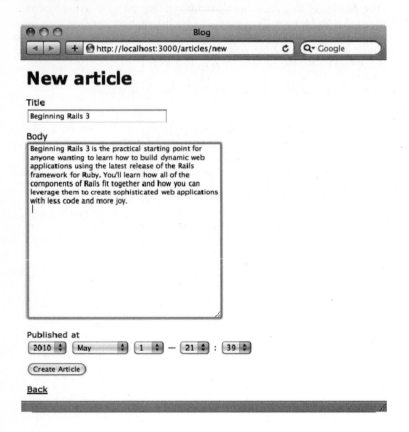

Figure 3-3. *Adding an article*

Notice that every time you add an article, you're redirected back to the index action, where you see all your articles listed. You can edit them, delete them, or create new ones. If you click the Show link, you're taken to the detail page for that article. You've got to admit, Rails gives you a lot of functionality for free.

Speed is the key benefit here. The scaffold generator allows you to quickly get something running, which is a great way to test your assumptions.

■ **CAUTION** Scaffolding comes with an important disclaimer. You shouldn't use it in production. It exists to help you do exactly what you just did: get something running.

Adding More Fields

Now that you can see the model represented in the browser, let's add some more fields to make it a little more interesting. Whenever you need to add or modify database fields, you should do so using a migration. In this case, let's add the excerpt and location fields to the articles table.

You didn't need to generate the last migration (the one you used to create the articles table), because the model generator took care of that for you. This time around, you can use the migration generator. It works just like the model and controller generators, which you've seen in action. All you need to do is give the migration generator a descriptive name for the transformation:

```
$ rails generate migration add_excerpt_and_location_to_articles
excerpt:string location:string
```

invoke	active_record
create	db/migrate/20100223232337_add_excerpt_and_location_to_articles.rb

As you've already seen, the generator creates a migration class in db/migrate prefixed by a number identifying when the migration was created. If you open the 20100223232337_add_excerpt_and_location_to_articles.rb file, you see the migration class with the code shown in Listing 3-4. As with the model generator, which prefilled the migration to some extent, passing field names and types as options to the migration generator prefills the generated class for you as long as you refer to the correct table name at the end of the migration name—in this case, to_articles.

Listing 3-4. The db/migrate/20100223232337_add_excerpt_and_location_to_articles.rb File

```ruby
class AddExcerptAndLocationToArticles < ActiveRecord::Migration
  def self.up
    add_column :articles, :excerpt, :string
    add_column :articles, :location, :string
  end

  def self.down
    remove_column :articles, :excerpt
    remove_column :articles, :location
  end
end
```

Looking at the add_column method, the first argument is the table name (articles), the second is the field name, and the third is the field type. Rails also fills in the self.down method to reverse the changes that this migration makes. Although it's unlikely at this point that you want to remove these fields, it's a good idea to maintain reversibility. The remove_column method is the opposite of add_column. The only difference in its arguments is that you don't need to specify the field type.

With this new migration in place, use the Rake task to apply it and make the changes to the database:

```
$ rake db:migrate
```

```
== AddExcerptAndLocationToArticles: migrating ===================================

-- add_column(:articles, : excerpt, :string)

   -> 0.0236s

-- add_column(:articles, : location, :text)

   -> 0.0013s

== AddExcerptAndLocationToArticles: migrated (0.0164s) ==========================
```

If all goes according to plan, the articles table has two new fields. You could edit the view templates in the app/views/articles folder to add form elements for the new fields, but instead let's call the generator again (you learn about views in Chapter 6):

```
$ rails generate scaffold Article title:string location:string excerpt:string
body:text published_at:datetime --skip-migration
```

Press Y when asked if you want to overwrite some files, and you're finished, as you can see in Figure 3-4.

Figure 3-4. Additional fields added to the new article form

This exposes one of the issues of this type of scaffolding: when you generate new versions of the scaffold files, you run the risk of overwriting custom changes you may have made.

Adding Validations

You may wonder what happens if you try to save a new article without giving it any information. Try doing that: Rails doesn't care. Actually, it's the Article model that doesn't care. This is because in Rails, the rules for data integrity (such as required fields) are the responsibility of the model.

To add basic validation for required fields, open the Article model in app/models/article.rb, and add the validation method shown in Listing 3-5 inside the class body.

Listing 3-5. Validation Added to the app/models/article.rb File: http://gist.github.com/312871

```
class Article < ActiveRecord::Base
  validates :title, :presence => true
  validates :body, :presence => true
end
```

Save the file, and try creating an empty article again. Instead of saving the record, Rails displays a formatted error message, as shown in Figure 3-5.

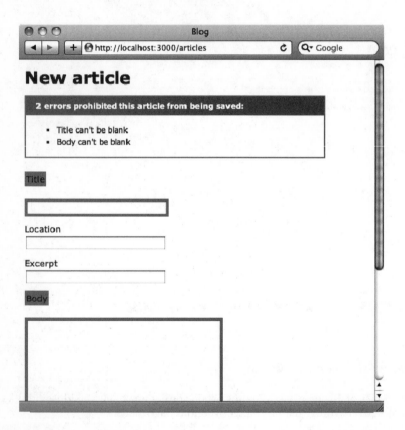

Figure 3-5. Error messages for an article

If you've done any web development before, you know that validating fields is a major nuisance. Thankfully, Rails makes it easy.

■ **NOTE** Notice that you don't need to restart the web server when you make changes to your project files in the app/ directory. This is a convenience provided by Rails when running in development mode.

Chapter 5 goes through all the specifics of model validations. For now, you're using only the most primitive methods of protecting your data. It shouldn't surprise you that Active Record is capable of much more involved validations, such as making sure a numeric value is entered, validating that data is in the correct format using regular expressions, and ensuring unique values, among other checks.

■ **NOTE** *Regular expressions* (*regex* for short) are expressions that describe patterns in strings. They're generally used to give a concise description of a set without having to list all elements. Like most programming languages, Ruby has built-in support for regular expressions.

Generated Files

Now that you've seen the pages in action, let's look at the articles controller again. As you can see in Listing 3-6, the controller is now chock-full of actions. There's one for each of index, show, new, create, edit, update, and destroy—the basic CRUD (Create, Read, Update and Delete) actions.

Listing 3-6. The app/controllers/articles_controller.rb File

```ruby
class ArticlesController < ApplicationController
  # GET /articles
  # GET /articles.xml
  def index
    @articles = Article.all

    respond_to do |format|
      format.html # index.html.erb
      format.xml  { render :xml => @articles }
    end
  end

  # GET /articles/1
  # GET /articles/1.xml
  def show
    @article = Article.find(params[:id])

    respond_to do |format|
      format.html # show.html.erb
      format.xml  { render :xml => @article }
    end
  end
```

```ruby
  # GET /articles/new
  # GET /articles/new.xml
  def new
    @article = Article.new

    respond_to do |format|
      format.html # new.html.erb
      format.xml  { render :xml => @article }
    end
  end

  # GET /articles/1/edit
  def edit
    @article = Article.find(params[:id])
  end

  # POST /articles
  # POST /articles.xml
  def create
    @article = Article.new(params[:article])

    respond_to do |format|
      if @article.save
        format.html { redirect_to(@article,
:notice => 'Article was successfully created.') }
        format.xml  { render :xml => @article,
:status => :created, :location => @article }
      else
        format.html { render :action => "new" }
        format.xml  { render :xml => @article.errors,
:status => :unprocessable_entity }
      end
    end
  end

  # PUT /articles/1
  # PUT /articles/1.xml
  def update
    @article = Article.find(params[:id])

    respond_to do |format|
      if @article.update_attributes(params[:article])
        format.html { redirect_to(@article,
:notice => 'Article was successfully updated.') }
        format.xml  { head :ok }
      else
        format.html { render :action => "edit" }
        format.xml  { render :xml => @article.errors,
:status => :unprocessable_entity }
      end
    end
  end
```

```
# DELETE /articles/1
# DELETE /articles/1.xml
def destroy
  @article = Article.find(params[:id])
  @article.destroy

  respond_to do |format|
    format.html { redirect_to(articles_url) }
    format.xml  { head :ok }
  end
end
end
```

As you did in this chapter, after you've generated scaffolding, if you change your model, you have to regenerate it if you want your application to follow suit. Most of the time, however, you make the changes by hand and have a variation of the default scaffold.

It's important to realize why scaffolding exists and to be aware of its limitations. As you've just seen, scaffolding helps when you need to get something running quickly to test your assumptions. It doesn't take you very far in the real world, and eventually you end up replacing most (if not all) of it.

Explore the generated code, and see if you can figure out how it hangs together. Don't worry if you can't understand all of it—the chapters that follow discuss it in depth. With everything you know about Rails already, you should be able to piece together most of it.

Try changing a few things to see what happens. If you inadvertently break something, you can always run the scaffolding generator again to revert to the original. Can you see how the views in app/views/articles are related to the actions? What about the response messages, like Article was successfully created? What happens when you change them? See if you can find where the error messages for failed validations are rendered. If you remove the message, does the record still get saved? You can learn a lot by exploring, so take as much time as you need.

Summary

This chapter started by outlining the basics of the sample application. Then, you rolled up your sleeves and created a database and configuration files. Based on the goals of the application, you began by creating the tables necessary to run the core of your Article model and got a first look at the simplicity and flexibility that migrations give the development process. The scaffolding allowed you to test your assumptions about the model and table you created by getting a firsthand look at it in action. You also took a first crack at adding in validations that ensure that you maintain the integrity of your data. The chapters that follow investigate these concepts in depth, starting with the first part of the MVC principle: models.

## CHAPTER 4

Working with a Database: Active Record

In the previous chapter, you took a whirlwind tour through creating a basic Rails application using the built-in scaffolding feature. You sketched out a basic model for a blog application and created the project databases. You used the built-in web server to run the application locally and practiced adding and managing articles from the web browser. In this chapter, you take a more in-depth look at how things work, starting with what is arguably the most important part of Rails: Active Record.

You may recall from Chapter 1 that Active Record is the Ruby object-relational mapping library that handles database abstraction and interaction for Rails. Whether you realized it or not, in the previous chapter, all access to the database—adding, editing, and deleting articles—happened through the magic of Active Record.

If you're not sure what exactly object-relational mapping is, don't worry. By the end of this chapter, you'll know. For now, it's best if you think of Active Record as being an intermediary that sits between your code and your database, allowing you to work with data effectively and naturally. When you use Active Record, you communicate with your database using pure Ruby code. Active Record translates the Ruby you write into a language that databases can understand.

This chapter teaches you how to use Active Record to talk to your database and perform basic operations. It introduces the concepts you need to know about communicating with databases and object-relational mapping. Then, you look at Active Record and walk through the techniques you need to know to effectively work with a database from Rails. If you don't have a lot of database experience under your belt, don't worry—working with databases through Active Record is a painless and even enjoyable experience. If you're an experienced database guru, you'll find that Active Record is an intelligent and efficient way to perform database operations without the need for low-level database-specific commands.

■ **NOTE** If you need to get the code at the exact point where you finished Chapter 3, download the zip file from `http://github.com/downloads/ccjr/blog/chapter04.zip` and extract it on your computer.

Introducing Active Record: Object-Relational Mapping on Rails

The key feature of Active Record is that it maps tables to classes, table rows to objects, and table columns to object attributes. This practice is commonly known as object-relational mapping (ORM). To be sure, Active Record isn't the only ORM in existence, but it may well be the easiest to use of the bunch.

One of the reasons Active Record is so easy to use is that almost no configuration is required to have it map a table to a class. You just need to create a Ruby class that's named after the table you want to map, and extend the Active Record Base class:

```
class Book < ActiveRecord::Base
end
```

Notice the part that reads < ActiveRecord::Base. The less-than sign indicates that the Book class on the left is a subclass of the one on the right, ActiveRecord::Base. In Ruby, when you extend a class like this, you automatically gain access to all the functionality in the parent class. There's a lot of code in the ActiveRecord::Base class, but you don't need to look at it. Your class merely extends it, and your work is finished.

Assuming Active Record knows how to find your database and that you have a table called books (note that the table name is plural, whereas the class name is singular), the table is automatically mapped. If you know your books table contains the fields title, publisher, and published_at, you can do this in any Ruby context:

```
book = Book.new

book.title = "Beginning Rails 3"
book.publisher = "Apress"
book.published_at = "2010-05-21"

book.save
```

These five lines write a new record to the books table. You gain a lot of ability by the simple act of subclassing! And that's why Active Record is easy to use. Notice how the table's fields (title, publisher, and published_at) can be read and written to using methods on the object you created (book). And you didn't need to tell Active Record what your fields were named, or even that you had any fields. It figured that out on its own. Of course, Active Record doesn't just let you create new records. It can also read, update, and delete records, plus a lot more.

Active Record is database-agnostic, so it doesn't care which database software you use, and it supports nearly every database out there. Because it's a high-level abstraction, the code you write remains the same no matter which database you're using. For the record (no pun intended), in this book you use SQLite. As explained in Chapter 2, SQLite is open source, easy to use, and fast, and it's the default database used for Rails development. (Along with the SQLite site, http://sqlite.org, the Wikipedia entry on SQLite is a good resource: http://en.wikipedia.org/wiki/SQLite.)

■ **NOTE** Rails is also ORM agnostic: it allows you to hook up your ORM of choice. The main ORM competitor for Active Record is DataMapper (`http://datamapper.org`), which you can use if you think Active Record has some deficiencies; however, we feel that sticking to the default ORM is the best way to learn.

What About SQL?

To be sure, you don't need Active Record (or any ORM) to talk to and manipulate your database. Databases have their own language: Structured Query Language (SQL), which is supported by nearly every relational database in existence. Using SQL, you can view column information, fetch a particular row or a set of rows, and search for rows containing certain criteria. You also use SQL to create, drop, and modify tables and insert, update, and destroy the information stored in those tables. The problem with SQL is that it's not object-oriented. If you want to learn the basic SQL syntax, look at Appendix B.

Object-oriented programming and relational databases are fundamentally different paradigms. The relational paradigm deals with relations and is mathematical by nature. The object-oriented paradigm, however, deals with objects, their attributes, and their associations to each other. As soon as you want to make objects persistent using a relational database, you notice something: there is a rift between these two paradigms—the so-called *object-relational gap*. An ORM library like Active Record helps you bridge that gap.

■ **NOTE** Active Record is based on a design pattern. *Design patterns* are standard solutions to common problems in software design. Well, it turns out that when you're working in an object-oriented environment, the problem of how to effectively communicate with a database (which isn't object-oriented) is quite common. Therefore, many smart people have wrapped their heads around the problem of how best to bring the object-oriented paradigm together with the relational database. One of those smart people is Martin Fowler, who, in his book *Patterns of Enterprise Application Architecture* (Addison-Wesley, 2002), first described a pattern that he called an Active Record. In the pattern Fowler described, a one-to-one mapping exists between a database record and the object that represents it. When Rails creator David Heinemeier Hansson sought to implement an ORM for his framework, he based it on Fowler's pattern.

Active Record lets you model real-world things in your code. Rails calls these real-world things *models*—the *M* in MVC. A model might be named `Person`, `Product`, or `Article`, and has a corresponding table in the database: `people`, `products`, or `articles`. Each model is implemented as a Ruby class and is stored in the app/models directory. Active Record provides the link between these classes and your tables, allowing you to work with what look like regular objects, which, in turn, can be persisted to the database. This frees you from having to write low-level SQL to talk to the database. Instead, you work with your data as if it were an object, and Active Record does all the translation into SQL behind the scenes. This means that in Rails, you get to stick with one language: Ruby.

■ **NOTE** Just because you're using Active Record to abstract your SQL generation doesn't mean SQL is evil. Active Record makes it possible to execute SQL directly whenever that's necessary. The truth is that raw SQL is the native language of databases, and there are some (albeit rare) cases when an ORM won't cut it.

Active Record Conventions

Active Record achieves its zero-configuration reputation by way of convention. Most of the conventions it uses are easy to grasp. After all, they're conventions, so they're already in wide use. Although you can override most of the conventions to suit the particular design of your database, you'll save a lot of time and energy if you stick to them.

Let's take a quick look at the two main conventions you need to know:

- Class names are singular; table names are plural.

- Tables contain an identity column named id.

Active Record assumes that the name of your table is the plural form of the class name. If your table name contains underscores, then your class name is assumed to be in *CamelCase*. Table 4-1 shows some examples.

Table 4-1. *Table and Class Name Conventions*

Table	Class
events	Event
people	Person
categories	Category
order_items	OrderItem

All tables are assumed to have a unique identity column named id. This column should be the table's *primary key* (a value used to uniquely identify a table's row). This is a fairly common convention in database design. (For more information on primary keys in database design, the Wikipedia entry has a wealth of useful information and links: http://en.wikipedia.org/wiki/Unique_key.)

The belief in convention over configuration is firmly entrenched in the Rails philosophy, so it should come as no surprise that there are more conventions at work than those listed here. You'll likely find that they all make good sense, and you can use them without paying much attention.

Introducing the Console

Ruby comes with a great little tool: an interactive interpreter called irb (for Interactive Ruby). Most of the time, you invoke irb using the console program that ships with Rails, but you can start up an irb session whenever you want by typing irb at the command prompt. The advantage of the console is that it enjoys the special privilege of being integrated with your project's environment. This means it has access to and knowledge of your models (and subsequently, your database).

You use the console as a means to get inside the world of your Article model and to work with it in the exact same way your Rails application would. As you see in a minute, this is a great way to showcase the capabilities of Active Record interactively.

You can execute any arbitrary Ruby code in irb and do anything you might otherwise do inside your Ruby programs: set variables, evaluate conditions, and inspect objects. The only essential difference between an interactive session and a regular old Ruby program is that irb echoes the return value of everything it executes. This saves you from having to explicitly print the results of an evaluation. Just run the code, and irb prints the result.

You can tell whenever you're inside an irb session by looking for the double greater-than sign (>>)— or a slightly different sign depending on your environment, which indicate the irb prompt, and the arrow symbol (=>), which indicates the response.

As you continue to progress with both Ruby and Rails, you'll find that irb is an essential tool. Using irb, you can play around with code and make sure it works as you expect before you write it into your programs.

If you've been following along with the previous chapters, then you should have a model called Article (in app/models/article.rb), and you've probably already entered some sample data when playing with scaffolding in the previous chapter. If not, make sure you get up to speed by reading Chapter 3 before moving on.

Let's load irb and start to experiment with the Article model. Make sure you're inside the blog application directory, and then type rails console on your command line. This causes the irb console to load with your application's *development* environment and leaves you at a simple prompt, waiting for you to enter some code:

```
$ rails console
Loading development environment.
>>
```

From the console, you can interrogate your Article model for information. For instance, you can ask it for its column names:

```
>> Article.column_names
=> ["id", "title", "body", "published_at", "created_at", "updated_at",
"excerpt", "location"]
```

Look at that! All your columns are presented as a Ruby array (you can tell by the fact that they're surrounded by square brackets). Another quick trick you may use often is to type just the name of your model class in the console to find out not only the column names, but also the data type of each column:

```
>> Article
=> Article(id: integer, title: string, body: text, published_at: datetime,
created_at: datetime, updated_at: datetime, excerpt: string, location: string)
```

You get the column_names class method courtesy of the ActiveRecord::Base class from which your Article class inherits. Actually, you get a lot of methods courtesy of ActiveRecord::Base. To see just how many, you can ask:

```
>> Article.methods.size
=> 518
```

That's a lot of methods! You may get a different number of methods depending on your environment. Don't worry—you don't need to memorize all of them; and most of them are private to Active Record and are used internally, so you never even use them. Also, Still, it's important, if for no other reason than to get a sense of what you get for free just by subclassing Active Record. Even though in this case ActiveRecord:: Base is considered the *superclass,* it sure makes your lowly Article class super, doesn't it? (Sorry, enough bad humor.)

A CRASH COURSE IN RUBY CLASS DESIGN

Object-oriented programming is all about objects. You create a class that encapsulates all the logic required to create an object, along with its properties and attributes, and use the class to produce new objects, each of which is a unique instance, distinct from other objects of the same class. That may sound a little abstract (and with good reason—abstraction, after all, is the name of the game), but if it helps, you can think of a class as being an object factory.

The obvious example is that of a car factory. Contained within a car factory are all the resources, tools, workers, and processes required to produce a shiny new car. Each car that comes off the assembly line is unique. The cars may vary in size, color, and shape, or they may not vary from each other much at all. The point is that even if two cars share the exact same attributes, they aren't the same car. You certainly wouldn't expect a change to the color of one car to affect all the others, would you? Well, in object-oriented programming, it's not much different. The class is the factory that produces objects, which are called *instances* of a class. From a single factory, an infinite number of objects can be produced:

```
class Car
end

car1 = Car.new
car2 = Car.new
```

car1 is a Car object, which is to say it's an instance of the class Car. Each car is a different object, created by the same factory. Each object knows which class it belongs to (which factory created it), so if you're ever in doubt, you can ask it:

```
car2.class #=> Car
```

Your Car class doesn't really do anything that useful—it has no attributes. So, let's give it some. You start by giving it a make—something like Toyota or Nissan. Of course, you need to define a way to read and write these attributes. You do this by creating aptly named *reader* and *writer* methods. Some object-oriented languages refer to these as *getters* and *setters*. The two sets of terms are pretty much interchangeable, but Ruby favors the former. Let's add a reader and writer for the make attribute:

```
class Car
  # A writer method. Sets the value of the @make attribute
  def make=(text)
    @make = text
  end

  # A reader method. Returns the value of the @make attribute
  def make
```

```
        @make
    end
end
```

The methods you just defined (`make()` and `make=()`) are instance methods. This is because they can be used only on instances of the class, which is to say, the individual objects that have been created from the class. To create a new instance of the `Car` class, you use the `new` constructor:

```
my_car = Car.new
```

That's all that's required to create a new instance of the class `Car` in a local variable called `my_car`. The variable `my_car` can now be considered a `Car` object. Although you have a new `Car` object, you haven't yet given it a `make`. If you use the reader method you created to ask your car what its make is, you see that it's `nil`:

```
my_car.make #=> nil
```

Apparently, if you want your car to have a `make`, you have to set it. This is where the writer method comes in handy:

```
my_car.make = 'Toyota'
```

This sets the value of the `make` attribute for your car to `Toyota`. If you had other `Car` objects, their `make`s would remain unchanged. You're setting the attribute only on the `my_car` object. Now, when you use the reader method, it confirms that the `make` attribute has been updated:

```
my_car.make #=> 'Toyota'
```

Of course, you can change the value any time you want:

```
my_car.make = 'Mazda'
```

And again, if you ask your `Car` object its `make`, it will tell you:

```
my_car.make #=> 'Mazda'
```

That's a simple example, but it illustrates a couple of very important points: Classes are used to create objects, and objects have attributes. Every object has a unique set of attributes, different from other objects of the same class.

The reason for this crash course in Ruby class design is to illustrate the point that modeling with Active Record is a lot like modeling with standard Ruby classes. If you decided to think of Active Record as being an extension to standard Ruby classes, you wouldn't be very far off. In practice, this fact makes using Active Record in Ruby quite natural. And because Active Record can reflect on your tables to determine which fields to map automatically, you need to define your attributes in only one place: the database. That's DRY (don't repeat yourself)! See Appendix A to learn more about Ruby's syntax, classes, and objects.

Active Record Basics: CRUD

Active Record is a big topic, so let's start with the basics. You've seen the so-called big four earlier, but here they are again: create, read, update, and delete, affectionately known as CRUD. In one way or another, most of what you do with Active Record in particular, and with databases in general, relates to CRUD. Rails has embraced CRUD as a design technique and as a way to simplify the modeling process. It's no surprise then that this chapter takes an in-depth look at how to do CRUD with Active Record.

Let's build on the blog application you started in the previous chapter. Although your application doesn't do much yet, it's at a stage where it's easy to demonstrate these concepts in a more concrete fashion.

This section uses the console, so keep it open as you work, and feel free to experiment as much as you want. The more experimentation you do, the deeper your understanding will be.

Creating New Records

You start by creating a new article in the database so you have something to work with. There are a few different ways to create new model objects, but they're all variations on the same theme. This section shows how each approach works and explains the often subtle differences between them.

Using the new Constructor

The most basic way to create a new model object is with the new constructor. If you read the crash-course sidebar on Ruby classes, you're sure to recognize it. If you didn't, then it's enough that you know new is the usual way to create new objects of any type. Active Record classes are no different. Try it now:

```
>> article = Article.new
=> #<Article id: nil, title: nil, body: nil, published_at: nil, created_at: nil,
updated_at: nil, excerpt: nil, location: nil>
```

All you're doing here is creating a new Article object and storing it in the local variable article. True to form, the console responds with the return value of the method, which in this case is a *string* representation of the model object. It may look a little funny, but this is what all Ruby objects look like when you inspect them. The response lists the attributes of the Article class. Starting here, you could call a few of the article variable methods. For example, the new_record? method tells you whether this object has been persisted (saved) to the database, and the attributes method returns a hash of the attributes that Active Record garnered by reflecting on the columns in the table:

```
>> article.new_record?
=> true
>> article.attributes
=> {"body"=>nil, "created_at"=>nil, "excerpt"=>nil, "location"=>nil,
"published_at"=>nil, "title"=>nil, "updated_at"=>nil}
```

Here, you're using *reader* methods, which read and return the value of the attribute in question. Because this is a brand-new record and you haven't given it any information, all your attributes are nil, which means they have no values. Let's remedy that now using (what else?) *writer* methods:

```
>> article.title = 'RailsConf'
=> "RailsConf"

>> article.body = 'RailsConf is the official gathering for Rails developers..'
=> "'RailsConf is the official gathering for Rails developers.."
```

```
>> article.published_at = '2010-02-27'
=> "2010-02-27"
```

■ **NOTE** A return of `nil` always represents nothing. It's a helpful little object that stands in the place of nothingness. If you ask an object for something and it returns `false`, then false is *something*, so it's not a helpful representation. As a nerdy fact, in logics, false and true are equal and opposite values, but they're values in the end. The same is true of zero (0). The number 0 isn't truly nothing—it's an actual representation of an abstract nothing, but it's still something. That's why in programming you have `nil` (or `null` in other languages).

Now, when you inspect your `Article` object, you can see that it has attributes:

```
>> article
=> #<Article id: nil, title: "RailsConf", body: "RailsConf is the official
 gathering for Rails devel...", published_at: "2010-02-27 00:00:00",
 created_at: nil, updated_at: nil, excerpt: nil, location: nil>
```

You still haven't written a new record. If you were to look at the `articles` table in the database, you wouldn't find a record for the object you're working with. (If you squint really hard at the preceding object-inspection string, notice that no `id` has been assigned yet.) That's because you haven't yet saved the object to the database. Fortunately, saving an Active Record object couldn't be any easier:

```
>> article.save
=> true
```

When you save a new record, a SQL INSERT statement is constructed behind the scenes. If the INSERT is successful, the `save` operation returns `true`; if it fails, `save` returns `false`. You can ask for a count of the number of rows in the table just to be sure that a record was created:

```
>> Article.count
=> 1
```

Sure enough, you have a new article! You've got to admit, that was pretty easy. (You may have created some articles during the scaffolding session. If so, don't be surprised if you have more than one article already.) Additionally, if you ask the article whether it's a `new_record?`, it responds with `false`. Because it's saved, it's not "new" anymore:

```
>> article.new_record?
=> false
```

Let's create another article. This time, omit all the chatter from the console so you can get a better sense of how the process plays out. You create a new object and place it in a variable, you set the object's attributes, and finally you save the record. Note that although you're using the local variable `article` to hold your object, it can be anything you want. Usually, you use a variable that indicates the type of object you're creating, like `article` or, if you prefer shorthand, just a:

```
>> article = Article.new

>> article.title      = "Introduction to SQL"
>> article.body     = "SQL stands for Structured Query Language, .."
>> article.published_at      = Date.today

>> article.save
```

■ **NOTE** Although writer methods look like assignments, they're really methods in disguise. `article.title = 'something'` is the functional equivalent of `article.title=('something')`, where `title=()` is the method. Ruby provides a little syntactic sugar to make writers look more natural.

Now you're rolling! You've already created a few articles and haven't had to write a lick of SQL. Given how easy this is, you may be surprised that you can do it in even fewer steps, but you can. Instead of setting each attribute on its own line, you can pass all of them to new at once. Here's how you can rewrite the preceding process of creating a new record in fewer lines of code:

```
>> article = Article.new(:title => "Introduction to Active Record",
:body => "Active Record is Rails's default ORM..", :published_at => Date.today)
>> article.save
```

Not bad, but you can do even better. The new constructor creates a new object, but it's your responsibility to save it. If you forget to save the object, it will never be written to the database.

Using the create Method

When you want to create an object and save it in one fell swoop, you can use the create method. Use it now to create another article:

```
>> Article.create(:title => "RubyConf 2010", :body => "The annual RubyConf will
take place in..", :published_at => '2010-05-19')
=> #<Article id: 4, title: "RubyConf 2010", body: "The annual RubyConf will take
place in..", published_at: "2010-05-19 00:00:00", created_at: "2010-05-01
23:17:19", updated_at: "2010-05-01 23:17:19", excerpt: nil, location: nil>
```

Instead of returning true or false, the create method returns the object it created—in this case, an Article object. You're actually passing a hash of attributes to the create method. Although hashes are normally surrounded by curly braces, *when a hash is the only argument to a Ruby method, the braces are optional.* You can just as easily create the attributes hash first and then give that to create:

```
>> attributes = { :title => "Rails Pub Nite", :body    => "Rails Pub Nite is every
3rd Monday of each month, except in December.", :published_at => "2010-05-19"}
=> {:title=>"Rails Pub Nite", :body=>"Rails Pub Nite is every
3rd Monday of each month, except in December.", :published_at=>" 2010-05-19"}
>>
```

```
=> #<Article id: 5, title: "Rails Pub Nite", body: "Rails Pub Nite is every 3rd
Monday of each month, e...", published_at: "2010-05-19 00:00:00",
created_at: "2010-05-01 23:36:07", updated_at: "2010-05-01 23:36:07",
excerpt: nil, location: nil>
```

Let's see how many articles you've created by doing a count:

```
>> Article.count
=> 5
```

You're getting the hang of this now. To summarize, when you want to create a new object and save it manually, use the new constructor; when you want to create and save in one operation, use create. You've already created five new records, which are plenty for now, so let's move on to the next step: finding records.

Reading (Finding) Records

Now that you have a few articles to play with, it's time to practice finding them. Every model class understands the find method. It's quite versatile and accepts a number of options that modify its behavior.

Let's start with the basics. find is a class method. That means you use it on the model class rather than an object of that class, just as you did the new and create methods. Like new and create, a find operation, if successful, returns a new object.

You can call find four ways:

- find(:id): Finds a single record by its unique id, or multiple records if :id is an array of ids

- find(:all) or its shortcut all: Finds all records in the table

- find(:first) or its shortcut first: Finds the first record

- find(:last) or its shortcut last: Finds the last record

The following sections go through the different ways to call find and explain how to use each.

Finding a Single Record Using an ID

The :id, :first and :last options mostly return a single record. The :id option is specific; you use it when you're looking for a specific record and you know its unique id. If you give it a single id, it either returns the corresponding record (if there is one) or raises an exception (if there isn't). If you pass an array of ids—like [4, 5]—as the parameter, the method returns an array with all records that match the passed in ids. The :first option is a little more forgiving; it returns the first record in the table, or nil if the table is empty, as explained in the next section.

You can find a single record using its unique id using find(:id). Here's how it works:

```
>> Article.find(3)
=> #<Article id: 3, title: "Introduction to Active Record", body: "Active Record
is Rails's default ORM..", published_at: "2010-05-01 04:00:00",
created_at: "2010-05-01 23:15:37", updated_at: "2010-05-01 23:15:37",
excerpt: nil, location: nil>
```

As you can see, you found the article with the id of 3. If you wanted to take a closer look at what was returned, you can store the result in a local variable:

```
>> article = Article.find(3)
=> #<Article id: 3 …>
>> article.id
=> 3
>> article.title
=> "Introduction to Active Record"
```

Here, you store the object that find returned in the local variable article. Then, you can interrogate it and ask for its attributes.

All this works because an article with the id 3 *actually exists*. If instead you search for a record that you know doesn't exist (say, 1037), Active Record raises an exception:

```
>> Article.find 1037
ActiveRecord::RecordNotFound: Couldn't find Article with ID=1037
…
```

Active Record raises a RecordNotFound exception and tells you it couldn't find any articles with the id of 1037. Of course it couldn't. You know that no such record exists. The lesson here is that you use find(:id) when you're looking for a specific record that you expect to exist. If the record doesn't exist, it's probably an error you want to know about; therefore, Active Record raises RecordNotFound.

RECOVERING FROM RECORDNOTFOUND ERRORS

When you use find with a single id, you expect the record to exist. How can you recover gracefully from a RecordNotFound exception if you need to? You can use Ruby's facility for error handling: begin and rescue. Here's how this works:

```
begin
   Article.find(1037)
rescue ActiveRecord::RecordNotFound
   puts "We couldn't find that record"
end
```

First, you open a begin block. Then, you cause a RecordNotFound error by deliberately searching for a record that you know doesn't exist. When the error occurs, Ruby runs the code you put inside the rescue part of the body, which prints a friendly message.

Finding a Single Record Using first

You can find the first record that the database returns by using the first method. This always returns exactly one item, unless the table is empty, in which case nil is returned:

```
>> Article.first
=> #<Article id: 1, title: "RailsConf", body: "RailsConf is the official
 gathering for Rails devel...", published_at: "2010-02-27 00:00:00",
```

```
created_at: "2010-05-01 23:12:09", updated_at: "2010-05-01 23:12:09",
excerpt: nil, location: nil>
```

Keep in mind that this isn't necessarily the first record in the table. It depends on the database software you're using and/or the default order in which you want your records to be retrieved. It's the equivalent of saying SELECT * FROM table LIMIT 1 in SQL. If you need to find a record and don't particularly care which record it is, first can come in handy. Note that first doesn't raise an exception if the record can't be found.

The last method works exactly the same as first; however, records are retrieved in the inverse order of first. For example, if records from articles are listed in chronological order for first, they're retrieved in inverse chronological order for last:

```
>> Article.last
=> #<Article id: 5, title: "Rails Pub Nite", body: "Rails Pub Nite is every 3rd
Monday of each month, e...", published_at: "2010-05-19 00:00:00",
created_at: "2010-05-01 23:36:07", updated_at: "2010-05-01 23:36:07",
excerpt: nil, location: nil>
```

Finding All Records

So far, you've looked at finding a single record. In each case, find, first, or last returns a single Article object. But what if you want to find more than one article? In your application, you want to display all the articles on the homepage.

If you run the all method, it returns all records for that class:

```
>> articles = Article.all
=> [#<Article id: 1,..> #<Article id: 2,..>, #<Article id: 3,..>,
#<Article id: 4,..> , #<Article id: 5,..>]
```

The square brackets in the response indicate that all has returned an array. You can confirm this by asking the articles variable what its class is:

```
>> articles.class
=> Array
```

Sure enough, articles tells you it's an Array. To be precise, it's an array of Article objects. Like all Ruby arrays, you can ask for its size:

```
>> articles.size
=> 5
```

Because articles is an array, you can access the individual elements it contains by using its *index*, which is numeric, starting at 0:

```
>> articles[0]
=> #<Article id: 1, title: "RailsConf", body: "RailsConf is the official
 gathering for Rails devel...", published_at: "2010-02-27 00:00:00",
 created_at: "2010-05-01 23:12:09", updated_at: "2010-05-01 23:12:09",
 excerpt: nil, location: nil>
```

And after you've isolated a single `Article` object, you can get at its attributes:

```
>> articles[0].title
=> "RailsConf"
```

What's happening here is that `all` produces an array, and you access the object at the `0` index and call the `title` method. You can also use the `first` method, which all arrays respond to, and get the same result, but with a little more natural syntax:

```
>> articles.first.title
=> "RailsConf"
```

If you want to iterate over the collection, you can use the each method, which, again, works with all arrays. Here, you loop over the array, extract each item into a variable called `article`, and print its `title` attribute using the puts command:

```
>> articles.each {|article| puts article.title}
RailsConf
Introduction to SQL
Introduction to Active Record
RubyConf 2010
Rails Pub Nite
=> [#<Article id: 1,..> #<Article id: 2,..>, #<Article id: 3,..>,
#<Article id: 4,..> , #<Article id: 5,..>]
```

Sometimes, you want your results ordered. For example, if you're listing all your articles, you probably want them listed chronologically. To do so, you can use the `order` method, which accepts as argument the name of the column or columns. For you SQL heroes, it corresponds to the SQL `ORDER` clause:

```
>> articles = Article.order("published_at")
=> [#<Article id: 1,..> #<Article id: 2,..>, #<Article id: 3,..>,
#<Article id: 4,..> , #<Article id: 5,..>]
>> articles.each {|article| puts article.published_at }
2010-02-27 00:00:00 UTC
2010-05-01 04:00:00 UTC
2010-05-01 04:00:00 UTC
2010-05-19 00:00:00 UTC
2010-05-19 00:00:00 UTC
=> [#<Article id: 1,..> #<Article id: 2,..>, #<Article id: 3,..>,
#<Article id: 4,..> , #<Article id: 5,..>]
```

Notice that when you call the `order` method, it returns an array object as you may have expected. One thing that happens on the background is that Active Record allows you to chain calls to multiple methods before sending the command to the database; so you can call `all`, followed by `order`, and some other methods we'll talk about in the next chapter, to create more precise database queries. Also, Active Record is smart enough to use *lazy loading*, a practice that only hits the database when necessary—in this example, when you call the each method.

By default, any column is ordered in ascending order (for example, 1–10, or *a*–*z*). If you want to reverse this to get descending order, use the `DESC` modifier (the same way you do in SQL, because the value of order parameter is really just a SQL fragment):

```
>> articles = Article.order ('published_at DESC')
=> [#<Article id: 4,..> #<Article id: 5,..>, #<Article id: 2,..>,
#<Article id: 3,..> , #<Article id: 1,..>]
>> articles.each {|article| puts article.published_at }
2010-05-19 00:00:00 UTC
2010-05-19 00:00:00 UTC
2010-05-01 04:00:00 UTC
2010-05-01 04:00:00 UTC
2010-02-27 00:00:00 UTC
=> [#<Article id: 4,..> #<Article id: 5,..>, #<Article id: 2,..>,
#<Article id: 3,..> , #<Article id: 1,..>]
```

Finding with Conditions

Although finding a record by its primary key is useful, it requires that you know the id to begin with, which isn't always the case. Sometimes you want to find records based on other criteria. This is where conditions come into play. Conditions correspond to the SQL WHERE clause. If you want to find a record by its title, you call the where method and pass a value that contains either a hash of conditions or a SQL fragment.

Here, you use a hash of conditions to indicate you want the first article with the title RailsConf:

```
>> Article.where(:title => 'RailsConf').first
=> #<Article id: 1, title: "RailsConf", body: "RailsConf is the official
 gathering for Rails devel...", published_at: "2010-02-27 00:00:00",
 created_at: "2010-05-01 23:12:09", updated_at: "2010-05-01 23:12:09",
 excerpt: nil, location: nil>
```

Because you use first, you get only one record (the first one in the result set, even if there is more than one result). If you instead use all, you get back a collection, even if the collection has only one item in it:

```
>> Article.where(:title => 'RailsConf').all
=> [#<Article id: 1, title: "RailsConf", body: "RailsConf is the official
 gathering for Rails devel...", published_at: "2010-02-27 00:00:00",
 created_at: "2010-05-01 23:12:09", updated_at: "2010-05-01 23:12:09",
 excerpt: nil, location: nil>]
```

Notice the square brackets, and remember that they indicate an array. More often than not, when you're doing a all operation, you expect more than one record in return. But all always produces an array, even if that array is empty:

```
>> Article.where(:title => 'Unknown').all
=> []
```

Using Dynamic Finders

It doesn't get any easier than dynamic finders. These finders are called *dynamic* because they use Ruby's method_missing functionality to automatically create methods that don't exist until runtime. Using dynamic finders, you can include the attribute you're looking for directly in the method name. This makes more sense when you see it in action:

```
>> Article.find_by_title('RailsConf')
=> #<Article id: 1, title: "RailsConf", …>
```

There are several variations of dynamic finders, which are summarized in the Table 4-2.

Table 4-2. *Dynamic Finders*

Finder	Example
find_by_*(cond)	find_by_title('RailsConf') # => Article
find_all_by_*(cond)	find_all_by_title('RailsConf') # => Array
find_by_*_and_*(cond1, cond2)	find_by_title_and_published_on('RailsConf', '2009-05-19') # => Article
find_all_by_*_and_*(cond1, cond2)	find_all_by_title_and_published_on('RailsConf', '2009-05-19') # => Array

Updating Records

Updating a record is a lot like creating a record. You can update attributes one at a time and then save the result, or you can update attributes in one fell swoop. When you update a record, a SQL UPDATE statement is constructed behind the scenes. First, you use a find operation to retrieve the record you want to update; next, you modify its attributes; and finally, you save it back to the database:

```
>> article = Article.first
>> article.title = "Rails 3 is great"
>> article.published_at = Time.now
>> article.save
=> true
```

This should look pretty familiar by now. The only real difference between this process and the process of creating a new record is that instead of creating a brand-new row, you fetch an existing row. You update the attributes the exact same way, and you save the record the same way. Just as when you create a new record, when save operates on an existing record, it returns true or false, depending on whether the operation was successful.

When you want to update an object's attributes and save it in a single operation, you use the update_attributes method. Unlike when you create a new record with create, because you're updating a record, you need to fetch that record first. That's where the other subtle difference lies. Unlike create, which is a class method (it operates on the class, not on an object), update_attributes is an instance method. Instance methods work on objects, or instances of a class. Here's an example:

```
>> article = Article.first
>>  article.update_attributes(:title => "RailsConf2010",
```

```
:published_at => 1.day.ago)
=> true
```

Deleting Records

You're finally at the last component of CRUD: delete. When you're working with databases, you inevitably need to delete records. If a user cancels their order, or if a book goes out of stock, or even if you have an error in a given row, you may want to delete it. Sometimes you need to delete all rows in a table, and sometimes you want to delete only a specific row. Active Record makes deleting rows every bit as easy as creating them.

There are two styles of row deletion: destroy and delete. The destroy style works on the *instance*. It instantiates the object, which means it finds a single row first, and then deletes the row from the database. The delete style operates on the *class*, which is to say it operates on the table rather than a given row from that table.

Using destroy

The easiest and most common way to remove a record is to use the destroy method, which means the first thing you need to do is find the record you want to destroy:

```
>> article = Article.last
>> article.destroy
=> #<Article id: 5, title: "Rails Pub Nite", body: "Rails Pub Nite is every 3rd
Monday of each month, e...", published_at: "2010-05-19 00:00:00",
created_at: "2010-05-01 23:36:07", updated_at: "2010-05-01 23:36:07",
excerpt: nil, location: nil>
```

If you're interested, the SQL that Active Record generates in response to the destroy operation is as follows:

```
DELETE FROM articles WHERE id = 5;
```

As a result, the article with the id of 5 is permanently deleted. But you still have the object hanging around in the variable article, so how can it really be gone? The answer is that although the object remains *hydrated* (retains all its attributes), it's *frozen*. You can still access its attributes, but you can't modify them. Let's see what happens if you try to change the location:

```
>> article.location = 'Toronto, ON'
RuntimeError: can't modify frozen hash
```

It appears that the deleted article is now a frozen hash. The object remains, but it's read-only, so you can't modify it. Given this fact, if you're going to delete the record, you don't really need to create an explicit Article object after all. You can do the destroy in a one-line operation:

```
>> Article.last.destroy
```

Here, the object instantiation is implicit. You're still calling the destroy instance method, but you're not storing an Article object in a local variable first.

You can still do better. You can use the class method destroy, which does a find automatically. As with find and create, you can use destroy directly on the class (that is, you don't create an object first). Because it operates on the table and not the row, you need to help it by telling it which row or rows you want to target. Here's how you delete the article with the id 1:

```
>> Article.destroy(1)
=> [#<Article id: 1, title: "RailsConf", body: "RailsConf is the official
 gathering for Rails devel...", published_at: "2010-02-27 00:00:00",
 created_at: "2010-05-01 23:12:09", updated_at: "2010-05-01 23:12:09",
 excerpt: nil, location: nil>]
```

Sometimes, you want to destroy more that one record. Just as with find, you can give destroy an array of primary keys whose rows you want to remove. Use square brackets ([]) to indicate that you're passing an array:

```
>> Article.destroy([2,3])
=> [#<Article id: 2, ..>, #<Article id: 3, ..>]
```

Even though ActiveRecord::Base.destroy is a class method, it instantiates each object before destroying it. You can tell this by looking at its source:

```
def destroy(id)
  if id.is_a?(Array)
    id.map { |one_id| destroy(one_id) }
  else
      find(id).destroy
  end
end
```

Here, you can see that if the received argument is an array, destroy iterates over the array and calls the same destroy method once for each item in the array. This effectively causes it to take the else path of the conditional, which performs a find first (instantiating the object) and then calls the instance version of destroy. Neat, huh? That pretty much covers destroy.

Using delete

The second style of row deletion is delete. Every Active Record class has class methods called delete and delete_all. The delete family of methods differ from destroy in that they don't instantiate or perform callbacks on the object they're deleting. They remove the row immediately from the database.

Just like find and create, you use delete and delete_all directly on the class (that is, you don't create an object first). Because the method operates on the table and not the row, you need to help it by telling it which row or rows you want to target:

```
>> Article.delete(4)
=> 1
```

Here, you specify a single primary key for the article you want to delete. The operation responds with the number of records removed. Because a primary key uniquely identifies a single record, only one record is deleted.

Just as with `find`, you can give `delete` an array of primary keys whose rows you want to delete. Use square brackets (`[ ]`) to indicate that you're passing an array:

```
>> Article.delete([5, 6])
=> 0
```

■ **NOTE** Unlike `find`, which is capable of collecting any arguments it receives into an array automatically, `delete` must be supplied with an array object explicitly. So, although `Model.find(1,2,3)` works, `Model.delete(1,2,3)` fails with an argument error (because it's really receiving three arguments). To delete multiple rows by primary key, you must pass an actual array object. The following works, because it's a single array (containing three items) and thus a single argument: `Model.delete([1,2,3])`.

Deleting with Conditions

You can delete all rows that match a given condition with the `delete_all` class method. The following deletes all articles before a certain date:

```
>> Article.delete_all("published_at < '2011-01-01'")
>> 0
```

The return value of `delete_all` is the number of records deleted.

■ **CAUTION** If you use `delete_all` without any arguments, it deletes all rows in the table, so be careful! Most of the time, you pass it a string of conditions.

When Good Models Go Bad

So far, you've been nice to your models and have made them happy by providing just the information they need. But in the previous chapter, you provided *validations* that prevented you from saving bad records to the database. Specifically, you told the `Article` model that it should never allow itself to be saved to the database if it isn't given a `title` and `body`. Look at the `Article` model, shown in Listing 4-1, to recall how validations are specified.

Listing 4-1. The app/models/article.rb File

```
class Article< ActiveRecord::Base
  validates :title, :presence => true
  validates :body, :presence => true
end
```

You may have noticed in your generated scaffolding that you use a helper method called errors.full_messages to print out a helpful error message. That helper isn't black magic; it's a bit of code that asks the model associated with the form for its list of errors (also referred to as the *errors collection*) and returns a nicely formatted block of HTML to show the user.

■ **NOTE** You may have noticed that you call methods in Ruby with a dot (.) For instance, you say @article.errors to get the error collection back. However, Ruby documentation has an idiomatic convention of using the # symbol along with the class name to let the reader know that there is a method it can call on an object. For example, on the Article class, you can use the method @article.title as Article#title, because it's something that acts on a particular @article but not the Article class itself. You've also seen that you can write the code Article.count, because you don't need to know about a particular @article, but only Article objects in general. Keep this convention in mind when you're reading Ruby documentation.

The secret to this is that every Active Record object has an automatic attribute added to it called errors. To get started, create a fresh Article object:

```
>> article = Article.new
=> #<Article id: nil, title: nil, body: nil, published_at: nil, created_at: nil,
updated_at: nil, excerpt: nil, location: nil>
>> article.errors.any?
=> false
```

This seems odd: you know this new article should have errors, because it's invalid—you didn't give it a title or a body. This is because you haven't triggered the validations yet. You can cause them to occur a couple of ways. The most obvious way is to attempt to save the object:

```
>> article.save
=> false
```

Every time you've used save before, the model has happily chirped true back to you. But this time, save returns false. This is because before the model allows itself to be saved, it runs through its gauntlet of validations, and one or more of those validations failed.

You would be right to guess that if you tried article.errors.any? again, it would return true:

```
>> article.errors.any?
=> true
```

Let's interrogate the errors collection a little more closely with the full_messages method:

```
>> article.errors.full_messages
=> ["Title can't be blank", "Body can't be blank"]
```

Voilà! Look how helpful the model is being. It's passing back an array of error messages.

If there is only one attribute that you care about, you can also ask the errors collection for a particular attribute's errors:

```
>> article.errors.on(:title)
=> "can't be blank"
```

Notice that because you tell it which attribute you're looking for, the message returns a slightly different result than before. What if you ask for an attribute that doesn't exist or doesn't have errors?

```
>> article.errors.on(:nonexistent)
=> nil
```

You get back nil, which lets you know that you didn't find anything.

Another helpful method is size, which, as your saw earlier, works with all arrays:

```
>> article.errors.size
=> 2
```

Saving isn't the only way you can cause validations to run. You can ask a model object if it's valid?:

```
>> article.valid?
=> false
```

If you try that on a new object, the errors collection magically fills up with your pretty errors.

Summary

In this chapter, you've become familiar with using the console to work with models. You've learned how to create, read, update, and destroy model objects. Also, you've briefly looked into how to see the simple errors caused by the validations you set up on your model in the previous chapter.

The next chapter discusses how to create relationships (called *associations*) between your models, and you begin to see how Active Record helps you work with your data in extremely powerful ways. It also expands on the concept of validations and shows how you can do a lot more with validates. You see that Rails provides a bevy of prewritten validators and an easy way to write your own customized validators.

■ ■ ■

## CHAPTER 5

Advanced Active Record: Enhancing Your Models

The previous chapter introduced the basics of Active Record and how to use it. This chapter delves more deeply into Active Record and teaches you how to enhance your models.

Model enhancement is a general term. It refers to endowing your models with attributes and capabilities that go beyond what you get from subclassing `ActiveRecord::Base`. A model contains all the logic that governs its citizenship in the world of your application. In the model, you can define how it interacts with other models, what a model should accept as a minimum amount of information for it to be considered valid, and other abilities and responsibilities.

Models need to relate to each other. In the real world, bank accounts have transactions, books belong to authors, and products have categories. These relationships are referred to as *associations*, and Active Record makes them easy to work with. Models also have requirements. For instance, you can't have a transaction without an amount—it might break your system if someone tried to have an empty transaction. So, Active Record gives you easy ways to tell a model what it should expect in order to be saved to the database.

This chapter teaches you how to programmatically enhance your models so they're more than just simple maps of your tables. To demonstrate the concepts, you build on the blog application you started in Chapter 3, so keep it handy if you want to follow along with the examples.

■ **NOTE** If you need to get the code at the exact point where you finished Chapter 4, download the zip file from `http://github.com/downloads/ccjr/blog/chapter05.zip` and extract it on your computer.

Adding Methods

Let's begin with a brief review of Active Record basics. At the simplest level, Active Record works by automatically wrapping database tables whose names match the plural, underscored version of any classes that inherit from `ActiveRecord::Base`. For example, if you want to wrap the users table, you create a subclass of `ActiveRecord::Base` called User, like this:

```
class User < ActiveRecord::Base
end
```

That's all you really need to have Active Record map the users table and get all the basic CRUD functionality described in Chapter 4. But few models are actually this bare.

So far, you've left your model classes unchanged. That's a good thing, and it speaks to the power and simplicity of Active Record. However, it leaves something to be desired. Most of the time, your models need to do a lot more than just wrap a table.

■ **NOTE** If you're familiar with SQL, you're probably feeling that Active Record provides only simple-case solutions and can't handle complicated cases. That's entirely untrue. Although SQL is useful for highly customized database queries, most Rails projects rarely need to touch SQL, thanks to some clever tricks in Active Record.

The primary way in which you enhance models is by adding methods to them. This is referred to as adding *domain logic*. With Active Record, all the logic for a particular table is contained in one place: the model. This is why the model is said to *encapsulate* all the domain logic. This logic includes access rules, validations, relationships, and, well, just about anything else you feel like adding.

In addition to all the column-based reader and writer methods you get by wrapping a table, you're free to define your own methods on the class. An Active Record subclass isn't much different from a regular Ruby class; about the only difference is that you need to make sure you don't unintentionally overwrite any of Active Record's methods (find, save, or destroy, for example). For the most part, though, this isn't a problem.

Let's look at a simple example. You often need to format data, rather than accessing a model attribute in its raw form. In the blog application, you want to be able to produce a formatted, long title that includes the title of the article and its date. To accomplish this, all you need to do is define a new instance method called long_title that performs the concatenation of those attributes and produces a formatted string. Add the code shown in Listing 5-1 just before the last end statement in the app/models/article.rb file.

Listing 5-1. Custom long_title Method, in app/models/article.rb: http://gist.github.com/323787

```
class Article< ActiveRecord::Base
  validates :title, :presence => true
  validates :body, :presence => true

  def long_title
    "#{title} - #{published_at}"
  end
end
```

You've just created an instance method on the model; that is, you've told the Article model that it's now endowed with a new attribute called long_title. You can address long_title in the same way as you would any other method on the class. Open an irb session and try this on the console. From the terminal window, make sure you're inside the blog application directory, then start up the Rails console with the following command:

```
$ rails console
```

This should drop you at a simple irb prompt with two right arrows and a blinking cursor; this may look a bit different based on your environment. From here, you create a new article and use it to call the long_title method:

```
>> Article.create :title => 'Advanced Active Record', :published_at => Date.today,
:body => 'Models need to relate to each other. In the real world, ...'
=> #<Article id: 6, title: "Advanced Active Record", …>
>> Article.last.long_title
=> "Advanced Active Record - 2010-05-02 04:00:00 UTC"
```

There is no difference between the methods Active Record creates and those you define. Here, instead of asking the model for one of the attributes garnered from the database column names, you define your *own* method called long_title, which does a bit more than the standard title method.

The methods you add to your models can be as simple as returning true or false or as complicated as doing major calculations and formatting on the object. The full power of Ruby is in your hands to do with as you please.

Don't worry if you don't feel comfortable adding your own methods to models just yet. The important part to note from this section is that Active Record models are regular Ruby classes that can be augmented, modified, played with, poked, and turned inside out with sufficient Ruby-fu. Knowing this is extremely helpful in being able to pull back the curtain and understand the advanced features of Active Record.

FAT MODELS

Some people may be made nervous by the long_title method you just created. They may see it as a violation of the MVC paradigm. They may ask, "Isn't formatting code supposed to be in the view?" In general, the answer is yes. However, it often helps to have models that act as intelligent objects. If you ask a model for some information about itself, it's natural to assume that it can give you a decent answer that doesn't require a large amount of work later on to figure out what it means. So, small formatted strings and basic data types that faithfully represent the data in the model are good things to have in your code.

An intelligent model like this is often called *fat*. Instead of performing model-related logic in other places (that is, in controllers or views), you keep it in the model, thus making it fat. This makes your models easier to work with and helps your code stay DRY.

A basic rule of thumb while trying to stay DRY is that if you find yourself copying and pasting a bit of code, it may be worth your time to take a moment and figure out if there is a better way to approach the problem. For instance, if you had kept the Article#long_title formatting outside the model, you might have needed to repeat the same basic string-formatting procedure every time you wanted a human-friendly representation of an article's title. Then again, creating that method is a waste of time if you're going to use it in only one place in the application and never again.

This is where programmer experience comes in. As you learn and mature in your Rails programming, you'll find it easier and easier to figure out where stuff is supposed to go. If you're always aiming for a goal of having the most maintainable and beautiful code you can possibly write, your projects will naturally become easier to maintain.

Next, you look at another common form of model enhancement: associations. Active Record's associations give you the ability to define in simple terms how models relate to and interact with each other.

Using Associations

It's a lowly application that has only one table. Most applications have many tables, and these tables typically need to relate to each other in one way or another. *Associations* are a common model enhancement that let you relate tables to each other.

Associations are natural constructs that you encounter all the time in the real world: articles have comments, stores have products, magazines have subscriptions, and so on. In a relational database system, you relate tables using a *foreign key reference* in one table to the *primary key* of another table.

■ **NOTE** The terms *relationship* and *association* can be used pretty much interchangeably. However, when this book refers to *associations*, it generally means the association on the Active Record side, as opposed to the actual foreign-key relationships at the database level.

Let's take the example of articles and comments. In a situation where a given article can have any number of comments attached to it, each comment *belongs to* a particular article. Figure 5-1 demonstrates the association from the database's point of view.

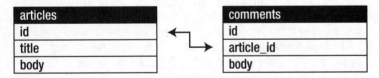

Figure 5-1. *The relationship between the* articles *and* comments *tables*

The example in Figure 5-1 uses a column named article_id in the comments table to identify the related article in the articles table. In database-speak, comments holds a *foreign-key reference* to articles.

By Rails convention, the foreign-key column is the singular, lowercase name of the target class with _id appended. So, for products that belong to a particular store, the foreign key is named store_id; for subscriptions that belong to magazines, the foreign key is named magazine_id; and so on. Here's the pattern:

```
#{singular_name_of_parent_class}_id
```

Table 5-1 shows a few more examples, just to drive this concept home.

Table 5-1. Sample Foreign-Key References

Model	Table	Foreign Key to Reference This Table
Article	articles	article_id
Person	people	person_id
Friend	friends	friend_id
Category	categories	category_id
Book	books	book_id

Whenever you need one table to reference another table, remember to create the foreign-key column in the table doing the referencing. That's all your table needs before you can put Active Record's associations to work.

Declaring Associations

As you've probably come to expect by now, Active Record makes working with associations easy. You don't need to get down to the bare metal of the database very often. As long as you understand the concept of primary and foreign keys and how to create basic relationships in your tables, Active Record does the proverbial heavy lifting, converting foreign-key relationships into rich object associations. This means you get to access associated objects cleanly and naturally using Ruby:

```
article.comments
store.products
magazine.subscriptions
```

After the relationships are defined in your database tables, you use a set of macro-like class methods in your models to create associations. They look like this:

- has_one

- has_many

- belongs_to

- has_and_belongs_to_many

Here's a quick example. The Message model declares a has_many relationship with Attachment; Attachment returns the favor by declaring that each of its objects belongs to a particular Message:

```
class Message < ActiveRecord::Base
  has_many :attachments
end

class Attachment < ActiveRecord::Base
```

```
    belongs_to :message
end
```

Given these instructions, Active Record expects to find a table called attachments that has a field in it called message_id (the foreign-key reference). It uses this association to let you say things like Message.first.attachments and get an array (or a *collection*) of Attachment objects that belong to the first Message in the database. Moreover, you can work with your associations in both directions. So, you can say Attachment.first.message to access the Message to which the first Attachment belongs. It sounds like a mouthful, but when you get the hang of it, it's quite intuitive.

Whenever you declare an association, Active Record automatically adds a set of methods to your model that make dealing with the association easier. This is a lot like the way in which Active Record creates methods based on your column names. When it notices that you've declared an association, it dynamically creates methods that enable you to work with that association. The following sections go through the different types of association and describe how to work with them. You also learn about the various options you can use to fine-tune associations.

Creating One-to-One Associations

One-to-one associations describe a pattern where *a row in one table is related to exactly one row in another table.*

Suppose that in your blog application, you have users and profiles, and each user has exactly one profile. Assume you have User and Profile models, and the corresponding users and profiles tables have the appropriate columns. You can tell your User model that it *has one* Profile and your Profile model that it *belongs to* a User. Active Record takes care of the rest. The has_one and belongs_to macros are designed to read like regular English, so they sound natural in conversation and are easy to remember. Each represents a different side of the equation, working in tandem to make the association complete.

■ **NOTE** Part of the Rails philosophy about development is that the gap between programmers and other project stakeholders should be bridged. Using natural language, such as *has one* and *belongs to*, in describing programmatic concepts helps bridge this gap, providing a construct that everyone can understand.

Adding the User and Profile Models

When you started the blog application, you decided to let anyone create new articles. This worked fine when only one person was using the system; but you want this to be a multiple-user application and let different people sign up, sign in, and start writing their own articles separately from one another.

Let's fire up the generator and create the User model:

```
$ rails generate model User email:string password:string
```

Just as you saw in the previous chapter, the model generator creates, among other things, a model file in app/models and a migration in db/migrate. Open db/migrate/20100306205458_create_users.rb, and you should see the now-familiar code in Listing 5-2.

Listing 5-2. Migration to Create the users Table, db/migrations/20100306205458_create_users.rb

```
class CreateUsers < ActiveRecord::Migration
  def self.up
    create_table :users do |t|
      t.string :email
      t.string :password

      t.timestamps
    end
  end

  def self.down
    drop_table :users
  end
end
```

This is standard migration fare. In the self.up definition, you use the create_table method to create a new users table. The new table object is *yielded* to the block in the variable, t, on which you call the string method to create each column. Along with the standard email field, you specify a password field, which you use for authentication, as explained in the "Reviewing the Updated Models" section later in this chapter. The primary key, id, is created automatically, so there's no need to specify it here.

As you probably noticed, the User model is extremely simple: it only contains information that allows the user to authenticate into the application. Some users may want to add a lot more detail about themselves and would love the ability to enter personal information such as birthday, bio, favorite color, Twitter account name, and so on. You can create a Profile model to hold such information outside the scope of the User model. Just as you did for the User model, use the generator again:

```
$ rails generate model Profile user_id:integer name:string birthday:date
bio:text color:string twitter:string
```

You also have a migration file for the Profile model in db/migrate/20100306210440_create_profiles.rb—feel free to take a peek. Notice the existence of the foreign key user_id in the profiles schema. Also recall that you don't need to specify primary keys in migrations because they're created automatically.

Now, all you need to do is run the migrations and create the new tables using the db:migrate Rake task. Run the migrations with the following command:

```
$ rake db:migrate
```

```
==  CreateUsers: migrating =====================================================

-- create_table(:users)

   -> 0.0019s

==  CreateUsers: migrated (0.0020s) ============================================
```

```
==  CreateProfiles: migrating ====================================================

-- create_table(:profiles)

   -> 0.0027s

==  CreateProfiles: migrated (0.0035s) ==========================================
```

With the table and foreign keys in place, Listings 5-3 and 5-4 show how to declare the one-to-one association on the User and Profile models.

Listing 5-3. The User Model, app/models/user.rb: http://gist.github.com/323944

```
class User < ActiveRecord::Base
  has_one :profile
end
```

Listing 5-4. The Profile Model, app/models/profile.rb: http://gist.github.com/323946

```
class Profile < ActiveRecord::Base
  belongs_to :user
end
```

The has_one declaration on the User model tells Active Record that it can expect to find one record in the profiles table that has a user_id matching the primary key of a row in the users table. The Profile model, in turn, declares that each of its records belongs_to a particular User.

Telling the Profile model that it belongs_to :user is saying, in effect, that each Profile object references a particular User. You can even go so far as to say that User is the parent and Profile is the child. The child model is dependent on the parent and therefore references it. Figure 5-2 demonstrates the has_one relationship.

has_one

User has_one :profile
Profile belongs_to :user

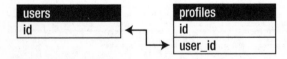

Figure 5-2. The one-to-one relationship between users and profiles

Let's get inside a console session (rails console) and see how this comes together. If you have a console session opened, run the reload! command in the console session to make sure it loads the newly generated models. Follow along to create objects and relate them to one another. First, create a user and a profile as follows:

```
>> reload!
Reloading...
>> user = User.create(:email => 'user@example.com', :password => 'secret')
=> #<User id: 1, email: "user@example.com", password: "secret",
 created_at: "2010-05-02 15:10:07", updated_at: "2010-05-02 15:10:07">
>> profile = Profile.create(:name => 'John Doe',
:bio => 'Ruby developer trying to learn Rails')
=> #<Profile id: 1, user_id: nil, name: "John Doe", birthday: nil,
bio: "Ruby developer trying to learn Rails", color: nil, twitter: nil,
created_at: "2010-05-02 15:10:55", updated_at: "2010-05-02 15:10:55">
```

▪ **NOTE** The `reload!` method reloads the Rails application environment within your console session. You need to call it when you make changes to existing code. It's exactly as if you had restarted your console session—all the variables you may have instantiated are lost.

Although you've successfully created a new user and a new profile, you haven't yet associated them with each other. If you ask the user object for its profile, it responds with `nil`:

```
>> user.profile
=> nil
```

To make the association happen, you specify it like any regular assignment on the user object and then call save, like so:

```
>> user.profile = profile
=> #<Profile id: 1, user_id: 1, name: "John Doe", birthday: nil,
bio: "Ruby developer trying to learn Rails", color: nil, twitter: nil,
created_at: "2010-05-02 15:10:55", updated_at: "2010-05-02 15:10:55">
>> user.save
=> true
```

Assignment is assignment—whether it's a `name` attribute to which you're assigning the value Joe or an association method to which you're assigning an object. Also notice that the profile's user_id attribute is updated to the value of `user.id`: this is what bonds both objects together. Now, when you ask the user object for its profile, it happily responds with one:

```
>> user.profile
=> #<Profile id: 1, user_id: 1, name: "John Doe", birthday: nil,
bio: "Ruby developer trying to learn Rails", color: nil, twitter: nil,
created_at: "2010-05-02 15:10:55", updated_at: "2010-05-02 15:10:55">
```

That's all there is to it. Although this is pretty good, you can do a bit better. You can create and save the profile in one shot and have it perform the association automatically, like this:

```
>> user.create_profile :name => 'Jane Doe', :color => 'pink'
=> #<Profile id: 2, user_id: 1, name: "Jane Doe", birthday: nil,
bio: nil, color: "pink", twitter: nil, created_at: "2010-05-02 15:18:57",
```

```
updated_at: "2010-05-02 15:18:57">
```

Using the `create_profile` method to create a new profile initializes the `Profile` object, sets its foreign key to `user.id`, and saves it to the database; at the same time, it sets the previous profile object's—the one named "John Doe"—`user_id` field to nil. This works for any `has_one` association, no matter what it's named. Active Record automatically generates the `create_#{association_name}` method for you. So, if you had a `Employee` model set up with an association like `has_one :address`, you would get the `create_address` method automatically.

These alternatives for doing the same thing may seem confusing, but they're really variations on the same theme. In all cases, you're creating two objects (the parent and the child) and telling them about one another. Whether you choose to do this in a multistep operation or all on one line is entirely up to you.

Earlier, you learned that declaring a `has_one` association causes Active Record to automatically add a suite of methods to make working with the association easier. Table 5-2 shows a summary of the methods that are added when you declare a `has_one` and `belongs_to` relationship between `User` and `Profile`, where `user` is a `User` instance.

Table 5-2. *Methods Added by the* `has_one` *Association in the User/Profile Example*

Method	Description
`user.profile`	Returns the associated (`Profile`) object; nil is returned if none is found
`user.profile=(profile)`	Assigns the associated (`Profile`) object, extracts the primary key, and sets it as the foreign key
`user.profile.nil?`	Returns true if there is no associated `Profile` object
`user.build_profile(attributes={})`	Returns a new `Profile` object that has been instantiated with attributes and linked to user through a foreign key but hasn't yet been saved
`user.create_profile(attributes={})`	Returns a new `Profile` object that has been instantiated with attributes and linked to user through a foreign key and that has already been saved

Although you're using the `User.has_one :profile` example here, the rules work for any object associated to another using `has_one`. Here are some examples, along with sample return values:

```
user.profile #=> #<Profile id: 2, user_id: 1, …>
user.profile.nil? #=> false
user.build_profile(:bio => 'eats leaves') #=> #<Profile id: nil, user_id: 1, …>
user.create_profile(:bio => 'eats leaves') #=> #<Profile id: 3, user_id: 1, …>
```

The `has_one` declaration can also include an options hash to specialize its behavior if necessary. Table 5-3 lists the most common options. For a complete list of all options, consult the Rails API

documentation
(http://api.rubyonrails.org/classes/ActiveRecord/Associations/ClassMethods.html#M001834).

Table 5-3. Common has_one Options

Option	Description	Example
:class_name	Specifies the class name of the association. Used when the class name can't be inferred from the association name.	has_one :profile, :class_name => 'Account'
:conditions	Specifies the conditions that the associated object must meet in order to be included as a WHERE SQL fragment.	has_one :profile, :conditions => "active = 1"
:foreign_key	Specifies the foreign key used for the association in the event that it doesn't adhere to convention of being the lowercase, singular name of the target class with _id appended.	has_one :profile, :foreign_key => 'account_id'
:order	Specifies the order in which the associated object is picked as an ORDER BY SQL fragment.	has_one :profile, :order => "created_at DESC"
:dependent	Specifies that the associated object should be removed when this object is. If set to :destroy, the associated object is deleted using the destroy method. If set to :delete, the associated object is deleted without calling its destroy method. If set to :nullify, the associated object's foreign key is set to NULL.	has_one :profile, :dependent => :destroy

Creating One-to-Many Associations

One-to-many associations describe a pattern where *a row in one table is related to one or more rows in another table*. Examples are an Email that has many Recipients, or a Magazine that has many Subscriptions.

Up until now, your articles have been orphaned—they don't belong to anyone. You remedy that now by associating users with articles. In your system, each article belongs to a user, and a user may have many articles. Figure 5-3 illustrates this association.

has_many

User has_many :articles
Article belongs_to :user

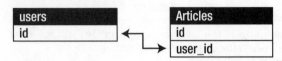

Figure 5-3. The one-to-many relationship between users and articles

Associating User and Article Models

Just as you associated users and profiles, you want to have a similar relationship between users and articles. You need to add a foreign key user_id in the articles table that points to a record in the users table.

Fire up the migration generator:

```
$ rails generate migration add_user_id_to_articles user_id:integer
```

Open db/migrate/20100306221123_add_user_id_to_articles.rb, and you should see the code in Listing 5-5.

Listing 5-5. Migration to Add user_id Field, db/migrate/20100306221123_add_user_id_to_articles.rb

```ruby
class AddUserIdToArticles < ActiveRecord::Migration
  def self.up
    add_column :articles, :user_id, :integer
  end

  def self.down
    remove_column :articles, :user_id
  end
end
```

Pay attention to the user_id column in the self.up section. It's the foreign-key reference column you've heard so much about. Also note that its type is :integer. That's important, because it's referring to a numeric id.

Now, all you need to do is run the migration using the db:migrate Rake task. Run the migration with the following command:

```
$ rake db:migrate
```

```
==  AddUserIdToArticles: migrating ==============================================

--  add_column(:articles, :user_id, :integer)

   -> 0.0012s

==  AddUserIdToArticles: migrated (0.0015s) =====================================
```

With the foreign key in place, Listings 5-6 and 5-7 show how you declare the one-to-many association in your Article and User models. Add these to the relevant models.

Listing 5-6. belongs_to Declaration in app/models/article.rb: http://gist.github.com/323981

```
class Article < ActiveRecord::Base
  validates :title, :presence => true
  validates :body, :presence => true

  belongs_to :user

  def long_title
    "#{title} - #{published_at}"
  end
end
```

Listing 5-7. has_many Declaration in app/models/user.rb: http://gist.github.com/323982

```
class User < ActiveRecord::Base
  has_one :profile
  has_many :articles
end
```

That's all there is to it. This bit of code has endowed your Article and User models with a lot of functionality.

■ **NOTE** For has_one and has_many associations, adding a belongs_to on the other side of the association is always recommended. The rule of thumb is that the belongs_to declaration always goes in the class with the foreign key.

Creating a New Associated Object

Your associations are in place; so, let's get back into the code to put what you've learned to the test. Do this exercise on the console: either run `rails console` to start a new console session, or type `reload!` if you still have a console window open from the previous section.

Let's test whether the association between users and articles is set up correctly. If it is, you should be able to ask the user object for its associated `articles`, and it should respond with a collection. Even though you haven't created any articles for this user yet, it should still work, returning an empty collection:

```
>> reload!
Reloading...
=> true
>> user = User.first
=> #<User id: 1, email: "user@example.com", password: "secret",
created_at: "2010-05-02 15:10:07", updated_at: "2010-05-02 15:10:07">
>> user.articles
=> []
```

Great! The has_many association is working correctly, and User instances now have an `articles` method, which was created automatically by Active Record when it noticed the has_many declaration.

Let's give this user some articles. Enter the following commands:

```
>> user.articles << Article.first
=> [#<Article id: 6, …, user_id: 1>]
>> user.articles.size
=> 1
>> user.articles
=> [#<Article id: 6, …, user_id: 1>]
```

By using the `<<` (append) operator, you attach `Article.first` onto your user object. When you use `<<` with associations, it automatically saves the new association. Some things in Active Record don't happen until you say save, but this is one of the examples where that part is done automatically.

What did that do exactly? Let's look into the article and find out:

```
>> Article.first.user_id
=> 1
```

See how this article's user_id points to the user with an id of 1? This means you've successfully related the two objects. You can even ask an `Article` instance for its user:

```
>> Article.first.user
=> #<User id: 1, email: "user@example.com", password: "secret",
created_at: "2010-05-02 15:10:07", updated_at: "2010-05-02 15:10:07">
```

Voilà! Your models can really start to express things now. The has_many and belongs_to declarations create more methods, as you did earlier with the `long_title` method. Let's look at what else these happy little helpers brought along to the party. Table 5-4 shows a summary of the methods that are added when you declare a has_many and belongs_to relationship between User and Article. (user represents a User instance.)

Table 5-4. Methods Added by the has_many Association in the User and Article Models

Method	Description
`user.articles`	Returns an array of all the associated articles. An empty array is returned if no articles are found.
`user.articles=(articles)`	Replaces the `articles` collection with the one supplied.
`user.articles << article`	Adds one or more articles to the collection, and saves their foreign keys.
`user.articles.delete(articles)`	Removes one or more articles from the collection by setting their foreign keys to `NULL`.
`user.articles.empty?`	Returns true if there are no associated `Article` objects for this user.
`user.articles.size`	Returns the number of associated `Article` objects for this user.
`user.article_ids`	Returns an array of associated article ids.
`user.articles.clear`	Clears all associated objects from the association by setting their foreign keys to `NULL`.
`user.articles.find`	Performs a `find` that is automatically scoped off the association; that is, it finds only within items that belong to `user`.
`user.articles.build(attributes={})`	Returns a new `Article` object that has been instantiated with attributes and linked to user through a foreign key but hasn't yet been saved. Here's an example: `user.articles.build(:title => 'Ruby 1.9')`.
`user.articles.create(attributes={})`	Returns a new `Article` object that has been instantiated with attributes and linked to user through a foreign key and has already been saved. Here's an example: `user.articles.create(:title => 'Hoedown')`.

You're using the `User.has_many :articles` example here, but the rules work for any object associated with another using `has_many`. Here are some examples, along with sample return values:

```
>> user.articles
=> [#<Article id: 6, …>]
>> user.articles << Article.new(:title => 'One-to-many associations',
:body => 'One-to-many associations describe a pattern ..')
=> [#<Article id: 6, …>, #<Article id: 7, …>]
>> user.article_ids
=> [6, 7]
>> user.articles.first
=> #<Article id: 6, …>
>> user.articles.clear
=> []
>> user.articles.count
 => 0
>> Article.count
 => 2
>> user.articles.create :title => 'Associations',
:body => 'Active Record makes working with associations easy..'
=> #<Article id: 8, …>
```

You can also pass in options to your association declaration to affect the way you work with those associations. Table 5-5 lists some of the most common options.

Table 5-5. Common has_many Options

Option	Description	Example
:class_name	Specifies the class name of the association. Used when the class name can't be inferred from the association name.	has_many :articles, :class_name => 'Post'
:conditions	Specifies the conditions that the associated objects must meet in order to be included as a WHERE SQL fragment.	has_many :articles, :conditions => "active = 1"
:foreign_key	Specifies the foreign key used for the association in the event that it doesn't adhere to convention of being the lowercase, singular name of target class with _id appended.	has_many :articles, :foreign_key => 'post_id'
:order	Specifies the order in which the associated objects are returned as an ORDER BY SQL fragment.	has_many :articles, :order => "published_at DESC"
:dependent	Specifies that the associated objects should be removed when this object is. If set to :destroy, the associated objects are deleted using the destroy method. If set to :delete, the associated objects are deleted without calling their destroy method. If set to :nullify, the associated objects' foreign keys are set to NULL.	has_many :articles, :dependent => :destroy

There's much more to has_many associations than can possibly be covered here, so be sure to check out the Rails API documentation (http://api.rubyonrails.org/classes/ActiveRecord/Associations/ClassMethods.html#M001833) for the full scoop.

Applying Association Options

It's time to apply what you've learned to your domain model. Specifically, you use the :order option to apply a default order to the User.has_many :articles declaration, and you use the :dependent option to make sure when you delete a user, all their articles are deleted as well.

Specifying a Default Order

When you access a user's articles, you want to make sure they come back in the *order* in which they've been published. Specifically, you want the oldest to be at the bottom of the list and the furthest in the future to be at the top. You can do this by configuring the has_many association with a default order using the :order option. Add the :order option to the has_many :articles declaration, as shown in Listing 5-8.

Listing 5-8. :order Option Added to has_many: http://gist.github.com/324010

```
class User < ActiveRecord::Base
  has_one :profile
  has_many :articles, :order => 'published_at DESC'
end
```

You give the name of the field that you want to order by, and then you say either ASC (ascending) or DESC (descending) to indicate the order in which the results should be returned. Because time moves forward (to bigger numbers), you want to make sure you're going back in time, so you use the DESC keyword here.

■ **NOTE** ASC and DESC are SQL keywords. You're actually specifying a *SQL fragment* here, as discussed in the "Advanced Finding" section later in this chapter.

You can also specify a secondary order by adding a comma between arguments. Let's say you wanted to sort by the title of the article *after* you sort by the date. If two articles have been published on the same day, they are ordered first by the date and then by the lexical order of the title. Listing 5-9 shows the article title added to the :order option.

Listing 5-9. Adding the Title to the :order Option for has_many: http://gist.github.com/324019

```
class User < ActiveRecord::Base
  has_one :profile
  has_many :articles, :order => 'published_at DESC, title ASC'
end
```

Notice that you use ASC for ordering on the title. This is because as letters go up in the alphabet, their value goes up. So, to sort alphabetically, use the ASC keyword.

Specifying Dependencies

Frequently, dependencies exist between models. For instance, in your blog application, if you delete users, you want to make sure they don't have articles in the system. Said another way, an Article is dependent on its User. You can let Active Record take care of this for you automatically by specifying the :dependent option to your association. Listing 5-10 shows all the options to has_many :articles, including the :dependent option.

Listing 5-10. :dependent Option Added to has_many: http://gist.github.com/324020

```
class User < ActiveRecord::Base
  has_one :profile
  has_many :articles, :order => 'published_at DESC, title ASC',
                      :dependent => :destroy
end
```

By passing in the symbol :destroy, you say not only that articles are dependent, but also that when the owner is deleted, you want to call the destroy method on every related article. This ensures that any *_destroy callbacks on the article instances are called (the chapter talks about callbacks later, in the "Making Callbacks" section). If you want to skip the callbacks, you can use the :delete option in place of :destroy, which deletes the records directly via SQL.

Let's say you want to set the foreign-key column (user_id) to NULL in the articles table, instead of completely destroying the article. Doing so essentially orphans the articles. You can do this by using the :nullify option in place of :destroy. If you don't use the :dependent option, and you delete a user with associated articles, you break foreign-key references in your articles table. For this application, you want to keep the as :nullify option, as per Listing 5-11.

Listing 5-11. :dependent Option Set to :nullify: http://gist.github.com/324023

```
class User < ActiveRecord::Base
  has_one :profile
  has_many :articles, :order => 'published_at DESC, title ASC',
                      :dependent => :nullify
end
```

Creating Many-to-Many Associations

Sometimes, the relationship between two models is many-to-many. This describes a pattern where *two tables are connected to multiple rows on both sides*. You use this in the blog application to add categories to articles. If you wanted to allow only one category to be selected for a given article, you could use has_many. But you want to be able to apply multiple categories.

Think about this for a minute: an article can have many categories, and a category can have many articles—where does the belongs_to go in this situation? Neither model belongs to the other in the traditional sense. In Active Record–speak, this kind of association is has_and_belongs_to_many (often referred to as habtm for short).

The `has_and_belongs_to_many` association works by relying on a join table that keeps a reference to the foreign keys involved in the relationship. The join table sits between the tables you want to join: articles and categories. Not surprisingly, then, the join table in this case is called `articles_categories`. Pay particular attention to the table name. It's formed from the names of each table in alphabetical order, separated by an underscore. In this case, the a in articles comes before the c in categories—hence, `articles_categories`. Figure 5-4 illustrates this relationship.

has_and_belongs_to_many

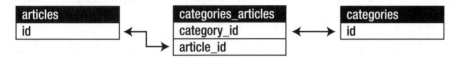

Category has_and_belongs_to_many :articles
Article has_and_belongs_to_many :categories

Figure 5-4. *The many-to-many relationship between articles and categories*

Let's start by adding the `Category` model. This is a simple matter of generating the model, consisting of just a `name` column. Run the following command inside your application root:

```
$ rails generate model Category name:string
```

Look at the generated migration in db/migrate/20100307001138_create_categories.rb; it's pretty familiar territory at this point. You need another migration to create the join table. Do that now by running the following command:

```
$ rails generate migration create_articles_categories
```

Remember that when you use `create_table` inside a migration, you don't need to specify the primary key, because it's created automatically. Well, in the case of a join table, you don't want a primary key. This is because the join table isn't a first-class entity in its own right. Creating tables without primary keys is the exception and not the rule, so you need to explicitly tell `create_table` that you don't want to create an id. Take a close look at the call to `create_table` in Listing 5-12. You pass in option `:id => false`, which prevents `create_table` from creating the primary key; also, you add the appropriate fields.

Listing 5-12. The db/migrate/20100307002156_create_articles_categories.rb File:

http://gist.github.com/324042

```
class CreateArticlesCategories < ActiveRecord::Migration
  def self.up
    create_table :articles_categories, :id => false do |t|
      t.references :article
      t.references :category
    end
  end
end
```

```
  def self.down
    drop_table :articles_categories
  end
end
```

You use the references method in the create_table block instead of using integer. It's just another notation that uses the association name as parameter instead of a field name; so, t.references :article is the same as t.integer :article_id. Feel free to pick the syntax you prefer. Go ahead and run the migrations:

```
$ rake db:migrate
```

```
==  CreateCategories: migrating ================================================

-- create_table(:categories)

   -> 0.0032s

==  CreateCategories: migrated (0.0034s) =======================================



==  CreateArticlesCategories: migrating ========================================

-- create_table(:articles_categories, {:id=>false})

   -> 0.0011s

==  CreateArticlesCategories: migrated (0.0013s) ===============================
```

With the Category model and the join table in place, you're ready to let Active Record in on your association. Open the Article and Category models, and add the has_and_belongs_to_many declarations to them, as shown in Listings 5-13 and 5-14.

Listing 5-13. has_and_belongs_to_many Declaration in app/models/article.rb:

http://gist.github.com/324055

```
class Article < ActiveRecord::Base
  validates :title, :presence => true
  validates :body, :presence => true

  belongs_to :user
  has_and_belongs_to_many :categories

  def long_title
    "#{title} - #{published_at}"
  end
end
```

Listing 5-14. has_and_belongs_to_many Declaration in app/models/category.rb:

http://gist.github.com/324057

```
class Category < ActiveRecord::Base
  has_and_belongs_to_many :articles
end
```

Seeding Data

As part of creating an application skeleton, Rails added a file called db/seeds.rb, which defines some data you always need in your database. The seeds file contains Ruby code, so you can use the classes and methods—including associations—available in your models, such as create and update. Open it and create one user and a few categories so that it looks like Listing 5-15.

Listing 5-15. The db/seeds.rb File: http://gist.github.com/324072

```
user = User.create :email => 'mary@example.com', :password => 'guessit'
Category.create [{:name => 'Programming'},
                 {:name => 'Event'},
                 {:name => 'Travel'},
                 {:name => 'Music'},
                 {:name => 'TV'}]
```

That should do nicely. You can load your seed data using the Rake task db:seed:

```
$ rake db:seed
```

If you need to add more default categories later, you can append them to the seed file and reload it. If you want to rerun the seed data, the trick is that the seeds file doesn't know whether the records already in the database have to be cleaned up; running rake db:seed again adds all records one more time, and you end up with duplicate user and categories. You should instead call rake db:setup, which re-creates the database and adds the seed data as you may expect.

You can also use fixtures to perform this same task of loading sample data for your application. Fixtures are a textual representation of database records, used for testing. Chapter 10 talks more about fixtures.

Let's give this a test run. Get your console ready, reload!, and run the following commands:

```
>> article = Article.last
=> #<Article id: 8, title: "Associations", …>
>> category = Category.find_by_name('Programming')
=> #<Category id: 1, name: "Programming", ..>
>> article.categories << category
=> [#<Category id: 1, name: "Programming", ..>]
>> article.categories.any?
=> true
>> article.categories.size
=> 1
```

Here, you automatically associate a category with an article using the << operator. You can even do this from the category's side of the association. Try the following:

```
>> category.articles.empty?
=> false
>> category.articles.size
=> 1
>> category.articles.first.title
=> "Associations"
```

You just did the opposite of the previous test. has_and_belongs_to_many works in both directions, right? So, you found your category and asked it for its first article titled "Associations", because that's what you associated in the other direction, too.

Using has_and_belongs_to_many is a very simple way to approach many-to-many associations. However, it has its limitations. Before you're tempted to use it for more than associating categories with articles, note that it has no way of storing additional information on the join. What if you want to know *when* or *why* someone assigns a category to an article? This kind of data fits naturally in the *join table*. Rails includes another type of association called has_many :through, which allows you to create rich joins like this.

Creating Rich Many-to-Many Associations

Sometimes, when you're modeling a many-to-many association, you need to put additional data on the join model. But because Active Record's has_and_belongs_to_many uses a join table (for which there is no associated model), there's no model on which to operate. For this type of situation, you can create *rich* many-to-many associations using has_many :through. This is really a combination of techniques that end up performing a similar but more robust version of has_and_belongs_to_many.

The basic idea is that you build or use a full model to represent the join table. Think about the blog application: articles need to have comments, so you create a Comment model and associate it with Article in a one-to-many relationship using has_many and belongs_to. You also want to be able to retrieve all the comments added to users' articles. You could say that users have many comments that belong to their articles, or users have many comments through articles. Figure 5-5 illustrates this relationship.

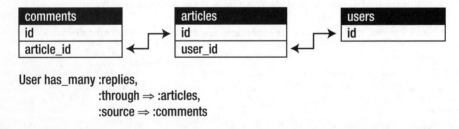

User has_many :replies,
            :through ⇒ :articles,
            :source ⇒ :comments

Figure 5-5. The rich many-to-many relationship between comments and users, through articles

Let's generate the model and migration for the Comment model:

```
$ rails generate model comment article_id:integer name:string email:string body:text
```

```
      invoke    active_record

      create    db/migrate/20100308213941_create_comments.rb

      create    app/models/comment.rb

      invoke    test_unit

      create    test/unit/comment_test.rb

      create    test/fixtures/comments.yml
```

Migrate by issuing the rake db:migrate command:

```
$ rake db:migrate
```

```
==  CreateComments: migrating ==================================================

-- create_table(:comments)

   -> 0.0016s

==  CreateComments: migrated (0.0017s) =========================================
```

Update your models to reflect the one-to-many association between comments and articles. Listings 5-16 and 5-17 show the updated Comment and Article models.

Listing 5-16. The Comment model in app/models/comment.rb: http://gist.github.com/325793

```
class Comment < ActiveRecord::Base
  belongs_to :article
end
```

Listing 5-17. The Article Model in app/models/article.rb: http://gist.github.com/325796

```
class Article < ActiveRecord::Base
  validates :title, :presence => true
  validates :body, :presence => true

  belongs_to :user
  has_and_belongs_to_many :categories
```

```
  has_many :comments

  def long_title
    "#{title} - #{published_at}"
  end
end
```

Nothing is new here—what you implement is very similar to the users and articles relationship you saw earlier, but instead of a user having many articles, an article has many comments.

Let's get back to the relationship between users and comments. You need to tell your user model that a user has many comments through its articles. Basically, you use the article model as a join table between users and comments. You achieve the linking using the has_many :through method. Listing 5-18 shows the updated User model.

Listing 5-18. The has_many :through Declarations in app/models/user.rb:

http://gist.github.com/325809

```
class User < ActiveRecord::Base
  has_one :profile
  has_many :articles, :order => 'published_at DESC, title ASC',
                      :dependent => :nullify
  has_many :replies, :through => :articles, :source => :comments
end
```

Notice that you rework how you name associations. One aspect of the Rails philosophy is that you should always be questioning and refactoring your code to work with best practices. In this incarnation, comments that users receive on their articles are called replies.

As an added benefit, has_many :through allows you to easily have nice names for your associations. The :source option lets you define the source name of the association. In this case, the replies are the articles' comments, so you set the :source option accordingly.

Let's play with this on the console to see how it works—don't forget to reload!. You first find the first user, find their first article, and create a comment on it. Then, you see that comment directly from the user object:

```
>> user = User.first
=> #<User id: 1, email: "user@example.com", …>
>> user.replies.empty?
=> true
>> article = user.articles.first
=> #<Article id: 8, title: "Associations", …, user_id: 1>
>> article.comments.create(:name => 'Guest',
:email => 'guest@example.com', :body => 'Great article!')
=> #<Comment id: 1, article_id: 8, name: "Guest", …>
>> user.replies
=> [#<Comment id: 1, article_id: 8, name: "Guest", …>]
>> user.replies.size
=> 1
```

Advanced Finding

Chapter 4 covered using the find class method in Active Record. This section expands on different find operations using the where method. Building advanced finder methods is one of the most important things you do with your models.

Using the where Method

The most basic condition style is the hash syntax. Active Record takes the Hash passed to the where method and turns the keys into column names and the values into parameters to match. The hash syntax is useful only if you're trying to find an exact match. Run the following command in a console window to try out the hash syntax:

```
>> Article.where(:title => 'Advanced Active Record')
=> [#<Article id: 6, title: "Advanced Active Record", …>]
```

The hash syntax works well for straightforward where operations where you use only ANDs to join together the conditions (that is, all conditions must match). However, sometimes you need more flexibility than exact matches.

Using a SQL Fragment

To specify conditions, you can pass in a SQL fragment as a string that is sent directly to the query. You need to have a pretty decent knowledge of SQL to use this kind of syntax; but it provides a lot of flexibility, and you can create arbitrarily complex SQL fragments if you're a SQL ninja.

Try the same find operation as in the previous section, but using a pure SQL condition fragment:

```
>> Article.where("title = 'Advanced Active Record'")
=> [#<Article id: 6, title: "Advanced Active Record", …>]
```

Let's try something more complicated that only SQL is able to do:

```
>> Article.where("created_at > '23-03-2010' OR body NOT LIKE '%model%'")
=> [#<Article id: 7, title: "One-to-many associations", …>,
#<Article id: 8, title: "Associations", …>]
```

Instead of using the = sign, you use the greater-than (>) symbol to make sure the date occurs after March 23, 2010. This is followed by the SQL OR operator, which says "if this first part isn't a match, then try the right-hand side and give it a second chance at matching." Therefore, you check the right-hand side only if the left-hand side fails. If an item fails the created_at match, you check to see if the body is NOT LIKE code. You can think of OR as a more permissive joining operator. It only cares that one of the conditions is a match. OR has a sister named AND, which requires that both conditions are true:

```
>> Article.where("created_at > '23-03-2010' AND body NOT LIKE '%model%'")
=> []
```

You also use the SQL LIKE (modified using NOT, for negation) operator, which allows you to make partial matches. Normally, when using =, SQL requires that the string match *perfectly*. However, LIKE is more permissive and allows partial matches when used with the % wildcard. The % symbols are SQL wildcard characters that apply in LIKE clauses. A % at the beginning of a pattern says that the pattern must match at the end of the field (the beginning can be any sequence of characters); a % at the end means that the pattern must match at the beginning, where the end can be any sequence of characters. Using a % on both sides of the pattern means that it must match anywhere in the field. Using %model% means that the word *model* must occur somewhere (anywhere) in the body of the article. In the previous example, you don't want articles that have the word *model*; therefore, an article with the sentence "I don't have your match" is accepted as a match.

As you can see, this usage has all the flexibility of SQL, but it also has SQL's natural limitations. For instance, you may need to find information based on what the user passes into the application via the request parameters in your application (the next chapter covers request parameters). If you aren't careful, that data can be very dangerous to your application, because it's open to SQL injection attacks. In such an attack, a user submits malicious code that tricks your database server into doing far more than you intended. For more information about SQL injection, check out the Wikipedia article at http://en.wikipedia.org/wiki/SQL_injection. Fortunately, Rails gives you a way to avoid such threats—using the array condition syntax, which performs correctly quoted replacements.

Using an Array Condition Syntax

The array condition syntax gives you the ability to specify conditions on your database calls in a safer way than using SQL syntax. Also, you don't need to worry so much about SQL specifics like quoting and other concerns, because it does automatic conversions for you on the inputs you give it. This is how it protects against SQL injection—it ensures that the substituted values are safely quoted, thereby preventing malicious users from injecting arbitrary SQL into your queries.

The following example requires the use of a nice little Ruby method called Time.now. Basically, it returns a Time object that is set to the current time. Let's see if you can find all the articles that were published before today:

```
>> Article.where("published_at < ?", Time.now)
=> [#<Article id: 6, title: "Advanced Active Record", …>]
```

It doesn't look like much was published before today. Instead of writing in the date, you put a ? in the spot where you'd normally write the value you want to find. The where method takes the second element in the array, Time.now, and replaces it where the first ? appears. Additionally, the array syntax automatically takes your time and converts it into something that your database likes. You can invoke the to_sql method after the where method to inspect the issued SQL statement:

```
>> Article.where("published_at < ?", Time.now).to_sql
=> "SELECT      \"articles\".* FROM          \"articles\"
WHERE     (published_at < '2010-05-02 16:27:51.059277')"
```

You give it a Time object, and it turns the object into the format that pleases your database. If you had passed it a string, it wouldn't have converted. You can even pass some information from another model:

```
>> Article.where("created_at = ?", Article.last.created_at)
   ⇨   [#<Article id: 8, title: "Associations", …>]
```

That condition returns all the articles created at the same moment as the last article. You can pass as many conditions as you want, as long as they occur in the same order as the question marks:

```
>> Article.where("created_at = ? OR body LIKE ?", Article.last.created_at, 'model')
=> [#<Article id: 8, title: "Associations", …>]
```

MONITORING THE LOGS

You can see the SQL statements issued by your application in the file `log/development.log`. It's often useful to monitor what the server is doing. You may have already noticed that when you run `rails server`, it tells you about what is going on in your application. However, different web servers (depending on what you've installed) give different outputs, some more descriptive than others.

Fortunately, Rails prints all of its activities to a log file. If you look in your `log` directory, you see `log/development.log`. This is the file where all the activities of your application are output. If you're running in production mode, the log file is `log/production.log`.

This file is written to live by your server. Sometimes it's useful (especially on a live server) to monitor the events occurring on your server. If you're on a UNIX system, you can run the command `tail -f log/development.log` to get a live feed from your logs. If you're on a Windows system, you can find several applications that behave like `tail` with a quick Google search.

During debugging, it can be useful to output messages to the log to see what's going on with your application. Almost anywhere in your application, you can do this:

```
logger.debug "This will only show in development"
logger.warn "This will show in all environments"
```

Both of these messages print directly to the `log` file and can be extremely useful for figuring out what is happening with your server.

The main disadvantage with the array syntax is that it can become confusing to remember the order of the elements you're passing in for the conditions.

Instead of adding a list of things at the end of the array, you can pass in a hash and change the question marks to actual named replacements. This can help you keep the order of your arguments straight:

```
>> Article.where("title LIKE :search OR body LIKE :search",
{:search => '%association%'})
=> [#<Article id: 7, title: "One-to-many associations", …>,
#<Article id: 8, title: "Associations", …>]
```

As you can see, you can reuse the same term multiple places in your condition. If you were using the regular array syntax, you'd have to pass the same value '%association%' twice. This is especially useful if you have many, manyconditions.

Using Association Proxies

Association proxy is a fancy term for the ability to chain together multiple calls to Active Record. You've been using this technique throughout the book, but it hasn't received special mention. Here is a basic example of association proxies:

```
>> User.first.articles.all
=> [#<Article id: 8, title: "Associations", …>]
```

This code returns all the articles of the first user. The `all` method (off `articles`) is automatically scoped to the user, which is to say it finds articles that belong to that user. If you remember, `articles` is a `has_many` relationship on the `User` model. The cool part is that this isn't two queries to the database. It does all this in one request to the database.

Scoped finders are also more secure. Imagine a multiple-user system where data owned by one user shouldn't be accessible by another user. Finding an associated object (say, an article) by its `id` doesn't restrict it to articles owned by a particular user. You could pass in the `article_id` and the `user_id` as conditions, but that's sloppy and error-prone. The correct way to do this is to scope all find operations off the user in question. For example, assuming you have a `User` object stored in the variable `current_user`, `current_user.articles.find(1)` ensures that the article with `id` 1 is returned only if it belongs to the `current_user`.

Anyone who has done database work will realize that this incredibly simple syntax is far easier than the SQL queries that need to be created to achieve similar results. If you play around with these chains, you can check out the log to see the SQL that's generated—be happy that you didn't have to write it yourself!

This technique doesn't just apply to finding. You can use it to automatically assign ownership with `build` and `create` constructors by setting the appropriate foreign keys. Consider the following example, which creates a new article for the `current_user`. It automatically sets the article's `user_id` to that of the current user:

```
current_user.articles.create(:title => 'Private', :body => 'Body here..')
```

This is much better than the alternative, which is to go through the `Article` model directly and set the user_id as an attribute (`Article.create(:user_id => current_user.id)`. As a rule, whenever you need to restrict find operations to an owner, or if you're assigning ownership, you should use the power of the association proxy.

Other Finder Methods

Active Record ships with other finder methods that complements the `where` method and can be used on their own as well. Table 5-6 lists some of those methods with a brief description and a quick example.

Table 5-6. *Some Active Record Finder Methods*

Method	Description	Example
where(conditions)	Specifies the conditions in which the records are returned as a WHERE SQL fragment	Article.where("title = 'Advanced Active Record'")
order	Specifies the order in which the records are returned as an ORDER BY SQL fragment	Article.order("published_at DESC")
limit	Specifies the number of records to be returned as a LIMIT SQL fragment	Article.limit(1)
joins	Specifies associated tables to be joined in as a JOIN SQL fragment	Article.joins(:comments)
includes	Specifies associated tables to be joined and loaded as Active Record objects in a JOIN SQL fragment	Article.includes(:comments)

You've used the where method before. Let's take the rest for a spin:

```
>> Article.all
=> [#<Article id: 6, title: "Advanced Active Record", …>,
#<Article id: 7, title: "One-to-many associations", …>,
#<Article id: 8, title: "Associations", …>]
>> Article.order("title ASC")
=> [#<Article id: 6, title: "Advanced Active Record", …>,
#<Article id: 8, title: "Associations", …>,
#<Article id: 7, title: "One-to-many associations", …>]
>> Article.limit(1)
=> [#<Article id: 6, title: "Advanced Active Record", …>]
>> Article.order("title DESC").limit(2)
=> [#<Article id: 7, title: "One-to-many associations", …>,
#<Article id: 8, title: "Associations", …>]
```

You first retrieve a list of articles with all; then, you retrieve all articles ordered alphabetically by their title using the order method. After that, you retrieve a single article using the limit method. Finally, you chain the limit method to order to retrieve a couple of articles after sorting them. All methods listed in Table 5-6 are chainable; when you chain finder methods to each other, Rails combine their specifics to form a single query to the database.

Default Scope

As you write applications, you may notice that you repeat certain conditions many times throughout your code. For the blog application, it would make sense to display categories in alphabetical order, as the user would expect. Rails provides a technique called *scope* to encapsulate commonly used find operations. Rails doesn't enforce a default order; it lets the database take care of sorting the results, which in most cases is done on the primary key id. Let's look at how your Category records are returned now:

```
>> Category.all
=> [#<Category id: 1, name: "Programming", …>, #<Category id: 2, name: "Event", …>,
#<Category id: 3, name: "Travel", …>, #<Category id: 4, name: "Music", ..>,
#<Category id: 5, name: "TV", …>]
```

As you can see, categories are returned according to their primary key id. Let's make sure categories are always listed alphabetically, regardless of the conditions you use for the query. The code in Listing 5-19 tells the Category class that you always want records to be ordered by the name field.

Listing 5-19. default_scope Declaration in app/models/category.rb: http://gist.github.com/325932

```
class Category < ActiveRecord::Base
  has_and_belongs_to_many :articles

  default_scope order('categories.name')
end
```

Notice that what you pass to the default_scope method is identical to the order method call in the previous section. As you may expect, you can pass any finder method to default_scope. Let's see the order in which your categories are retrieved now:

```
>> reload!
Reloading...
>> Category.all
=> [#<Category id: 2, name: "Event", …>, #<Category id: 4, name: "Music", …>,
#<Category id: 1, name: "Programming", …>, #<Category id: 5, name: "TV", …>,
#<Category id: 3, name: "Travel", …>]
```

As you can see, your categories are sorted alphabetically by default.

■ **NOTE** When specifying the order for the default scope, you use the fully qualified name categories.name instead of just name. Whenever you use associations to retrieve categories, Rails runs a SQL command to join categories with other tables, which may also have a name field; using the table name makes sure your database always knows the field you really want to sort by.

Named Scope

The default scope is useful. But in most cases, the only code you want to have there is default ordering for your application, because adding a condition to default_scope would make that condition be applied every time. For queries that you run often, you should create named scopes that make your code easier to read and maintain.

Let's create two named scopes: the first one lists all the articles with a published_at date and is named :published; the second scope lists all the articles without a published_at date and is named :draft. You create both scopes using the scope method, which takes the name of the scope as its first parameter and a finder method call as its second. Listing 5-20 shows the updated Article model.

Listing 5-20. Named Scopes Declarations in app/models/article.rb: http://gist.github.com/325944

```ruby
class Article < ActiveRecord::Base
  validates :title, :presence => true
  validates :body, :presence => true

  belongs_to :user
  has_and_belongs_to_many :categories
  has_many :comments

  scope :published, where("articles.published_at IS NOT NULL")
  scope :draft, where("articles.published_at IS NULL")

  def long_title
    "#{title} - #{published_at}"
  end
end
```

As in a regular where method, you can use arrays as parameters. In fact, you can chain finder methods with other named scopes. You define the recent scope to give you articles recently published: first you use the published named scope, and then you chain to it a where call (see Listing 5-21).

Listing 5-21. Recent Named Scope Declaration in app/models/article.rb:

http://gist.github.com/326095

```ruby
class Article < ActiveRecord::Base
  validates :title, :presence => true
  validates :body, :presence => true

  belongs_to :user
  has_and_belongs_to_many :categories
  has_many :comments

  scope :published, where("articles.published_at IS NOT NULL")
  scope :draft, where("articles.published_at IS NULL")
  scope :recent, lambda { published.where("articles.published_at > ?",
1.week.ago.to_date)}
```

```
  def long_title
    "#{title} - #{published_at}"
  end
end
```

■ **NOTE** `lambda` is a keyword in Ruby that defines a self-contained stand-alone method, which is executed only when you invoke it. You use `lambda` in the `recent` scope declaration to make sure the `1.week.ago.to_date` statement is executed only when you call the `recent` scope on your model.

To make scopes even more useful, you can define scopes that can receive parameters, instead of hard-coding the values you want to query with. You need search functionality that allows the end user to look up articles by title; so, let's add another scope called `where_title` that accepts an argument and searches by it (see Listing 5-22).

Listing 5-22. where_title Named Scope Declaration in app/models/article.rb:

http://gist.github.com/326098

```
class Article < ActiveRecord::Base
  validates :title, :presence => true
  validates :body, :presence => true

  belongs_to :user
  has_and_belongs_to_many :categories
  has_many :comments

  scope :published, where("articles.published_at IS NOT NULL")
  scope :draft, where("articles.published_at IS NULL")
  scope :recent, lambda { published.where("articles.published_at > ?",
1.week.ago.to_date)}
  scope :where_title, lambda { |term| where("articles.title LIKE ?", "%#{term}%") }

  def long_title
    "#{title} - #{published_at}"
  end
end
```

Now that you've added those scopes, let's see them in action in a console session. When you look at the results of running the methods, you get an English-like syntax that makes the code easy to read and expand. Pay special attention to the line that uses `Article.draft.where_title("one")`, which shows how you chain scopes to get the exact data you want:

```
>> reload!
Reloading...
>> Article.published
=> [#<Article id: 6, title: "Advanced Active Record", …>]
>> Article.draft
```

```
=> [#<Article id: 7, title: "One-to-many associations", …>,
#<Article id: 8, title: "Associations", …>]
>> Article.recent
=> [#<Article id: 6, title: "Advanced Active Record", …>]
>> Article.draft.where_title("one")
=> [#<Article id: 7, title: "One-to-many associations", …>]
>> Article.where_title("Active")
=> [#<Article id: 6, title: "Advanced Active Record", …>]
```

Applying Validations

It's probably a safe bet that you don't want every field in your tables to be optional. Certain fields need to be required, terms of service agreements need to be accepted, and passwords need to be confirmed. That's just the way it is when you're building web applications, and Rails understands this. Consider this example of an Account model:

```
class Account < ActiveRecord::Base
  validates :login, :presence => true
  validates :password,  :confirmation => true
  validates :terms_of_service, :acceptance => true
end
```

Like associations, validations are sets of high-level macros that let you selectively apply common validation requirements to your model's attributes. In this section, you create a full set of validations for your blog application, and you see first-hand how easy it is to perform basic validations with Active Record. You start by applying some of the built-in validations, and then you build a couple custom validation methods.

Using Built-in Validations

Rails has myriad built-in validators, all of which are accessible through the validates method. You learn about some of the options the validates method accepts as you apply them to your blog application. Check the API for details of all the Rails validators (http://api.rubyonrails.org/classes/ActiveModel/Validations/ClassMethods.html#M001995).

As a reference as you get started, you can pass two common options into any built-in validator. These are described in Table 5-7.

Table 5-7. *Default Options for All Validators*

Option	Description	Example
:message	Specifies the error message shown if validation fails.	:message => "too long"
:on	Specifies when this validation happens. The default is :save. Other options are :create and :update.	:on => :create

Validating That a Value Has Been Entered

You can use the :presence option to make sure a user has entered *something* into a field. This is very useful in many cases. You have those validations in the Article model for the title and body fields as shown in Listing 5-23.

Listing 5-23. validates :presence => true Method in app/models/article.rb

```ruby
class Article < ActiveRecord::Base
  validates :title, :presence => true
  validates :body, :presence => true

  belongs_to :user
  has_and_belongs_to_many :categories
  has_many :comments

  scope :published, where("articles.published_at IS NOT NULL")
  scope :draft, where("articles.published_at IS NULL")
  scope :recent, lambda { published.where(["articles.published_at > ?",
1.week.ago.to_date])}
  scope :where_title, lambda { |term| where("articles.title LIKE ?", "%#{term}%") }

  def long_title
    "#{title} - #{published_at}"
  end
end
```

The default message is "can't be blank."

Validating That a Value Is Unique

Often, you want to make sure a certain field is unique. The :uniqueness option validates whether the value of the specified attribute is unique across the system. You use this method in the User model to make sure each e-mail is unique, as shown in Listing 5-24.

Listing 5-24. validates :uniqueness => true Method in app/models/user.rb:

http://gist.github.com/326128

```ruby
class User < ActiveRecord::Base
  validates :email, :uniqueness => true

  has_one :profile
  has_many :articles, :order => 'published_at DESC, title ASC',
                      :dependent => :nullify
  has_many :replies, :through => :articles, :source => :comments
end
```

When the record is created, a check is performed to make sure no record exists in the database with the given value for the specified attribute email (that maps to a column). When the record is updated, the same check is made, but disregarding the record itself. The default error message is "#{*value*} has already been taken."

The :uniqueness option can also validate whether the value of the specified attributes are unique based on multiple scope parameters. For example, you can use it to make sure a teacher can be on the schedule only once per semester for a particular class:

```
class Schedule < ActiveRecord::Base
  validates :teacher_id, :uniqueness => { :scope => [:semester_id, :class_id] }
end
```

Validating Length or Size

Sometimes you want to validate the length, or size, of a field entry. You can do this by using the :length option. You use this method in the User model to specify a valid number of characters for an e-mail address, as shown in Listing 5-25. The option for specifying a size range is :within.

Listing 5-25. validates :length Method in app/models/user.rb: http://gist.github.com/326138

```
class User < ActiveRecord::Base
  validates :email, :uniqueness => true, :length => { :within => 5..50 }

  has_one :profile
  has_many :articles, :order => 'published_at DESC, title ASC',
                      :dependent => :nullify
  has_many :replies, :through => :articles, :source => :comments
end
```

If you want to ensure only the minimum or maximum, you can use the :minimum or :maximum option. Table 5-8 lists the most common :length option's options.

Table 5-8. Options for validates :length

Option	Description
:minimum	Specifies the minimum size of the attribute
:maximum	Specifies the maximum size of the attribute
:is	Specifies the exact size of the attribute
:within	Specifies the valid range (as a Ruby Range object) of values acceptable for the attribute
:allow_nil	Specifies that the attribute may be nil; if so, the validation is skipped
:too_long	Specifies the error message to add if the attribute exceeds the maximum

Option	Description
:too_short	Specifies the error message to add if the attribute is below the minimum
:wrong_length	Specifies the error message to add if the attribute is of the wrong size
:message	Specifies the error message to add if :minimum, :maximum, or :is is violated

Validating the Format of an Attribute

The :format option checks whether a value is in the correct format. Using this method requires familiarity with regular expressions (regex) or being able to steal other people's regular expressions. The classic example (and the one you need) is e-mail. Update the validates method as shown in Listing 5-26.

Listing 5-26. validates :format Method in app/models/user.rb: http://gist.github.com/326146

```
class User < ActiveRecord::Base
  validates :email, :uniqueness => true,
                    :length => { :within => 5..50 },
                    :format => { :with => /^[^@][\w.-]+@[\w.-]+[.][a-z]{2,4}$/i }

  has_one :profile
  has_many :articles, :order => 'published_at DESC, title ASC',
                      :dependent => :nullify
  has_many :replies, :through => :articles, :source => :comments
end
```

Don't be put off by how complicated this looks. You pass in the :with option and a regex object to say what patterns you want to match.

■ **TIP** If you want to learn more about using regular expressions, you can find many tutorials and books on the subject. One good reference is *Regular Expression Recipes* (Apress, 2004).

Validating Confirmation

Whenever a user changes an important piece of data (especially the password), you may want the user to confirm that entry by typing it again. This is the purpose of the :confirmation option. When you use this helper, you create a new virtual attribute called #{*field_name*}_confirmation. Add this to the User model for password confirmation, as shown in Listing 5-27.

Listing 5-27. validates :confirmation Method in app/models/user.rb: http://gist.github.com/326153

```
class User < ActiveRecord::Base
  validates :email, :uniqueness => true,
                    :length => { :within => 5..50 },
                    :format => { :with => /^[^@][\w.-]+@[\w.-]+[.][a-z]{2,4}$/i }
  validates :password, :confirmation => true

  has_one :profile
  has_many :articles, :order => 'published_at DESC, title ASC',
                      :dependent => :nullify
  has_many :replies, :through => :articles, :source => :comments
end
```

The password attribute is a column in the users table, but the password_confirmation attribute is virtual. It exists only as an in-memory variable for validating the password. This check is performed only if password_confirmation isn't nil and runs whenever the object is saved.

Other Validations

The validates method accepts some other options too; Table 5-9 summarizes the ones that haven't been covered.

Table 5-9. *Other Options for the validates Method*

Option	Description
:numericality	Validates that the field is a numeric value
:inclusion	Validates that the field value is inside the specified range
:exclusion	Validates that the field value is out of the specified range
:acceptance	Validates the acceptance of a boolean field

Building Custom Validation Methods

In the blog application, you'd like to make sure no one creates a comment for an article that hasn't been published yet. First, you need to create a method so you can ask an Article if its published_at field is null or not by using the present? method which returns true if a values exists, and false otherwise. This method is useful outside validations, because you may want to indicate on the administration interface later whether an article has been published. Let's add that method now and call it published?. Add the code shown in Listing 5-28 to the Article model.

Listing 5-28. Adding the published? Method in app/models/article.rb: http://gist.github.com/326170

```
class Article < ActiveRecord::Base
  validates :title, :presence => true
  validates :body, :presence => true

  belongs_to :user
  has_and_belongs_to_many :categories
  has_many :comments

  scope :published, where("articles.published_at IS NOT NULL")
  scope :draft, where("articles.published_at IS NULL")
  scope :recent, lambda { published.where("articles.published_at > ?",
1.week.ago.to_date)}
  scope :where_title, lambda { |term| where("articles.title LIKE ?", "%#{term}%") }

  def long_title
    "#{title} - #{published_at}"
  end

  def published?
    published_at.present?
  end
end
```

This gets you a step closer to your goal. When building validations, Active Record gives you nice objects called *errors* to use. Whenever you want to add a validation error to the list of errors, you just say errors.add(column_name, error_message). So, let's implement a method called article_should_be_published in the Comment class that uses this functionality, as shown in Listing 5-29.

Listing 5-29. Adding the article_should_be_published Method in app/models/comment.rb: http://gist.github.com/326177

```
class Comment < ActiveRecord::Base
  belongs_to :article

  def article_should_be_published
    errors.add(:article_id, "is not published yet") if article
&& !article.published?
  end
end
```

This checks whether you should apply the error by evaluating the if statement. If that if statement is true, you want to add an error into the errors object. Note that before you test whether the article is published, you make sure article isn't nil. This is so your test doesn't throw an error. If article is nil, that should be handled by another validator: the validates method with the :presence option.

How do you tell Active Record that this method should be run before a save? You use the validate class method and pass it a symbol with the name of the method. At the top of your Comment class, add the code shown in Listing 5-30. Note that we also expect comments to have values for name, email and body; so, we add a presence validation call.

Listing 5-30. validate Method in app/models/comment.rb: http://gist.github.com/326183

```
class Comment < ActiveRecord::Base
  belongs_to :article

  validates :name, :email, :body, :presence => true
  validate :article_should_be_published

  def article_should_be_published
    errors.add(:article_id, "is not published yet") if article
&& !article.published?
  end
end
```

This lets Active Record know to pay attention to your new article_should_be_published method. In Chapter 10, you write tests to make sure this is working. But you can also go to the console—if you have it open already, don't forget to reload!—and try to create an invalid object to see if it reports errors for you. The easiest way to get to errors in an Active Record object is with comment.errors.full_messages, as shown here:

```
>> article = Article.draft.first
=> #<Article id: 7, title: "One-to-many associations", …>
>> comment = article.comments.create :name => 'Dude',
:email => 'dude@example.com', :body => 'Great article!'
=> #<Comment id: nil, article_id: 7, name: "Dude", email: "dude@example.com",
body: "Great article!", created_at: nil, updated_at: nil>
>> comment.errors.full_messages
=> ["Article is not published yet"]
```

Making Callbacks

You often want to have things happen during the life cycle of the model. Certain actions need to happen during certain events pertaining to a particular model. For instance, what if you want to send an e-mail to your administrator whenever someone cancels their account? Or perhaps you want to make sure to create a new model because some other model was also created. Sometimes, certain actions in the life of a model should execute associated actions.

To implement this, Active Record has *callbacks*. Six callbacks are commonly used in Active Record models:

- before_create

- after_create

- before_save

- after_save

- before_destroy

- after_destroy

As you can see, the names of the Rails callbacks describe their purpose. When you create a method with any of these names in your model, the method is called automatically by the model during the time the name suggests. For instance, if you make a before_save method, that method is called right before the model object is saved.

Any callback that starts with before_ can stop the execution chain if it returns false. For instance, if you define the following before_create, you ensure that this model object will *never* be created:

```
def before_create
  false
end
```

This can be a "gotcha" later if you're doing something like an assignment of false to a variable. If you're ever confused why a model won't save, check your before filters.

In the blog application, you'd like to make sure that when a user creates a comment, an e-mail is automatically sent to the article author. Although you don't send an e-mail here, this chapter goes over the steps required to put together code to eventually send the e-mail in Chapter 9. To set this up, you add an after_create method to the Comment class that will eventually have the code to send an e-mail. Add the method shown in Listing 5-31 to the Comment model.

Listing 5-31. after_create Method in app/models/comment.rb: http://gist.github.com/326205

```
class Comment < ActiveRecord::Base
  belongs_to :article

  validates :name, :email, :body, :presence => true
  validate :article_should_be_published

  def article_should_be_published
    errors.add(:article_id, "is not published yet") if article
&& !article.published?
  end

  def after_create
    puts "We will notify the author in Chapter 9"
  end
end
```

You use the code you want to be executed directly in the code of the after_create method. This is nice and simple, but you should probably use the pattern as you do for validate in Listing 5-30, where you pass in a symbol that references the method to run when the validation is performed. This helps keep the code readable and easier to augment in the future, because you can supply an arbitrary number of methods to run on a callback, separated by a comma. Name the method email_article_author, and tell Active Record to run it after a record is created, as shown in Listing 5-32.

Listing 5-32. email_article_author Method Specified as an after_create Callback in

app/models/comment.rb: http://gist.github.com/326211

```
class Comment < ActiveRecord::Base
  belongs_to :article

  validates :name, :email, :body, :presence => true
```

```
  validate :article_should_be_published

  after_create :email_article_author

  def article_should_be_published
    errors.add(:article_id, "is not published yet") if article
&& !article.published?
  end

  def email_article_author
    puts "We will notify #{article.user.email} in Chapter 9"
  end
end
```

Active Record provides many more callbacks than are mentioned here, but those listed at the beginning of this section are the ones we find ourselves using often. Some of the others are used in extremely rare cases (for instance, after_initialize, which is called after an object is initialized). These callbacks can help you with just about anything you need to do during the life cycle of a model. They're part of smart models, which know how to deal with their own birth, life, and death.

Observers

As you saw in the previous section about callbacks, you can add a lot of code to tie up functionality between classes when specific events occur. However, as you add logic to a model to support callbacks, the model code tends to become cluttered, which increases the model's complexity.

In the previous example, you can argue that the Comment model shouldn't care if an e-mail has to be sent; this seems to be logic that isn't relevant to the model. Rails provides the option of using *observers*, which are classes that respond to the same callbacks models do, but in a separate class, so they don't clutter the model.

To see an observer in action, reimplement the e-mail to send snippets into an observer:

```
$ rails generate observer Comment
```

invoke	active_record
create	app/models/comment_observer.rb
invoke	test_unit
create	test/unit/comment_observer_test.rb

Now that the CommentObserver class has been created, you can open it and add the same code that's in the Comment class (see Listing 5-33). The only difference is that the code is no longer executed within the context of a comment object, so the added comment is passed as a parameter to the after_create method. At this point, you also need to remove the email_article_author method and its after_create call from the Comment class (see Listing 5-34).

Listing 5-33. Current CommentObserver Class in app/models/comment_observer.rb:

```
http://gist.github.com/326236
class CommentObserver < ActiveRecord::Observer
  def after_create(comment)
    puts " We will notify the author in Chapter 9"
  end
end
```

Listing 5-34. Current app/models/comment.rb: http://gist.github.com/326238

```
class Comment < ActiveRecord::Base
  belongs_to :article

  validates :name, :email, :body, :presence => true
  validate :article_should_be_published

  def article_should_be_published
    errors.add(:article_id, "is not published yet") if article
&& !article.published?
  end
end
```

Before you can see this code in action, you have to tell Rails that you want the `CommentObserver` class to be triggered by the Active Record callbacks of the `Comment` class. To do that, make sure your config/application.rb file looks like Listing 5-35, and restart your application.

Listing 5-35. Current config/application.rb: http://gist.github.com/326246

```
require File.expand_path('../boot', __FILE__)

require 'rails/all'

# If you have a Gemfile, require the gems listed there, including any gems
# you've limited to :test, :development, or :production.
Bundler.require(:default, Rails.env) if defined?(Bundler)

module Blog
  class Application < Rails::Application
    # Activate observers that should always be running
    config.active_record.observers = :comment_observer
    # Configure the default encoding used in templates for Ruby 1.9.
    config.encoding = "utf-8"
    # Configure sensitive parameters which will be filtered from the log file.
    config.filter_parameters += [:password]
  end
end
```

Updating the User Model

You still need to do a little work on your User model. You can apply many of the techniques described in this chapter, such as custom methods to allow you to perform user authentication, and validation methods to make sure your data stays clean.

When you created the user migration (Listing 5-2), you added a field called password. This field stores a plain-text password—which, if you think about it, isn't very secure. It's always a good idea to encrypt any sensitive data so it can't be easily read by would-be intruders. You deal with the encryption in the User model itself, but the first thing you do is rename the field in the database from password to hashed_password. This is so you can create a custom accessor called password with which to set the password while maintaining a field to store the encrypted version in the database. The plain-text password is never saved.

To accomplish this, you create a migration. From the terminal, issue the following command to create the new migration:

```
$ rails generate migration rename_password_to_hashed_password
```

Next, fill in the migration as shown in Listing 5-36.

Listing 5-36. Migration to Rename password to hashed_password in
db/migrate/20100309052120_rename_password_to_hashed_password.rb: http://gist.github.com/326261

```
class RenamePasswordToHashedPassword < ActiveRecord::Migration
  def self.up
    rename_column :users, :password, :hashed_password
  end

  def self.down
    rename_column :users, :hashed_password, :password
  end
end
```

Run the migration using the rake db:migrate command, as follows:

```
$ rake db:migrate
```

```
==  RenamePasswordToHashedPassword: migrating =================================

--  rename_column(:users, :password, :hashed_password)

    -> 0.0558s

==  RenamePasswordToHashedPassword: migrated (0.0560s) ========================
```

Next, update your User model so that it looks like Listing 5-37. You program all the user-authentication methods you need for allowing users to log in. Let's look at the code first and then see in detail what you've done.

Listing 5-37. Current User Model in app/models/user.rb: http://gist.github.com/326271

```ruby
require 'digest'
class User < ActiveRecord::Base
  attr_accessor :password

  validates :email, :uniqueness => true,
                    :length => { :within => 5..50 },
                    :format => { :with => /^[^@][\w.-]+@[\w.-]+[.][a-z]{2,4}$/i }
  validates :password, :confirmation => true,
                       :length => { :within => 4..20 },
                       :presence => true,
                       :if => :password_required?

  has_one :profile
  has_many :articles, :order => 'published_at DESC, title ASC',
                      :dependent => :nullify
  has_many :replies, :through => :articles, :source => :comments

  before_save :encrypt_new_password

  def self.authenticate(email, password)
    user = find_by_email(email)
    return user if user && user.authenticated?(password)
  end

  def authenticated?(password)
    self.hashed_password == encrypt(password)
  end

  protected
    def encrypt_new_password
      return if password.blank?
      self.hashed_password = encrypt(password)
    end

    def password_required?
      hashed_password.blank? || password.present?
    end

    def encrypt(string)
      Digest::SHA1.hexdigest(string)
    end
end
```

Whenever you store something sensitive like a password, you should encrypt it. To encrypt the password in your User model, you use a simple algorithm called a *hash* that creates a random-looking string from the provided input. This hashed output can't be turned back into the original string easily, so even if someone steals your database, they will have a prohibitively difficult time discovering your users' passwords. Ruby has a built-in library called Digest that includes many hashing algorithms.

Let's go through the additions to the User model:

- require 'digest': You start by requiring the Digest library you use for encrypting the passwords. This loads the needed library and makes it available to work with in your class.

- attr_accessor :password: This defines an accessor attribute, password, at the top of the class body. It tells Ruby to create reader and writer methods for password. Because the password column doesn't exist in your table anymore, a password method isn't created automatically by Active Record. Still, you need a way to set the password before it's encrypted, so you make your own attribute to use. This works like any model attribute, except that it isn't persisted to the database when the model is saved.

- before_save :encrypt_new_password: This before_save callback tells Active Record to run the encrypt_new_password method before it saves a record. That means it applies to all operations that trigger a save, including create and update.

- encrypt_new_password: This method should perform encryption only if the password attribute contains a value, because you don't want it to happen unless a user is changing their password. If the password attribute is blank, you return from the method, and the hash_password value is never set. If the password value isn't blank, you have some work to do. You set the hashed_password attribute to the encrypted version of the password by laundering it through the encrypt method.

- encrypt: This method is fairly simple. It uses Ruby's Digest library, which you included on the first line, to create an SHA1 digest of whatever you pass it. Because methods in Ruby always return the last thing evaluated, encrypt returns the encrypted string.

- password_required?: When you perform validations, you want to make sure you're validating the presence, length, and confirmation of the password only if validation is required. And it's required only if this is a new record (the hashed_password attribute is blank) or if the password accessor you created has been used to set a new password (password.present?). To make this easy, you create the password_required? predicate method, which returns true if a password is required or false if it's not. You then apply this method as an :if condition on all your password validators.

- self.authenticate: You can tell this is a class method because it's prefixed with self (it's defined on the class *itself*). That means you don't access it via an instance; you access it directly off the class, just as you would find, new, or create (User.authenticate, not @user = User.new; @user.authenticate). The authenticate method accepts an e-mail address and an unencrypted password. It uses a dynamic finder (find_by_email) to fetch the user with a matching e-mail address. If the user is found, the user variable contains a User object; if not, it's nil. Knowing this, you can return the value of user if, and only if, it isn't nil and the authenticated? method returns true for the given password (user && user.authenticated?(password)).

- authenticated?: This is a simple predicate method that checks to make sure the stored hashed_password matches the given password after it has been encrypted (via encrypt). If it matches, true is returned.

117

Let's play with these new methods from the console so you can get a better idea of how this comes together:

```
>> user = User.first
=> #<User id: 1, email: "user@example.com", ..>
>> user.password = 'secret'
=> "secret"
>> user.password_confirmation = 'secret'
=> "secret"
>> user.save
=> true
>> user.hashed_password
=> "e5e9fa1ba31ecd1ae84f75caaa474f3a663f05f4"
>> User.authenticate('user@example.com', 'secret')
=> #<User id: 1, email: "user@example.com", …>
>> User.authenticate('user@example.com', 'secret2')
=> nil
>> second_user = User.last
=> #<User id: 2, email: "mary@example.com", …>
>> second_user.update_attributes(:password => 'secret',
:password_confirmation => 'secret')
=> true
>> User.authenticate('mary@example.com', 'secret')
=> #<User id: 2, email: "mary@example.com", …>
```

When you ask the User model to authenticate someone, you pass in the e-mail address and the plain-text password. The authenticate method hashes the given password and then compares it to the stored (hashed) password in the database. If the passwords match, the User object is returned, and authentication was successful. When you try to use an incorrect password, nil is returned. In Chapter 7, you write code in your controller to use these model methods and allow users to log in to the site. For now, you have a properly built and secure back end for the way users authenticate.

With the validation in the User model, the db/seeds.rb file also needs to be updated to make sure it follows the rules expected in the model. While we are at it, we also add some code to create a few articles. Update your db/seeds.rb file so that it looks like Listing 5-38.

Listing 5-38. Current Seeds File in db/seeds.rb: http://gist.github.com/387374

```
user = User.create :email => 'mary@example.com',
                   :password => 'guessit',
                   :password_confirmation => 'guessit'
Category.create [{:name => 'Programming'},
                {:name => 'Event'},
                {:name => 'Travel'},
                {:name => 'Music'},
                {:name => 'TV'}]
user.articles.create :title => 'Advanced Active Record',
            :body => "Models need to relate to each other. In the real world, ..",
            :published_at => Date.today
user.articles.create :title => 'One-to-many associations',
            :body => "One-to-many associations describe a pattern ..",
            :published_at => Date.today
```

```
user.articles.create :title => 'Associations',
                :body => "Active Record makes working with associations easy..",
                :published_at => Date.today
```

Reviewing the Updated Models

You've made a lot of changes to your models, so let's make sure we're on the same page before you move on. Look at the Article, Category, and Comment models in Listings 5-39, 5-40, and 5-41, and make sure yours match.

Listing 5-39. Current Article Model in app/models/article.rb

```
class Article < ActiveRecord::Base
  validates :title, :presence => true
  validates :body, :presence => true

  belongs_to :user
  has_and_belongs_to_many :categories
  has_many :comments

  scope :published, where("articles.published_at IS NOT NULL")
  scope :draft, where("articles.published_at IS NULL")
  scope :recent, lambda { published.where("articles.published_at > ?",
1.week.ago.to_date)}
  scope :where_title, lambda { |term| where("articles.title LIKE ?", "%#{term}%") }

  def long_title
    "#{title} - #{published_at}"
  end

  def published?
    published_at.present?
  end
end
```

Listing 5-40. Current Category Model in app/models/category.rb

```
class Category < ActiveRecord::Base
  has_and_belongs_to_many :articles

  default_scope order('categories.name')
end
```

Listing 5-41. Current Comment Model in app/models/comment.rb

```
class Comment < ActiveRecord::Base
  belongs_to :article

  validates :name, :email, :body, :presence => true
  validate :article_should_be_published
```

```
  def article_should_be_published
    errors.add(:article_id, "is not published yet") if article
&& !article.published?
  end
end
```

Summary

After reading this chapter, you should have a complete understanding of Active Record models. The chapter covered associations, conditions, validations, callbacks, and observers at breakneck speed. Now the fun part starts. In the next chapter, you get to use all the groundwork established in this chapter to produce the web interface for the data structures you've created. This is when you get to reap the benefits of your hard work.

## CHAPTER 6

Action Pack: Working with the View and the Controller

When you type a URL into your browser's address bar and press Enter, a few things happen behind the scenes. First, the URL is translated into a unique address by which the server that hosts the application can be identified. The request is then sent to that server, which begins a chain of events that culminates in a response. The response is usually, but not always, in the form of an HTML document, which is essentially a text document full of special codes that your browser understands and can render visually on your screen. At this point, the request cycle is complete, and the browser waits for further input from you. If you click a link somewhere on the page or type a new URL in the address bar, the cycle begins all over again: the request is sent, the server processes it, and the server sends back the response.

When you make a request to a Rails application, this request cycle is the responsibility of a component of Rails called Action Pack. The Action Pack library is an integral component of the Rails framework and one that you need to be familiar with if you intend to master Rails.

This chapter begins with an overview of Action Pack. Then, you get to work using it in your sample blog application.

■ **NOTE** If you need to get the code at the exact point where you finished Chapter 5, you can download the zip file from `http://github.com/downloads/ccjr/blog/chapter06.zip` and extract it in your computer.

Action Pack Components

You've been introduced to the MVC pattern, but if you need a refresher, here it is. The *model* is your application's world, most often represented by database objects like articles, comments, and subscribers. The *controller* is the grand orchestrator, dealing with requests and issuing responses. The *view* is the code that contains instructions for rendering visual output for a browser, like HTML.

Armed with this refresher, you may be able to guess what roles are played by Action Pack. This isn't a test, so here's the answer: Action Pack is the controller and the view. The controller performs the logic, and the view renders the template that is given back to the requesting browser. Not surprisingly, two of the modules that make up Action Pack are named accordingly: Action Controller and Action View.

At this point, you may be wondering why the view and the controller are wrapped up in a single library, unlike models, which have a library of their own. The answer is subtle and succinct: controllers and views are very closely related. The pages that follow paint a more complete picture of both the role and the relationship of controllers and views, how they work, and how they work together to create and control the interface of a Rails application.

Action Controller

Controllers orchestrate your application's flow. Every time a user requests a page, submits a form, or clicks a link, that request is handled—in one way or another—by a controller. When you're programming your application, you spend a lot of time building controllers and giving them instructions on how to handle requests.

The concept of controllers can sometimes be difficult for newcomers to grasp. Even if you've built web applications before, say in ASP or PHP, you may not be used to this form of separation, where the mechanics of flow are controlled by a separate entity and not embedded in the pages themselves.

Let's look at the example of the CD player in a car to illustrate the concept of controllers. The player is required to respond to certain events, such as the user pressing the Play button, fast forwarding, or rewinding a track. When you push a button, you expect something to happen—you've made a request, and you wait for the subsequent response.

If your CD player was a Rails application, the instructions for what to do when a certain event takes place, such as the pressing of the Eject button, would be contained in a controller. If you were to sketch it on paper, it might look something like this:

- CD Player
- Play
- Stop
- Fast-forward
- Rewind
- Eject

These events, or actions, describe what the player should be capable of *doing*. Obviously, each of these actions would need to be programmed to do something with the disc inside the player. When someone presses Eject, you would first call on the stop action (if the disc is playing) and then arrange for the player to spit out the disc. You would code all the instructions for dealing with an eject event into the controller—specifically, inside the eject action. The same would apply for play, fast-forward, and rewind.

It's worth noting that this type of logic has nothing to do with the CD itself, nor does it have anything to do with the music on the CD. If this were a Rails application, the CD would be the model. It can be used independently of the player. In fact, it can be used in all sorts of players, not just the one in your car.

The stereo in your car is probably capable of more than just playing CDs. Most stereos have a radio receiver built in as well. The radio would have its own set of events that would likewise need to be handled. These actions might include things like changing stations, setting presets, and switching between AM and FM. To keep things well organized, you would probably want to group these actions inside their own controller, separate from the CD controller. After all, the radio and the CD player do different things.

When you're dealing with a Rails application, it's not much different. You separate the things that you need your application to do with an object from the object itself. Even when you're not dealing directly with an object (adjusting the volume on your car stereo has little to do with either the CD in the player or the station on the radio), you still handle the event inside a controller.

Each controller in Rails is designed as a Ruby class. Without getting too technical, Listing 6-1 shows how the CD player example would look if it were a Ruby class.

Listing 6-1. `CDPlayer` Class

```ruby
class CDPlayer
  def play
  end

  def stop
  end

  def fast_forward
  end

  def rewind
  end

  def eject
  end
end
```

Inside the `CDPlayer` class, you define a method for each action, or each thing you want your CD player to be able to do. So, if you were to send the message "play" to an instance of the `CDPlayer` class, it would know how to handle it (of course, because the `play` method is empty in this example, nothing would happen). On the other hand, if you sent the message "pause," Ruby would raise an exception and tell you that the method wasn't found. If you wanted `CDPlayer` objects to respond to that message, you would need to add a method called (you guessed it) pause.

All the methods in this class are public, which means they can be invoked by anyone. You don't need to do anything special to a method to make it public. *Unless otherwise declared, all methods in a Ruby class are public by default.* If you were to mark an action as private, though, it could be used only internally by the class. For example, if the `stop` method were private, it would raise a `NoMethodError` if you called it from outside the `CDPlayer` class. However, the `eject` method is free to call on `stop`, because it does so internally. Although the usefulness of this feature will become apparent as you continue to learn about controllers, consider this: if your CD player needed to display the time remaining for a given track, it might need to perform a few calculations to figure that out. You might create a method for doing these internal calculations, but would you want that method to be accessible from the outside? Would you have a button called Calculate on your player?

It's time for a working definition: *Action Controllers are Ruby classes containing one or more public methods known as actions.* Each action is responsible for responding to a request to perform some task. A typical controller is most often a collection of actions that relate to a specific area of concern. For example, consider the blog application you've been building in the previous chapters. The controller that manages articles has the class name `ArticlesController` and has action methods for listing, creating, reading, updating, and deleting articles.

The example of the CD player worked well to illustrate the basic concept of controllers, it won't take you much further when dealing with web applications. If you were really dealing with a CD player, you would press Play, the disc would start playing, and that would be the end of it. But because Rails was specifically designed for building web applications, it makes a fair number of assumptions about what you want your actions to do when they're finished firing. Chief among these is the rendering of a view.

Imagine that you're reading a list of posts on someone's blog. You click the title of a post, and you expect to be taken to a new screen that shows you just that post. You requested an action (show), and in response, you receive a new screen. This happens all the time in the world of web applications: when you click a link, you expect to go to a new page.

In Rails, it's the general case that when actions have completed their work, they respond by rendering a view. The concept of actions rendering views is so common that Rails has internalized it as a convention: *unless otherwise stated, when an action is finished firing, it renders a view.* How does Rails know what view to render if you don't tell it? It looks for a view whose name matches that of the requested action. This should give you some insight as to why Action Controller and Action View are bundled together in Action Pack. Because of the way controller actions relate to views, a few other mechanisms facilitate their communication, all of which are covered shortly.

Action View

The Action View library is the second half of Action Pack. Given that controllers are responsible for handling the request and issuing a response, views are responsible for rendering the output of a response in a way a browser (or any other user agent) can understand. Let's say you request the index action from the ArticlesController. After performing the logic to retrieve a list of articles, the controller hands off to the view, which formats the list of articles to make them look pretty. The controller then collects the results of the render, and the HTML is sent back to the browser, thus completing the request cycle.

Although the controller and the view are separate entities, they need to communicate with each other. The primary mechanism by which they do this is through shared variables. These shared variables are called *instance variables* and are easy to spot in Ruby because they're prefixed with the @ symbol. Keep this in mind as you look at the view example in Listing 6-2, which uses an instance variable called @articles to produce an article listing.

Listing 6-2. An Example View

```
<html>
  <body>
    <ul>
      <% for article in @articles %>
        <li><%= article.title %></li>
      <% end %>
    <ul>
  </body>
</html>
```

■ **NOTE** Listing 6-2 uses a for loop, but there are a few different ways to iterate over a collection of objects. This book covers them as you move along.

Even without knowing any Ruby, you should be able to guess what this code does: it iterates over the collection of articles stored in the variable @articles and prints the title of each between HTML list-item (<li>) tags. If @articles contained three articles whose titles were One, Two, and Three, respectively, the preceding code would be compiled to the following:

```
<html>

  <body>

    <ul>

      <li>One</li>

      <li>Two</li>

      <li>Three</li>

    <ul>

  </body>

</html>
```

You may wonder where the variable @articles came into being. If you guessed in the controller, you would be right. The controller sets up instance variables that the view can access. In this case, the controller created a variable called @articles, and the view was given automatic access to it. Notice that the view doesn't perform any logic to fetch the list of articles; it relies on the controller to have set up the variable and performs the display logic necessary to turn the collection into a browser-ready HTML list.

Embedded Ruby

The codes you see mixed into the HTML markup are Ruby. Because templates that are capable of dealing only with static HTML wouldn't be very useful, Action View templates have the benefit of being able to use Embedded Ruby (ERb) to programmatically enhance them.

Using ERb, you can embed Ruby into your templates and give them the ability to deal with data from the controller to produce well-formed HTML representations. ERb is included in the Ruby standard library, and Rails makes extensive use of it. You trigger ERb by using embeddings such as <% %> and <%= %> in your template files to evaluate or print Ruby code, respectively. If you've ever worked with ASP, JSP, or PHP, this style of embedding should be familiar to you.

In the example in the preceding section, the loop is constructed within *evaluation embedding* tags (<% %>), and the article's title is printed using *output embedding* tags (<%= %>). Pay close attention to the subtle difference between the two embedding types: output embedding includes an equal sign; regular embedding doesn't. When you use output embedding, you're effectively saying, *print the results of the Ruby code when it's evaluated*. Regular embedding doesn't print results; it evaluates whatever is between the tags and goes on its merry way. If you mistakenly omit the equal sign, no errors are raised, but nothing is printed either. You have a set of empty list tags.

> ■ **NOTE** Following the Model behaviour, Rails is modular and can be used with other templating libraries. A popular alternative is the Haml–http://haml-lang.com–template language used by many Rails developers.

Helpers

The terms of the MVC are fairly strict in the way they advocate the separation of components. Controllers really shouldn't concern themselves with the generation of view code, and views shouldn't concern themselves with anything but the simplest of logic. Although it's possible to use ERb to execute arbitrary Ruby code inside a view, and although controllers are certainly capable of generating markup, it's generally considered in violation of the MVC pattern to do so. This is where helpers come in to play.

Action Pack's *helpers* do exactly what their name implies: they help views by providing a convenient location to encapsulate code that would otherwise clutter the view and violate the terms of the MVC. They offer a middle ground between controllers and views and help to keep your application organized and easy to maintain.

If you think about it, ERb tags really aren't the best place for performing complex logic, and templates can quickly become unwieldy when creating markup programmatically. For this reason, Action Pack includes a large suite of built-in helpers for generating all sorts of HTML fragments—from creating forms and formatting dates, to making hyperlinks and image tags. And when the built-in helpers aren't enough, you can write your own. Each controller gets its own helper module that's mixed in automatically, ready to lend your templates a hand when they need it.

Routing

All the information pertaining to which controller and action to call on comes in the form of the request URL. Action Pack includes a specialized component called *routing*, which is responsible for dissecting the incoming URL and delegating control to the appropriate controller and action.

Every request that comes into your web application originates in the form of a URL. The routing system allows you to write the rules that govern how each URL is picked apart and handled.

A traditional URL contains the path to a file on the server, relative to the server's home directory. Here's an example:

```
http://example.com/articles/show.asp?id=1037
```

You can tell a lot from this URL. First, you know the server technology being used is Microsoft's ASP. Given that, you also know that this URL resolves to the show.asp script, which is inside the /articles directory. In this case, there is no URL rewriting going on; the mapping of the URL to the script that handles it is one to one.

The problem with this kind of mapping is that you have no control over the URL. The URL is coupled to the script. What if you want to invoke the show.asp script, but want the URL to read articles/detail.asp instead of show.asp? Or better yet, what if you don't want to expose the underlying script implementation (ASP) at all and use just articles/detail? There's no way. The lack of flexibility in this kind of URL mapping is a problem. If you ever need to change the name of the script being invoked, you instantly break all the URL references. This can be a major pain if you need to update all your code, especially if your pages are indexed by search engines.

Action Pack's routing solves this problem by decoupling the URL from the underlying program implementation. In Rails, the URL is related to the specific resource being requested, and it can be formatted to correctly identify that resource without having to conform to the name of the script that does the handling. When thought of in this way, URLs become part of the interface of an application, unrelated to the files that are ultimately invoked to process a request.

There are myriad reasons why a routing system is a good idea. Here are just a few of them:

- Decoupled URLs can convey meaning, becoming part of the interface.

- Clean, readable URLs are more user-friendly and easier to remember.

- URLs can be changed without affecting the underlying implementation.

Of course, like most things in Rails, the routing system is open to configuration; and one of the great benefits of routes is that because they're decoupled, they can be customized to create meaningful URLs without much effort. This chapter teaches you how to build and customize routes for your application, understand the default routes that Rails creates for you, create named routes, and use routes when creating links and redirects in your code.

RESTful Resources

Rails adapted RESTful design as a convention in Rails 1.2 onward. Representational State Transfer (REST) is a principle used mainly over the HTTP protocol to offer a better interface for client-server operations. This section first talks about the REST concept and then explains how Rails implemented it through RESTful controllers and resources.

The REST principle is based on working with information in the form of *resources*. Each piece of information is dealt with as a *resource*, each resource has a unique interaction point for every *action* that can be performed on it, and each interaction point (action) is normally represented using a URL and a request method.

For example, think of a blog, which is a collection of information resources. Every article is a resource, and every action you perform on it, such as read, edit, or delete, has its own interaction point, mainly identified by a URL and a request method.

HTTP protocol, which is the main web protocol you normally use in browsers, has several request methods. These four are the primary ones used in RESTful design:

- POST: Normally used to *submit* forms and *new* resource data

- GET: Mainly used to request a page to *view* a resource or more

- PUT: Used to modify specific resource

- DELETE: Used to delete a resource

Do those four methods remind you of anything? If you're thinking of CRUD, then you're right. Taking the main database operations create, read, update, and delete (CRUD) in REST design and tying them up with HTTP's main methods gives you what's called a *RESTful* web service.

RESTful web services are commonly used in APIs (referred to as REST APIs) by associating every CRUD method with its corresponding HTTP method:

- POST/Create: Creates of a resource

- GET/Read: Requests a specific resource or group of resources

- PUT/Update: Edits attributes of a resource

- DELETE/Delete: Deletes a resource

Rails implemented RESTful design for controllers by introducing the concept of resources. Every model in your application is dealt with via a controller as a resources set, and that RESTful controller has certain methods that handle your regular operations on that model. You examine that in depth after you understand the Action Pack request cycle.

The Action Pack Request Cycle

The entire request-to-response process is called the Action Pack *request cycle*. The request cycle consists of the following steps:

1. Rails receives a request from the outside world (usually a browser).

2. Routing picks apart the request to determine the controller and action to invoke.

3. A new controller object is instantiated, and an action method is called.

4. The controller interacts with the model (usually performing a CRUD operation).

5. A response is sent back to the browser, in the form of either a render or a redirect.

Figure 6-1 illustrates the process.

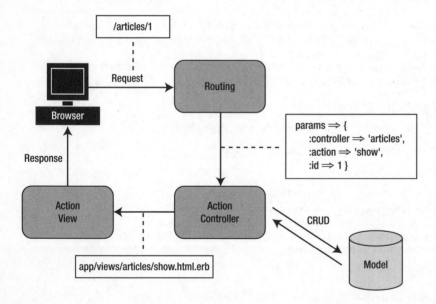

Figure 6-1. The Action Pack request cycle

Not long ago (and still today), developers used to construct *server pages*. Such a page had a bunch of code at the top of an otherwise static page, just above the opening HTML tag. The markup was littered with different sorts of code: it wasn't unusual to see the database being accessed, forms being processed, sessions being set, and all manner of logic being performed in-line. The web server was responsible for controlling the application—one page redirecting to another, running the code, and then dumping the results to the screen.

We won't get into the multitude of reasons why this is a bad idea, except to say that it presents the problem of coupling. In this scenario, the business logic and the view are mashed together, making the code more difficult to maintain and debug. ASP and PHP pages are notable offenders, and if you're coming from either of these camps, the concept of separating concerns may be foreign at first. Here's a way to think about it that may help. Imagine taking the code and logic from the top of each page and sticking it in one place, leaving only the HTML behind. Then, instead of using the web server to invoke each page as you would with a static site, have the web server call on a single dispatcher that finds the code you want to execute and calls it. The code it invokes—the file that contains the processing logic extracted from the server page—is called the controller. Instead of logic being divided among pages, it's divided into actions.

The single biggest advantage of this pattern is that the processing logic is decoupled from the view and safely contained in one place. As you see, it's a lot easier to work this way. The interplay between actions is considerably easier to visualize and understand when it isn't spread out over a host of locations. Your server pages become lightweight views, left to handle only the simplest of instructions, if any.

A Controller Walk-Through

Instead of boring you with more theory about controllers, views, and MVC, let's dig in and start writing some real-world code. You continue building your blog application, examining the finer points and the places where convention wins out over configuration. Along the way, this section touches on some of the most essential controller and view concepts. By the end of this walk-through, you should have a complete grasp of how the Rails request cycle works and a working example to refer to and expand on in the subsequent chapters. The purpose of this walk-through isn't to examine each and every aspect of Action Pack in detail, but rather to give you a practical overview of how the components—routes, controllers, helpers, views, layouts, and partials—work together to control your application and construct its interface.

Setting Up Routes

Links and URLs are important in web applications. They serve as the entry point to the application and contain all the information required to route an incoming request to the controller and action that will handle it. Before you get into the meat of understanding controllers and their actions, you need to spend a few minutes learning how to get from request to response. It all starts with routing.

Routing Basics

In Rails, all the rules for mapping URLs to controllers are a matter of configuration. You find the `routes.rb` file in the `config` directory. If you open that file in your editor now and examine it, you see lots of commented code with samples of routes you could possibly define. Look at the last commented line to understand how routes can be defined:

```
match ':controller(/:action(/:id(.:format)))'
```

Routes work based on pattern matching and can include variables to set directly within the pattern. Here, the pattern is a three-segment string partitioned by slashes (/) and containing variables to set, where the variables are prefixed by a colon (:). The first segment sets the :controller variable, the second the :action variable, and the third the :id and :format variables. These variables are used to determine the controller and action to invoke and the parameters to send along. The pattern is matched from left to right, and the variables are optional. If the :id variable is empty, only the controller and action are set. If the :action variable is empty, only the :controller variable are set, and so on.

Routing priority is based on the order in which routes exist in routes.rb, so that the first route defined has the highest priority. If an incoming URL matches the first route defined, the request is sent along, and no other routes are examined

Routes are commonly defined using the match method. The argument to match can either be a string pattern to match, as in the previous example, or a hash with string pattern as a key and another string that identifies the controller and action to be called.

Here's an example that matches a specific pattern and sets the controller and action in response:

```
match '/teams/home' => 'teams#index'
```

This route matches a URL like http://example.com/teams/home and routes the request to the index action on the teams controller. The name of the controller and action are separated by the # symbol. You can also set arbitrary parameters when using the route. For example, let's say you want to set a parameter called query that you can access and use in your controller:

```
match '/teams/search/:query' => 'teams#search'
```

This route matches a URL like http://example.com/teams/search/toronto, routing the request to the teams controller and the search action. The third segment in the URL is assigned to the :query parameter because you specify :query as an in-line variable.

Routes can be complex, and it's possible to apply conditions and other forms of logic to them. For the most part, though, you can get a lot of mileage from the general cases outlined here. The Rails API documentation (http://api.rubyonrails.org/classes/ActionController/Routing.html) contains details on using the more complex routing features.

Named Routes

One of the coolest things about routing in Rails is a feature known as *named routes*. You can assign a name to a given route to make referring to it in code easier. You still define the route the same way as a regular routes, but you need a new hash pair, where the key is :as and the value is the name of the route.

For example, let's take the search route defined in the previous section and turn it into a named route:

```
match '/teams/search/:query' => 'teams#search', :as => 'search'
```

With this definition in place, Rails creates helper methods that allow you to reference this particular route using its name: search_url and search_path. The *_url variant returns a full URL including the protocol and hostname (http://example.com/teams/search), whereas the *_path variant returns just the path (/teams/search).

Later, this chapter covers redirection methods and hyperlink-generation helpers. For now, note that you can use them with named routes:

```
link_to "Search", search_path
```

outputs

```
<a href="/teams/search">Search</a>
```

Named routes are shorter, DRYer, and impervious to changes made at the routing level. So, if you change the controller name from teams to cities, you don't need to update links that use the named route; for the unnamed version, you do.

RESTful Routes and Resources

Earlier, the discussion of RESTful design said that information is dealt with in the form of resources. Rails makes it easy for you to do that: for every action in your controller, you have an associated named route to call.

Resources are configured in the routes.rb file using the resources method. If you look at the routes file in your blog application, you see resources :articles at the top: it was added when you generated the articles scaffold in Chapter 3. The resources :articles method defines the following named routes for the articles controller:

```
article_path => /articles/:id

articles_path => /articles

edit_article_path => /articles/:id/edit

new_article_path => /articles/new
```

The resources method generated four named routes for you; but when you open the ArticlesController, you have seven actions (see Table 6-1). How can you access the remaining actions? Remember that when you learned about REST earlier, you saw that every operation is identified by both a URL *and* a request method. Using different request methods with the generated named routes, Rails routes them to the appropriate controller actions.

Table 6-1. Articles Named Routes

Request Method	Named Routes	Parameters	Controller Action
GET	articles_path		index
POST	articles_path	Record hash	create
GET	article_path	ID	show
PUT	article_path	ID and Record hash	update
DELETE	article_path	ID	destroy
GET	edit_article_path	ID	edit
GET	new_article_path		new

■ **NOTE** You can list all the available routes in your application by calling the `rake routes` command from the terminal.

By following the REST convention, instead of defining a named route for every action, you use the `resources` method in your routes file. To give some examples, if you want to access the `index` action in your articles controller, you go to `/articles` in your browser; the default request method when you type a URL in your browser is GET. What if you want to create a new article? You can do that by submitting a form to `/articles` with the default request method for forms, POST. To get a specific article, type `/articles/:id`, where `:id` is your article id. It's that simple.

Configuring Routes for the Blog Application

Let's configure the routes to be used in your blog application. You haven't built all the controllers and actions yet (you do that next), but that shouldn't stop you from getting the routes in place.

You can handle an empty request for the root of your application's domain using the `root` method. In the blog application, you want the root URL (`http://localhost:3000`) to connect to the list of articles. To accomplish this, you add a `root` declaration to your routes file and make it the first route. Make sure your `config/routes.rb` file looks like Listing 6-3 (note that all comments have been deleted).

Listing 6-3. The config/routes.rb File: http://gist.github.com/330822

```
Blog::Application.routes.draw do
  root :to => "articles#index"
  resources :articles
end
```

Speaking of web servers, because the server looks for matching static files located in the `/public` directory before invoking Rails, and because there's a default `index.html` file (it's the Rails welcome page you saw in Chapter 3), you need to delete it before your default route takes effect.

Static files, like those located in `/public`, are served by the web server independently of Rails. This means images, style sheets, and JavaScript files are all served in this manner, without any server-side processing (which, by the way, is why they're called *static*). Go ahead and delete `public/index.html`.

Now that you have some routes defined, let's move back to the articles controller and try to understand its actions and templates.

Revisiting the Scaffold Generator

You generated a scaffold for your articles in Chapter 3, and this scaffold generated a RESTful controller for the `Article` model in addition to all the required templates. The generator also added the resources declaration to your `route.rb` file. Listing 6-4 shows the `ArticlesController` that your scaffold generated.

Listing 6-4. app/controllers/articles_controller.rb

```
class ArticlesController < ApplicationController
  # GET /articles
```

```ruby
  # GET /articles.xml
  def index
    @articles = Article.all

    respond_to do |format|
      format.html # index.html.erb
      format.xml  { render :xml => @articles }
    end
  end

  # GET /articles/1
  # GET /articles/1.xml
  def show
    @article = Article.find(params[:id])

    respond_to do |format|
      format.html # show.html.erb
      format.xml  { render :xml => @article }
    end
  end

  # GET /articles/new
  # GET /articles/new.xml
  def new
    @article = Article.new

    respond_to do |format|
      format.html # new.html.erb
      format.xml  { render :xml => @article }
    end
  end

  # GET /articles/1/edit
  def edit
    @article = Article.find(params[:id])
  end

  # POST /articles
  # POST /articles.xml
  def create
    @article = Article.new(params[:article])

    respond_to do |format|
      if @article.save
        format.html { redirect_to(@article,
:notice => 'Article was successfully created.') }
        format.xml  { render :xml => @article,
:status => :created, :location => @article }
      else
        format.html { render :action => "new" }
        format.xml  { render :xml => @article.errors,
:status => :unprocessable_entity }
```

```ruby
        end
      end
    end

    # PUT /articles/1
    # PUT /articles/1.xml
    def update
      @article = Article.find(params[:id])

      respond_to do |format|
        if @article.update_attributes(params[:article])
          format.html { redirect_to(@article,
:notice => 'Article was successfully updated.') }
          format.xml  { head :ok }
        else
          format.html { render :action => "edit" }
          format.xml  { render :xml => @article.errors,
:status => :unprocessable_entity }
        end
      end
    end

    # DELETE /articles/1
    # DELETE /articles/1.xml
    def destroy
      @article = Article.find(params[:id])
      @article.destroy

      respond_to do |format|
        format.html { redirect_to(articles_url) }
        format.xml  { head :ok }
      end
    end
end
```

This may look like a lot of code to swallow, but in reality it's simple. The scaffold generator creates the articles controller with the default seven actions discussed earlier for RESTful controllers: index, show, new, edit, create, update, and destroy.

Before your action renders a view, you arrange for it to set an instance variable that the view can use. To refresh your memory, an instance variable is a special kind of Ruby variable that is unique to a given instance of a class, serving as a way for an object to maintain its state. Because views are, in essence, extensions of the controller object, they can access its instance variables directly (although not without some behind-the-scenes Ruby magic that Rails takes care of for you). For all intents and purposes, however, you can consider instance variables to be shared between controllers and views.

You can store any Ruby object in an instance variable, including strings, integers, models, hashes, and arrays. If you reexamine each action in the articles controller, notice that it always starts by setting an instance variable to be called later in that action's view. Let's take the index method as an example (see Listing 6-5).

Listing 6-5. The Index Action in app/controllers/articles_controller.rb

```
# GET /articles
# GET /articles.xml
def index
  @articles = Article.all

  respond_to do |format|
    format.html # index.html.erb
    format.xml  { render :xml => @articles}
  end
end
```

You define and set an instance variable named @articles, which holds the array of all your articles. Then, you call the respond_to method, which tells the index action how to respond to every supported format in your application.

Let's step back a bit. When you call the index method by typing the URL (http://localhost:3000/articles) into your browser—don't forget to start your local server using the rails server command—the request goes first to your routes file, where it's forwarded to the controller. Then, the controller responds to this request by setting an instance variable and rendering *something* back to the browser.

What the controller renders is based on what has been requested. Normally, it's an HTML page request, but it can also be an XML or an Ajax request. It's the responsibility of the respond_to method to define how to respond to each of those requests. In the index action, you accept two formats: HTML, where Rails renders the index template using the path (/articles); and XML, where Rails renders the articles in XML format using the path (/articles.xml).

Try that in the browser. Visit http://localhost:3000/articles to see the list of articles you know and saw earlier, and visit http://localhost:3000/articles.xml to see the result shown in Figure 6-2.

Figure 6-2. Output of http://localhost:3000/articles.xml

GET AN API FOR FREE

Using RESTful controllers in Rails gives you the ability to have an API for your application. An Application Programming Interface (API) is a set of functions that enables other applications to talk to your application. On the Web, this is normally done using XML, and REST is one of the main architectures used for that.

With Rails and its RESTful controllers, defining your API is a seamless process; basically, you just need to tell your controller to respond to XML requests, and you have an API. What's neat in Rails is that the scaffold generator adds the XML part by default to all your controller actions, providing you with an API for free.

Rendering Responses

When an action has completed, it attempts to render a template of the same name. That's the case with the index action just discussed: it renders the index.html.erb template by default. The same applies to edit, new and show actions. But sometimes you want to *render* something else.

If you look at the create and update actions, notice that if the @article.save succeeds, you redirect to the saved @article show page with a friendly message. However, if the save fails, you want to render the new or the edit template. If you didn't explicitly render those templates, the actions would fall through to their default behavior and attempt to render their default create and update templates, which don't exist.

The render method takes several options for its first argument: :text, :nothing, :inline, :template, :action, :xml, :json, :js, and :update.

■ **NOTE** The :update and :js responses are fairly specialized. You use them when you're rendering Ajax or JavaScript responses, as you learn in Chapter 8.

Redirecting

It may not sound like it, but a redirection is a response. Redirects don't happen on the server side. Instead, a response is sent to your browser that tells it to perform a redirection to another URL. The specifics of issuing a redirect aren't something you need to worry about, though, because Rails provides a specialized method to take care of the internals. That method is called redirect_to, and it's one you'll find yourself using a lot, so it's a good idea to get familiar with it.

The redirect_to method usually takes a URL as a parameter, which in most cases is represented by one of your routes. Let's say that you want to redirect the user to the articles' index page, and the path you use is articles_path—a route added by resources :articles in config/routes.rb; so, you execute redirect_to(articles_path). If you look at the destroy action, the user is redirected to articles_url after an article is deleted.

As you can see from the create and update actions, redirect_to can also take an object as a parameter, in which case it redirects to a path that represents that object. This means Rails uses a convention to translate objects to their show action named route. In this case, redirect_to(@article) is a shortcut equivalent to redirect_to(article_path(:id => @article)).

WHAT MAKES A CLASS AN ACTION CONTROLLER?

If you're the curious sort (and, of course, you are), you may wonder how ArticlesController, a seemingly normal Ruby class, becomes a full-fledged Action Controller. Well, if you look closely, notice that ArticlesController inherits from another class: ApplicationController. To get a better picture of what's going on, let's take a peek at the ApplicationController class in app/controllers/application_controller.rb:

```
class ApplicationController < ActionController::Base
  protect_from_forgery
end
```

The mystery is quickly solved. The simple controller becomes an Action Controller by subclassing the ApplicationController class, itself a subclass of ActionController::Base. This is an example of inheritance and is common in object-oriented programming. When one class subclasses another, it inherits all the behavior and methods of the parent. In the case of the articles controller, it inherits all the capabilities of the application controller. Likewise, ApplicationController inherits all the capabilities of *its* parent, ActionController::Base. The ActionController::Base class effectively endows your articles controller with its special abilities.

The application controller is the base from which all the controllers you make inherit. Because it's the parent of all controllers in your application, it's a great place to put methods that you want accessible in every controller.

By looking at the articles controller, you now understand the basic conventions and common concepts of how a RESTful controller normally behaves. You have seven default actions, and in every one of them you do the following:

- Set an instance variable to be used later in the rendered action or template

- Handle the response using the respond_to method to either do a render or redirect_to another path, depending on the behavior you want to achieve

Understanding Templates

The next step is to look at the actions' templates. Look in the app/views/articles directory, and you see five templates:

```
_form.html.erb

index.html.erb

show.html.erb

new.html.erb

edit.html.erb
```

The basic convention of Action Pack is as follows: *templates are organized by controller name, and a template with the same name as the action being invoked is rendered automatically.* You don't need to wire up anything. Merely by requesting an action from a controller, Rails renders the corresponding template in that controller's directory inside app/views/ that has the same name.

Let's try an example. Make sure your local web server is running (rails server), and open http://localhost:3000/articles/ in your browser. You see the articles index page shown in Figure 6-3.

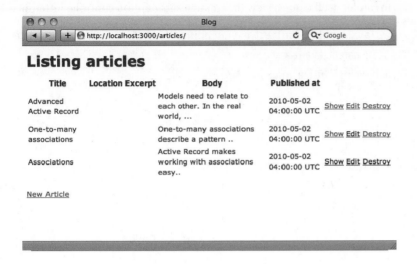

Figure 6-3. *Output of http://localhost:3000/articles*

The articles listing is actually rendered from app/views/articles/index.html.erb, which follows the convention discussed earlier. It's the articles controller, so it goes to the articles directory in app/views. After determining which controller to invoke, Rails proceeds to instantiate it and call its index method. Its default response after running the index action is to perform a render. Rails looks for a template named index.html.erb in the app/views/articles directory and loads it. The same applies to the show action: the show.html.erb template is rendered.

At this point, the request cycle is complete. If you refresh your browser, the cycle begins anew, and the same result is rendered. Notice how all the internals are taken care of for you. All you need to do is create an appropriately named route, controller, action, and view, stick them in the right place, and request the URL in your browser. Rails takes care of making sure everything is knitted together properly.

Before you go any further, use your browser's View Source command to see the HTML that was produced. If you know anything about HTML (and chances are you do), you'll quickly realize that some additional HTML code has been rendered around the code in index.html.erb; it came from a *layout*. Most web pages have headers, footers, sidebars, and other page elements that, when styled, make the page look pretty. Rails has a built-in facility for dealing with page layouts.

Working with Layouts

Rails uses layouts to interpolate the output of an individual template into a larger whole—a reversal of the common pattern of including a shared header and footer on every page (which, if you've done any work in languages like PHP and ASP, is all too familiar). The scaffold generator you ran in Chapter 3 created a layout file and placed it in app/views/layouts/application.html.erb. The application.html.erb layout is applied to all controllers. However, if you like your layout to apply to a specific controller, you can create a layout file named after the controller you want. For example, a layout that applies only to the articles controller should be created in app/views/layouts/articles.html.erb. That's the way it works in Rails. Just as an action tries to render itself using a view that matches its name, a controller attempts to use a layout that matches its name.

Open the app/views/layouts/application.html.erb in your editor. You should see something like the file shown in Listing 6-6.

Listing 6-6. The app/views/layouts/application.html.erb File

```
<!DOCTYPE html>
<html>
<head>
  <title>Blog</title>
  <%= stylesheet_link_tag :all %>
  <%= javascript_include_tag :defaults %>
  <%= csrf_meta_tag %>
</head>
<body>

<%= yield %>

</body>
</html>
```

At rendering time, the layout yields the results of the template fragment's execution in place. See the `<%= yield %>` bit that's highlighted in bold? That's the important part. Wherever you put the `yield` keyword is where your content goes.

One more thing to note: Rails is all about convention over configuration. Here, the convention is that a layout with the name application.html.erb is automatically applied to all templates unless an alternate is specified. This means that if you change the name of the layout as it stands, it won't be automatically applied. If you want to apply a different layout to a given controller, you can either have a layout named after the controller or specify it in the controller using the class method layout:

```
class ExampleController < ApplicationController
  layout 'my_layout' # Will use a layout in app/views/layouts/my_layout.html.erb
end
```

COMMON LAYOUT CONVENTIONS

A few conventions apply to working with layouts:

A layout named application.html.erb is applied automatically unless a more specific candidate exists or is explicitly specified in the controller.

A layout that matches the name of a controller is automatically applied if present. Controller-specific layouts take precedence over the application-level layout.

You can use the layout directive at the class level in any controller (that is, not inside an action) to set the layout for the entire controller: layout 'my_layout'.

> You can include a layout for a specific action with an explicit call to `render` inside the action: `render :layout => 'my_layout'`.
>
> Sometimes, you want to render an action without a layout. In that case, you can pass `false` in place of the layout name: `render :layout => false`.
>
> In practice, you usually use `application.html.erb` and rarely take advantage of the controller-specific layout functionality. On the occasions when you need to use a different layout for a particular controller, use the `layout` directive.

Looking at the Article Form

Let's look at the `new` template in action. The `new` action has a single purpose: to initialize and display the form for creating a new article. The actual creation of a new `Article` object is the responsibility of the `Article` model (remember the discussions of the model in Chapters 4 and 5), but it's orchestrated by the controller. Moreover, it needs data (like a title and body), which it must procure from somewhere. The `edit` action isn't any different, except that it finds and displays a form of an existing article object rather than a new one.

You can extract this information from HTML form elements placed in the view and handled in the controller. Open `new.html.erb` and `edit.html.erb`, which look like Listings 6-7 and 6-8.

Listing 6-7. Content of app/views/articles/new.html.erb

```
<h1>New article</h1>

<%= render 'form' %>

<%= link_to 'Back', articles_path %>
```

Listing 6-8. Content of app/views/articles/edit.html.erb

```
<h1>Editing article</h1>

<%= render 'form' %>

<%= link_to 'Show', @article %> |
<%= link_to 'Back', articles_path %>
```

Notice the similarity between the templates, especially the render `'form'` part highlighted in bold. The render method renders a partial named `form` in this context. The upcoming section "Staying DRY with Partials" talks more about partials; for now, let's focus on the content of the template in `app/views/articles/_form.html.erb` (see Listing 6-9).

Listing 6-9. Content of app/views/articles/_form.html.erb

```
<%= form_for(@article) do |f| %>
  <% if @article.errors.any? %>
  <div id="errorExplanation">
    <h2><%= pluralize(@article.errors.count, "error") %>
```

```
prohibited this article from being saved:</h2>
    <ul>
    <% @article.errors.full_messages.each do |msg| %>
      <li><%= msg %></li>
    <% end %>
    </ul>
  </div>
  <% end %>

  <div class="field">
    <%= f.label :title %><br />
    <%= f.text_field :title %>
  </div>
  <div class="field">
    <%= f.label :location %><br />
    <%= f.text_field :location %>
  </div>
  <div class="field">
    <%= f.label :excerpt %><br />
    <%= f.text_field :excerpt %>
  </div>
  <div class="field">
    <%= f.label :body %><br />
    <%= f.text_area :body %>
  </div>
  <div class="field">
    <%= f.label :published_at %><br />
    <%= f.datetime_select :published_at %>
  </div>
  <div class="actions">
    <%= f.submit %>
  </div>
<% end %>
```

You use form helpers for each of your fields. Visit the article's new page at
http://localhost:3000/articles/new in your browser, and you see that the helpers function to produce
a nicely formatted HTML form. Use your browser's View Source command to look at the HTML that was
generated. Here's part of the generated HTML:

```
<h1>New article</h1>



<form accept-charset="UTF-8" action="/articles" class="new_article"

id="new_article" method="post">

  <div style="margin:0;padding:0;display:inline">
```

```
  <input name="_snowman" type="hidden" value="&#9731;" />

  <input name="authenticity_token" type="hidden"

  value="Dhqp8NmXwgsAPMVHJPfoRWu8UJN1XurF8ngdzaksC48=" />

</div>


<div class="field">

  <label for="article_title">Title</label><br />

  <input id="article_title" name="article[title]" size="30" type="text" />

</div>

<div class="field">

  <label for="article_location">Location</label><br />

  <input id="article_location" name="article[location]" size="30" type="text" />

</div>

<div class="field">

  <label for="article_excerpt">Excerpt</label><br />

  <input id="article_excerpt" name="article[excerpt]" size="30" type="text" />

</div>

<div class="field">

  <label for="article_body">Body</label><br />

  <textarea cols="40" id="article_body" name="article[body]" rows="20"></textarea>

</div>

…

<div class="actions">
```

```
        <input id="article_submit" name="commit" type="submit" value="Create Article" />

    </div>

</form>
```

Note the way in which Rails formats the name attribute of each form element: *model[attribute]*. This helps when it comes to parsing the parameters from the form, as you see shortly. If you manually create your form elements (which you need to do sometimes), you can use this naming convention to make sure your form values are easy to parse in the controller. Most of the time, though, you use form helpers when working with forms, especially when you're dealing with Active Record objects. Let's spend some time discussing form helpers.

Using Form Helpers

One of the best things about working with templates in Rails is the presence of helpers. Rails comes with a bunch of helper methods that take the tedium out of generating the bits of HTML that your views need. Let's face it: nothing is more of a drag to build than HTML forms. Fortunately, Rails understands the plight of the web developer all too well and provides a suite of easy ways to build forms.

Two basic varieties of form helpers are available:

- FormHelper: Active Record–aware tag helpers for creating forms that hook into models.

- FormTagHelper: Helpers that output tags. They aren't integrated with Active Record. The names of these helpers are suffixed with _tag.

The FormHelper type is aware of Active Record objects assigned to the template; the FormTagHelper (note the Tag) type isn't. The advantage of the Active Record–aware, FormHelper, helpers is that they know how to populate themselves with data and can automatically be highlighted in the event of validation errors from the model. But not every form element you make corresponds directly to a model attribute. That's where the FormTagHelper group comes in handy. These have no special relationship with Active Record; they just output form tags.

In your article's form template (Listing 6-9), you use six helpers: form_for, label, text_field, text_area, datetime_select, and submit.

The form_for helper is of the FormHelper variety. It creates an HTML form tag for the passed object (@article, in this case) and places everything in the do..end block inside the resulting form. It also produces and sets a *form local variable* to the form block. The form local variable, in this case called f, is aware of the @article object and uses its attributes' names and values when calling the other form helpers: label, text_field, text_area, datetime_select, and submit.

By default, forms use the HTTP POST method. If you want to use a different method, you need to specify it manually using the :method option (for example, :method => :get). If you remember, POST is the request method you used for the create action in your RESTful designed controller.

GET VS. POST

The HTTP protocol defines several request methods, the most popular of which are GET and POST. Both are methods for requesting a web page; the difference is in how the request is sent. GET is the simpler of the two. It includes all the information about the request as part of the URL. POST sends information invisibly, which is to say, as part of the request header and not part of the URL. So, you can't type a POST request into your browser's location bar. Every time you request a web page via the location bar in your browser, you're using GET. When you submit a form, say to register on a web site, the form is submitted via a POST.

How do you know when to use which? The best way to think of this is to consider GET a read method. It should never do anything destructive, such as modifying a database record. POST, on the other hand, can be thought of as a write method. When you need to update or delete data, use POST.

Remember that you should never put a state-changing action behind a GET request. For more information, see http://www.w3.org/2001/tag/doc/whenToUseGet.html.

The label helper is a FormHelper method that outputs an HTML label tag for the provided attribute. Here's an example of the output for :title:

```
<label for="article_title">Title</label>
```

The text_field helper is of the FormHelper variety, meaning that it corresponds to Active Record objects. It creates an HTML input tag whose type is set to "text" and assigns it a name and an id that match the given object and method (title in this case). Here's what the rendered output looks like:

```
<input id="article_title" name="article[title]" size="30" type="text" />
```

The text_area helper is also of the FormHelper variety. It's similar to text_field, except it returns a text area instead of a text input. Here's what the HTML output looks like for the body field:

```
<textarea cols="40" id="article_body" name="article[body]" rows="20"></textarea>
```

The datetime_select helper is a FormHelper that outputs a set of HTML select tags to input a date and time value.

The submit helper is a FormHelper that creates an input element whose type is set to "submit". It accepts the name of the submit button as its first argument. If you don't provide a name to the submit method, it generates a name based on the @article object. For example, in the New Article form, the generated name is Create Article, whereas in the Edit Article form, the name is Update Article. Here's the HTML output from the example:

```
<input id="article_submit" name="commit" type="submit" value="Create Article" />
```

All these helpers (and, to be sure, most helpers in Rails) accept a hash of options as their last argument to customize the resulting HTML. For example, to give your `title` field a class of `large`, you write `f.text_field :title, :class => 'large'`, which adds the `class` attribute to the output:

```
<input class="large" id="article_title" name="article[title]"

size="30" type="text" />
```

You can pass arbitrary options in this way, all of which end up as attributes on the resulting tag. For example, to apply an in-line `style` attribute, you can use `:style => 'background: #fab444'`. Here's a list of some of the most common `FormHelper` helpers:

- `text_field`
- `hidden_field`
- `password_field`
- `file_field`
- `text_area`
- `check_box`
- `radio_button`

All these methods can be suffixed with `_tag` to create standard HTML tags (with no Active Record integration).

For a full list of `FormHelper` and `FormTagHelper` methods, consult the Rails API, where you can find a complete reference along with usage examples:

- http://api.rubyonrails.org/classes/ActionView/Helpers/FormHelper.html
- http://api.rubyonrails.org/classes/ActionView/Helpers/FormTagHelper.html

Now, back to your form. Let's see what happens when you submit it. (Make sure your server is still running.) Click the Create Article button, and you see the screen shown in Figure 6-4.

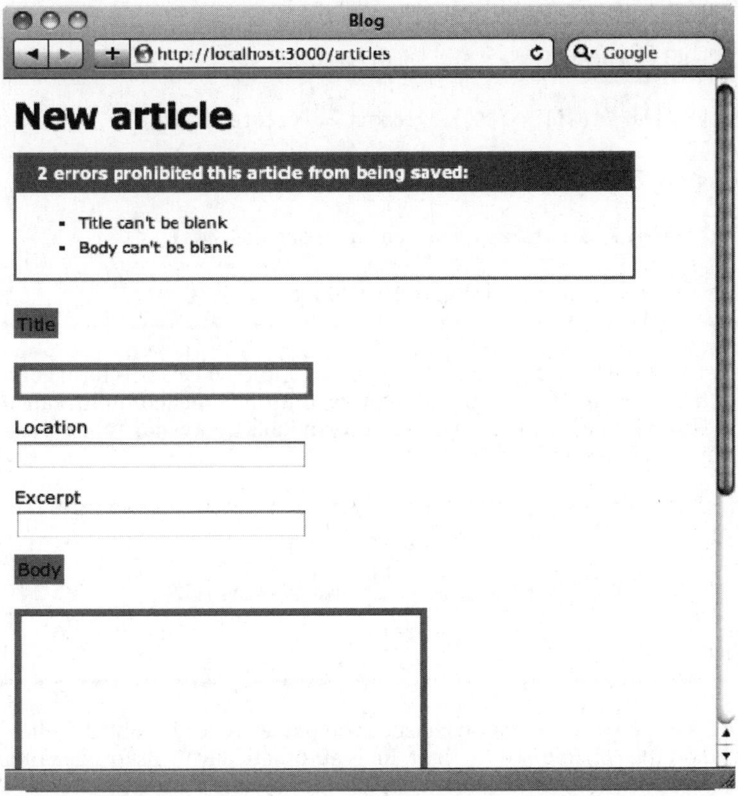

Figure 6-4. *New article form with validation errors*

What happened? Well, as the message says, Rails couldn't create an `article` for you. Of course it couldn't—you set validation rules in your `Article` model to prevent the creation of a new article object with an empty `title` or body field. But let's look at the output from the server running in the command prompt and see what happened:

```
Started POST "/articles" for 127.0.0.1 at 2010-03-12 22:54:43

  Processing by ArticlesController#create as HTML

  Parameters: {"_snowman"=>"",

"authenticity_token"=>"Dhqp8NmXwgsAPMVHJPfoRWu8UJN1XurF8ngdzaksC48=",
```

```
"article"=>{"title"=>"", "location"=>"", "excerpt"=>"", "body"=>"",

"published_at(1i)"=>"2010", "published_at(2i)"=>"5", "published_at(3i)"=>"2",

"published_at(4i)"=>"22", "published_at(5i)"=>"35"}, "commit"=>"Create Article"}

Rendered articles/_form.html.erb (55.9ms)

Rendered articles/new.html.erb within layouts/application.html.erb (65.4ms)

Completed in 179ms (Views: 71.2ms | ActiveRecord: 0.0ms) with 200
```

See the section titled Parameters above? You may recognize this as a Ruby hash. This hash contains all the form values you submitted. Notice that there's an entry for the button name (commit), called Create Article and for authenticity_token, which is used for security in Rails to prevent anonymous form posts. The article portion of the hash looks like this:

```
"article"=>{"title"=>"", "location"=>"", "excerpt"=>"", "body"=>"",

"published_at(1i)"=>"2010", "published_at(2i)"=>"5", "published_at(3i)"=>"2",

"published_at(4i)"=>"22", "published_at(5i)"=>"35
```

If you're thinking that this looks a lot like the options hashes you passed to article objects when you were working with Active Record on the console, you're right. Rails automatically turns form elements into a convenient hash that you can pass into your models to create and update their attributes. In a minute, you put this feature to use in the next action, create. First, let's take a deeper look at params.

Processing Request Parameters

Request parameters—whether they originate from requests of the GET or POST variety—are accessible via the params hash. To be specific, params is a method that returns a Hash object so you can access it using hash semantics. Hashes in Ruby are similar to arrays but are indexed by arbitrary keys—unlike arrays, which are indexed by number. (If you need a quick review of the Hash object, flip to Appendix A for a Ruby primer.)

The value of any request variable can be retrieved by its symbolized key. So, if there's a variable called id in the request parameters, you can access it with params[:id]. Just to drive this concept home, let's look at a sample URL and display the params hash that it populates. Point your browser to http://localhost:3000/articles?title=rails&body=great, and check the server output. You should see something similar to this:

```
Parameters: {"title"=>"rails", "body"=>"great"}
```

Revisiting the Controller

With an understanding of params under your belt, let's go back to your controller. The create action is the target of the form submission. The method code shown in Listing 6-10 is from the articles controller, just under the new method.

Listing 6-10. The Create Action in app/controllers/articles_controller.rb

```
# POST /articles
# POST /articles.xml
def create
  @article = Article.new(params[:article])

  respond_to do |format|
    if @article.save
      format.html { redirect_to(@article,
:notice => 'Article was successfully created.') }
      format.xml  { render :xml => @article,
:status => :created, :location => @article }
    else
      format.html { render :action => "new" }
      format.xml  { render :xml => @article.errors,
:status => :unprocessable_entity }
    end
  end
end
```

Let's walk through this. First, you initialize a new Article object with whatever attributes come in via the params hash, storing it in an instance variable named @article. Then, you try to save the object.

If the save is successful, you use a facility that Rails provides called the *flash* to set a message—by passing the :notice option to redirect_to—before redirecting to the show action on the same articles controller. The flash is a special kind of storage mechanism provided by Rails for convenience. It encapsulates the pattern of wanting to set a message on one action and have that message persist to the next, only to disappear after that action is rendered. This is useful for providing user feedback, as you do here to say "Article was successfully created." If you look at the show article file in app/views/articles/show.html.erb, you have access to the notice variable, allowing the message to be displayed:

```
<p class="notice"><%= notice %></p>
```

The flash message you set is available to the controller and action you redirect to (the show action on the articles controller). There are two special flash cases, notice and alert, that you can use just as you did in the previous example by passing them as arguments to redirect_to.

■ **NOTE** When you pass `:notice => "Article was successfully created"` to `redirect_to`, it's identical to calling `flash[:notice] = "Article was successfully created"` in a separate line. Also, when you retrieve, in any view template, the message using `notice`, you could as well use `flash[:notice]`. So, you can use any named key when calling `flash` because it's implemented as a Ruby hash. You store values in it based on a key. The key can be anything you like: you can use any symbol, such as `flash[:warning]` =, in your controller and later retrieve it in your views using the same `flash[:warning]` call.

If the save fails, you render the `new` action again so that any errors can be corrected.

Displaying Error Messages in Templates

Let's try submitting the form empty one more time to explore it again. Sure enough, the form doesn't save. Notice that you're still on the same screen and that the form elements are highlighted in red, as shown in Figure 6-4.

If you look at the HTML source, you see that the `input` and `label` tags are surrounded by `div` elements with the class name `fieldWithErrors`:

```
<div class="fieldWithErrors">

  <label for="article_title">Title</label>

</div><br />

<div class="fieldWithErrors">

  <input id="article_title" name="article[title]" size="30" type="text" value="" />

</div>
```

Rails does this automatically for any fields that fail validation. You can use these classes to style invalid elements.

■ **NOTE** The style rules that turn the invalid fields red are generated by the scaffold generator and are in `public/stylesheets/scaffold.css`. All static files, such as style sheets and images, are located in the `public` directory.

The formatted list of errors that appears at the top of the page is rendered using the code snippet below, which is a part of app/views/articles/_form.html.erb:

```
<% if @article.errors.any? %>
<div id="errorExplanation">
  <h2><%= pluralize(@article.errors.count, "error") %> prohibited this article from being
saved:</h2>
  <ul>
  <% @article.errors.full_messages.each do |msg| %>
    <li><%= msg %></li>
  <% end %>
  </ul>
</div>
<% end %>
```

Now that you understand this much, let's submit the form with valid data. If all goes according to plan, the new article should be created, and you're redirected to that article's show action, where you see the friendly notice message you set. Notice that if you refresh the page using your browser's Refresh button, the notice message disappears.

Edit and Update actions

The edit and update actions look almost identical to the new and create actions. The main difference is that instead of instantiating a new Article object, you fetch an existing one. You use Active Record's update_attributes method to update all the Article attributes with those from the params hash. If the update fails, update_attributes returns false, and your if statement takes the else path (see Listing 6-11).

Listing 6-11. The Update Action in app/controllers/articles_controller.rb

```
  # PUT /articles/1
  # PUT /articles/1.xml
  def update
    @article = Article.find(params[:id])

    respond_to do |format|
      if @article.update_attributes(params[:article])
        format.html { redirect_to(@article,
:notice => 'Article was successfully updated.') }
        format.xml  { head :ok }
      else
        format.html { render :action => "edit" }
        format.xml  { render :xml => @article.errors,
:status => :unprocessable_entity }
      end
    end
end
```

Revisiting the views

Let's get back to the views. If you look at the new and edit templates, you can't help but notice that they render almost the same HTML: only the header and navigation are slightly different. Remember from the RESTful discussion that the HTTP request methods for create and update should be POST and PUT, respectively. Rails once more takes care of that for you. You're rendering the same app/view/articles/_form.html.erb partial, but Rails knows the request method to use based on the @article variable passed to the form_for helper.

Try editing one of the articles. The URL should be something like http://localhost:3000/articles/1/edit; it looks similar to the new form, but with the record information already populated (see Figure 6-5).

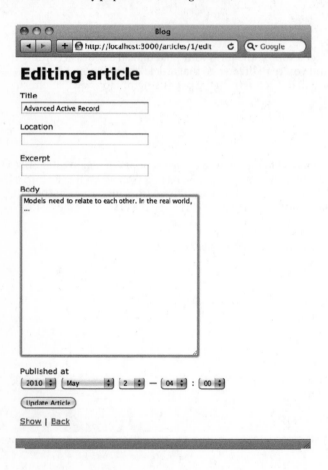

Figure 6-5. *Editing an existing article*

Thanks to the form_for helper, the form fields are populated with their respective @article attributes. If you try to submit this form and look at the output from the server running on the command prompt, you see the following:

```
Started POST "/articles/1" for 127.0.0.1 at 2010-05-02 19:20:37

  Processing by ArticlesController#update as HTML

Parameters: {"_snowman"=>"☃",

"authenticity_token"=>"Dhqp8NmXwgsAPMVHJPfoRWu8UJN1XurF8ngdzaksC48=",

"article"=>{"title"=>"Advanced Active Record", "location"=>"", "excerpt"=>"",

"body"=>"Models need to relate to each other. In the real world, ...",

"published_at(1i)"=>"2010", "published_at(2i)"=>"5", "published_at(3i)"=>"2",

"published_at(4i)"=>"04", "published_at(5i)"=>"00"},

"commit"=>"Update Article", "id"=>"1"}

  Article Load (0.3ms)  SELECT "articles".* FROM "articles"

WHERE ("articles"."id" = 1) LIMIT 1

  SQL (17.0ms)  UPDATE "articles" SET "excerpt" = '', "location" = '',

"updated_at" = '2010-05-02 23:20:37.950735' WHERE ("articles"."id" = 1)

Redirected to http://localhost:3000/articles/1

Completed 302 Found in 60ms
```

Notice the bold line: the update action of the articles controller was called as expected. Rails recognizes that the @article variable passed to form_for isn't a new record; therefore, it calls the update action for you. This is yet another example of convention over configuration in Rails.

Staying DRY with Partials

A typical web application is rife with view code and often suffers from a lot of needless duplication. The HTML forms for adding and modifying articles are good examples of forms that are very similar. Wouldn't it be nice if there was a way to reuse the common elements from one form in more than one place? That's where partial templates come in.

Partial templates, usually referred to as *partials*, are similar to regular templates, but they have a more refined set of capabilities. Partials are used quite often in a typical Rails application, because they help cut down on duplication and keep the code well organized. They follow the naming convention of being prefixed with an underscore, thus distinguishing them from standard templates (which are meant to be rendered on their own).

Rather than creating two separate forms, Rails keeps your code DRY by using a single partial and including it from both the new and edit templates. Let's look at the code from new.html.erb and edit.html.erb, shown in Listings 6-12 and 6-13.

Listing 6-12. The app/views/articles/new.html.erb File

```
<h1>New article</h1>

<%= render 'form' %>

<%= link_to 'Back', articles_path %>
```

Listing 6-13. The app/views/users/edit.html.erb File

```
<h1>Editing article</h1>

<%= render 'form' %>

<%= link_to 'Show', @article %> |
<%= link_to 'Back', articles_path %>
```

Let's take a closer look at the render method. When referencing the partial in the render method, you don't include the leading underscore:

```
<%= render 'form' %>
```

A single string argument is passed to the render method. The render method also accepts a second argument in a form of a hash. (Have you noticed yet that Rails is a big fan of the options hash?) The string argument is the partial's name. Upon seeing this, the render method searches the current directory for a file named _form.html.erb. Notice that you don't need to include the leading underscore or the file extension when specifying the partial's name; Rails knows to look for a file in the same directory as the calling template with a leading underscore.

Let's take a brief detour to discuss a few things about partials. One of the things that makes partials unique is a special convenience: automatic local variable assignment by way of convention over configuration. That's was a mouthful. The next section explains.

Local Variable Assignment in Partials

The render method accepts a hash of local variables as part of the options hash. This is an example of what a render partial with local variables looks like:

```
<%= render 'header', :title => 'My Blog' %>
```

Any number of local variables can be assigned this way, and any object can be set as the value. In the preceding example, the partial has access to the local variable title.

Rendering an Object Partial

Following the same convention of local variable assignment in partials, Rails makes it easier to render a partial that represents a specific object. For example, suppose you have the following render call in your code:

```
<%= render @article %>
```

Rails looks for a partial in app/views/articles/_article.html.erb and automatically assigns a local variable called article. It's a t shortcut for

```
<%= render 'article', :article => @article %>
```

Rendering a Collection of Partials

Another common pattern of t rendering partials renders a collection of objects. Rails has a convention for rendering collections where you pass the collection as the first argument of the render method; Rails automatically loops across this collection and renders the partial of every object inside that array accordingly. Here's an example:

```
<%= render @articles %>
```

This behaves exactly like the previous call, but it performs more magic under the hood. For example, if the @articles array contains different Active Record objects, such as two articles and two comments, the render call renders the right partial template for each of those objects. It renders /app/views/comments/_comment.html.erb for the comment objects and /app/views/articles/_article.html.erb for the article objects. It translates as follows:

```
<% @articles.each do |object| %>
  <%= render object %>
<% end %>
```

Summary

This chapter covered a lot of ground. It began with a general introduction to the components that compose Action Pack, the Rails library responsible for the controller and the view. Then, it launched into a controller walk-through, where you visited your scaffold-generated controller. In doing so, you learned about routes, what happens when you generate a scaffold, how actions relate to views, and how to work with layouts. You were introduced to Rails' form helpers, and you learned how easily forms integrate with Active Record objects. The chapter also introduced partials, and you learned how to keep your templates DRY and easy to maintain.

This chapter gave you your first taste of Rails outside the model. You now have a complete understanding of how Rails divides its concerns and a firsthand look at MVC in action. You started by modeling your domain in Chapters 4 and 5, and now you've completed the first iteration of building a web application around your domain.

You should be proud of yourself. At this stage, you know a lot about Rails. The next chapter builds on this knowledge, starting with more advanced topics like building a controller from scratch, sessions, and state, and sprucing up the application with some CSS.

CHAPTER 7

■ ■ ■

Advanced Action Pack

Now that you have a very good understanding of how the components of Action Pack work, it's time to dig a little deeper. You start by generating the user controller from scratch, writing its actions, and creating its templates. Then, you add some functionality to the blog application: you allow users to leave comments when reading an article and make sure only logged-in users have access to adding and editing content. Finally, you give your application some styling so it looks better and more like a real application.

■ **NOTE** If you need to get the code at the exact point where you finished Chapter 6, download the zip file from `http://github.com/downloads/ccjr/blog/chapter07.zip` and extract it on your computer.

Generating a Controller

It's time to create your first controller from scratch. If you haven't noticed already, Rails ships with generators for most common tasks, and controllers are no exception. The syntax for the controller generator is as follows:

```
$ rails generate controller ControllerName [actions] [options]
```

As a minimum, the controller generator takes the name of the controller as an argument, which you can specify using either CamelCase (sometimes called MixedCase) or underscore_case. The generator also takes an optional list of actions to generate. For every action you specify, you get an empty method stub in the controller and a template in app/views/#{controller_name}. To see a list of all available options, you can run the generator `rails generate controller` without arguments.

■ **TIP** The help output for the controller generator contains sample usage and options that you're sure to find interesting. All of the generators (and most UNIX commands, for that matter) respond to the `--help` argument (or variations thereof), so you're encouraged to try it whenever you're issuing a system command.

Generate the Users controller using the following command:

```
$ rails generate controller Users
```

create	app/controllers/users_controller.rb
invoke	erb
create	app/views/users
invoke	test_unit
create	test/functional/users_controller_test.rb
invoke	helper
create	app/helpers/users_helper.rb
invoke	test_unit
create	test/unit/helpers/users_helper_test.rb

Take the time to read the output of the generator so you get a sense of all the files that were just created. Notice where the templates are located: in the app/views directory, inside a subdirectory named after the controller. In this case, because your controller is called users, your templates go in app/views/users. Open the newly minted controller file in app/controllers/users_controller.rb and take a look: see Listing 7-1.

Listing 7-1. Users Controller in app/controllers/users_controller.rb

```
class UsersController < ApplicationController
end
```

■ **TIP** It's a convention in Rails that controller names should always be plural.

As you can see, all the generator gives you is an empty stub. If you want your users controller to do anything useful, you need to add a few actions and give it something to do. Let's add the actions you need to the controller now. Edit users_controller.rb so that it looks like Listing 7-2.

Listing 7-2. Updated app/controllers/users_controller.rb: http://gist.github.com/337147

```
class UsersController < ApplicationController
  def new
    @user = User.new
```

```
  end

  def create
    @user = User.new(params[:user])
    if @user.save
      redirect_to articles_path, :notice => 'User successfully added.'
    else
      render :action => 'new'
    end
  end

  def edit
    @user = User.find(params[:id])
  end

  def update
    @user = User.find(params[:id])
    if @user.update_attributes(params[:user])
      redirect_to articles_path, :notice => 'Updated user information successfully.'
    else
      render :action => 'edit'
    end
  end
end
```

You add four actions: new, create, edit, and update. The actions you add look very similar to the ones you saw in the articles controller in Chapter 6. The main difference is that you aren't using the respond_to block; therefore, Rails directly renders the default erb templates. Let's create those templates: Listings 7-3 and 7-4 show the new and edit templates.

Listing 7-3. New User Template in app/views/users/new.html.erb: http://gist.github.com/337207

```
<h1>New user</h1>

<%= render 'form' %>

<%= link_to 'Back', articles_path %>
```

Listing 7-4. Edit User Template in app/views/users/edit.html.erb: http://gist.github.com/337206

```
<h1>Editing user</h1>

<%= render 'form' %>

<%= link_to 'Back', articles_path %>
```

In both the new and edit templates, you render a form partial, which is expected to be in app/views/users/_form.html.erb. Create the form partial and make sure it looks like Listing 7-5.

Listing 7-5. User Form Partial in app/views/users/_form.html.erb: http://gist.github.com/337209

```
<%= form_for(@user) do |f| %>
  <% if @user.errors.any? %>
  <div id="errorExplanation">
    <h2><%= pluralize(@user.errors.count, "error") %>
prohibited this user from being saved:</h2>
    <ul>
    <% @user.errors.full_messages.each do |msg| %>
      <li><%= msg %></li>
    <% end %>
    </ul>
  </div>
  <% end %>

  <div class="field">
    <%= f.label :email %><br />
    <%= f.text_field :email %>
  </div>
  <div class="field">
    <%= f.label :password %><br />
    <%= f.password_field :password %>
  </div>
  <div class="field">
    <%= f.label :password_confirmation %><br />
    <%= f.password_field :password_confirmation %>
  </div>
  <div class="actions">
    <%= f.submit %>
  </div>
<% end %>
```

You use the same form helpers discussed in Chapter 6: `text_field` for text input and `password_field` for password inputs. Before you go to the browser to try what you've created, you need to add users as a resource in your routes file. Edit `config/routes.rb` so it looks like Listing 7-6.

Listing 7-6. Adding Users to routes.rb in config/routes.rb: http://gist.github.com/337211

```
Blog::Application.routes.draw do
  root :to => "articles#index"
  resources :articles
  resources :users
end
```

To see it all in action, try adding a new user by visiting `http://localhost:3000/users/new`. The form should look like Figure 7-1.

Figure 7-1. Adding a new user

Now you can create a new user, and you can also edit that user if you have the user's id. In fact, anyone can create and edit users at the moment; but shortly, you change the edit and update actions' implementation to make sure users can only edit their own profile.

Nested Resources

You added support for comments earlier, but only at the model level. You didn't implement a controller or view for the Comment model—and that's what you do now.

Comments are special because they aren't regular resources that you can implement in a regular RESTful controller, like articles or users. Comments are more dependent on an article; they never exist on their own because they're conceptually meaningless if they're not tied to an article.

Instead of defining comments as standalone resources as you did articles, you define them as nested resources of articles. Go to the routes file, and update the resources :article call to look like Listing 7-7.

Listing 7-7. Adding Comments to routes.rb in config/routes.rb: http://gist.github.com/338747

```
Blog::Application.routes.draw do
  root :to => "articles#index"
  resources :articles do
```

```
    resources :comments
  end
  resources :users
end
```

To define a nested resource, you use the resources method passed inside a block to the parent resource. Notice how resources :comments is passed as a block to the resources :articles call; therefore, comments become a nested resource of articles. The named routes for nested resources are different from standalone ones; they're built on top of a singular article named route, requiring an article id every time they're called. Table 7-1 lists the generated named routes for comments.

Table 7-1. Comments' Named Routes

Request Method	Nested Named Routes	Parameters	Controller Action
GET	article_comments_path	Article ID	index
POST	article_comments_path	Record hash	create
GET	article_comment_path	ID, article ID	show
PUT	article_comment_path	ID, article ID, and record hash	update
DELETE	article_comment_path	ID, article ID	destroy
GET	edit_article_comment_path	ID, article ID	edit
GET	new_article_comment_path	Article ID	new

Every time you call comment named routes, you must provide an article id. Let's generate the comments controller and see how you take care of that:

```
$ rails generate controller Comments
```

```
    create    app/controllers/comments_controller.rb

    invoke    erb

    create    app/views/comments

    invoke    test_unit

    create    test/functional/comments_controller_test.rb

    invoke    helper
```

create	app/helpers/comments_helper.rb
invoke	test_unit
create	test/unit/helpers/comments_helper_test.rb

Of the default seven actions for which Rails generates named routes, you need only two for comments: create and destroy. You don't need index, new, or show actions because comments are listed, shown, and added from the article's show page. You don't want to support editing or updating a comment, so you don't need edit or update either. Listing 7-8 shows how the comments controller looks with only those two actions.

Listing 7-8. Comments Controller in app/controllers/comments_controller.rb:

http://gist.github.com/338756

```ruby
class CommentsController < ApplicationController
  before_filter :load_article

  def create
    @comment = @article.comments.new(params[:comment])
    if @comment.save
      redirect_to @article, :notice => 'Thanks for your comment'
    else
      redirect_to @article, :alert => 'Unable to add comment'
    end
  end

  def destroy
    @comment = @article.comments.find(params[:id])
    @comment.destroy
    redirect_to @article, :notice => 'Comment deleted'
  end

  private
    def load_article
      @article = Article.find(params[:article_id])
    end
end
```

Notice the before_filter call at the beginning of the controller; it runs the method load_article before all the actions in your comments controller. That's all you need to know for now. This chapter talks more about filters shortly.

The load_article method does a simple task: it finds the article from the passed article_id and assigns it to the @article instance variable. Remember that you always have the article_id in your parameters because it's always included in your nested named routes. With load_article in before_filter, you always have @article loaded and accessible in your comments controller's actions and templates.

Also notice how you find and assign @comment: you do so using @article.comments. This way, you make sure you're dealing only with @article comments, and you don't create or delete comments from another article.

Now, let's update the views and create some templates. As mentioned earlier, you *list*, *show*, and add *new* comments from the article's show page; so, let's update the article show page, make it a little nicer, and then add new code to display comments. Listing 7-9 shows how app/views/articles/show.html.erb looks after the update.

Listing 7-9. Updated Article Show Template in app/views/articles/show.html.erb:

http://gist.github.com/338770

```
<%= render @article %>

<h3>Comments</h3>
<div id="comments">
  <%= render @article.comments %>
</div>

<%= render :file => 'comments/new' %>
```

That's a lot of cleaning. First, you extract displaying the attributes into a partial named app/views/articles/_article.html.erb, which you call using render @article. One of the benefits of creating a partial is that you can use it in other pages, such as the articles index page, which you implement shortly.

Notice that the flash notice is removed from the article show template. To make sure the flash messages show in any view template, you move it to the application layout in app/views/layouts/application.html.erb (see Listing 7-10).

Listing 7-10. Updated Application Layout Template in app/views/layouts/application.html.erb:

http://gist.github.com/388446

```
<!DOCTYPE html>
<html>
<head>
  <title>Blog</title>
  <%= stylesheet_link_tag :all %>
  <%= javascript_include_tag :defaults %>
  <%= csrf_meta_tag %>
</head>
<body>

<%= content_tag :p, notice, :class => 'notice' if notice.present? %>
<%= content_tag :p, alert, :class => 'alert' if alert.present? %>

<%= yield %>

</body>
</html>
```

Then, you list comments using the collection render on @article.comments. To refresh your memory, this loops through the article comments rendering the app/views/comments/_comment.html.erb partial for every comment.

Finally, you render the app/views/comments/new.html.erb template as a file; you could render it as a partial too, but it's more like a template than a partial. In some projects, you may need to render a regular template file—corresponding to an action—which may also be used like a partial in other parts of the application. In this case, to render the app/views/comments/new.html.erb file in the context of another template, you use render :file.

None of the files mentioned have been created yet. Let's do that now. Create app/views/articles/_article.html.erb, app/views/comments/_comment.html.erb, and app/views/comments/new.html.erb, as shown in Listings 7-11, 7-12, and 7-13, respectively.

Listing 7-11. Article Partial in app/views/articles/_article.html.erb: http://gist.github.com/338785

```erb
<%= div_for article do %>
  <h3>
    <%= link_to article.title, article %>
    <span class='actions'>
      <%= link_to "Edit", edit_article_path(article) %>
      <%= link_to "Delete", article, :confirm => "Are you sure?",
:method => :delete %>
    </span>
  </h3>
  <%= article.body %>
<% end %>
```

Listing 7-12. Comment Partial in app/views/comments/_comment.html.erb:

http://gist.github.com/338789

```erb
<%= div_for comment do %>
  <h3>
    <%= comment.name %> &lt;<%= comment.email %>&gt; said:
    <span class='actions'>
      <%= link_to 'Delete', article_comment_path(:article_id => @article,
:id => comment), :confirm => 'Are you sure?', :method => :delete %>
    </span>
  </h3>
  <%= comment.body %>
<% end %>
```

Listing 7-13. New Comment Template in app/views/comments/new.html.erb:

http://gist.github.com/338791

```erb
<%= form_for([@article, @article.comments.new]) do |f| %>
  <div class="field">
    <%= f.label :name %><br />
    <%= f.text_field :name %>
  </div>
  <div class="field">
    <%= f.label :email %><br />
    <%= f.text_field :email %>
```

```
  </div>
  <div class="field">
    <%= f.label :body %><br />
    <%= f.text_area :body %>
  </div>
  <div class="actions">
    <%= f.submit 'Add' %>
  </div>
<% end %>
```

The article and comment partials are pretty straightforward; aside from the markup, you display the attributes and link to actions. You also wrap the content inside a div_for helper, which renders a div element with a unique id for the object passed as a parameter.

The new comment form calls form_for: instead of passing a single object as you do for article when you call form_for(@article), you pass an array of both the article object @article and a new comment object by calling @article.comments.new. This is a short way to tell Rails that you're dealing with a nested resource. Calling form_for([@article, @article.comments.new]) is identical to

```
form_for(:comment, @article.comments.new,
:url => [@article, @article.comments.new])
```

which is also identical to

```
form_for(:comment, @article.comments.new,
:url => article_comments_path(:article_id => @article))
```

Passing the array of both the parent object and the nested child object translates into the corresponding nested named route. You can replace the named route path of the delete link in app/views/comments/_comment.html.erb with [@article, comment]. Change the comment partial to look like Listing 7-14.

Listing 7-14. Delete Link Changed in app/views/comments/_comment.html.erb:

http://gist.github.com/338801

```
<%= div_for comment do %>
  <h3>
    <%= comment.name %> &lt;<%= comment.email %>&gt; said:
    <span class='actions'>
      <%= link_to 'Delete', [@article, comment], :confirm => 'Are you sure?',
:method => :delete %>
    </span>
  </h3>
  <%= comment.body %>
<% end %>
```

Now that you've created the missing templates and added the required code to the controller, let's look at the browser and see how it looks in the article show page. Run your server, go to your browser, and click your way through to an article; you should see something very similar to Figure 7-2.

Figure 7-2. *Article show page with new comment form*

Try adding a few comments, and see how the form behaves. Congratulations! You just added comment support to your blog application using nested resources. Now that you have comments and users in the system, let's add some authorization logic to make sure only logged-in users can create and update articles.

Sessions and the Login/Logout Logic

The whole point of having users in your blog application is to allow them to create their *own* articles, and to do that you need to recognize them when they create an article. Web applications normally do that by using *sessions*. Let's talk a little more about that before you implement it in your application.

Lying in State

HTTP is *stateless*. In short, that means each and every request you make across the HTTP protocol is autonomous. The web server has no idea that it has talked to your browser before; each request is like a blind date. Given this tidbit of information, you may wonder how you can stay logged in to a given site. How can the application remember you're logged in if HTTP is stateless? The answer is that you fake state.

You've no doubt heard of browser cookies. In order to simulate state atop HTTP, Rails uses cookies. When the first request comes in, Rails sets a cookie on the client browser. The browser remembers the cookie locally and sends it along with each subsequent request. The result is that Rails is able to match the cookie that comes along in the request with session data stored on the server.

Rails ships with a few different session storage mechanisms. You can choose to store session data directly in the browser cookies (that is the default) or in the database, or you can write your own session store implementation. We like the database approach the best, because it fits well with Rails' architectural principles.

The Shared-Nothing Architecture

Rails is built on the principle of a shared-nothing architecture. *Shared-nothing* means that no piece of data is shared between the servers that host the application. Storing session data on the server would violate this principle.

Imagine that you store your session data on the file system of the server that runs your application. This works fine as long as you're using only one server for your application. But what happens when your site becomes busy and you decide that you need multiple servers to keep up with the traffic? You need to use a *load balancer*—a hardware or software layer that routes requests to one of several application servers to spread out the load. Say a request comes in to server 1, and you store some session data in the file system. Then server 1 gets busy, and the load balancer decides to send the next request to server 2. But the session data isn't on server 2; it's on server 1. This presents a dilemma. The shared-nothing architecture avoids this problem by keeping the state somewhere other than on the application server, such as the database, as shown in Figure 7-3.

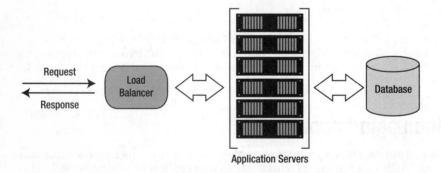

Figure 7-3. Shared-nothing architecture

■ **NOTE** Purists argue that this isn't really shared-*nothing*. After all, you're sharing the database server. But because a single database server can service dozens of application servers without a hitch, using it as a centralized storage location for session data is a worthy compromise.

Storing Sessions in the Database

The default cookie-based session storage mechanism "just works" with no configuration required. However, storing session data in the database is important enough that it's worth taking a brief detour to set up. Fortunately, Rails makes this an easy affair. A built-in Rake task called `db:sessions:create` makes a migration to create the sessions table. To run it, enter the following from your application's directory on the command line:

```
$ rake db:sessions:create
```

invoke	active_record
create	db/migrate/20100320204433_add_sessions_table.rb

This creates a migration to create the necessary sessions table in the database. All you need to do is run it:

```
$ rake db:migrate
```

Now that the sessions table has been created, you need to tell Rails that you want to use the database for session storage. This is matter of configuration and is therefore specified in the `config/initializers/session_store.rb` file. Open this file in your editor; the database session configuration options are already there, although they're commented out. Comment the `ActionController::Base.session` section, and remove the comment from the last line to activate the `active_record_store` option for sessions, as shown in Listing 7-15.

Listing 7-15. Activating active_record_store in config/initializers/session_store.rb:

http://gist.github.com/338898

```
# Be sure to restart your server when you modify this file.

# Blog::Application.config.session_store :cookie_store, :key => '_blog_session'

# Use the database for sessions instead of the cookie-based default,
# which shouldn't be used to store highly confidential information
# (create the session table with "rake db:sessions:create")
Blog::Application.config.session_store :active_record_store
```

You need to stop and start your web server for this change to take effect. Remember to use Ctrl+C to stop the server (and `rails server` to start it up again).

Using the Session

Secure in the knowledge that Rails will take care of all the low-level details of sessions for you, using the session object couldn't be easier. session is implemented as a hash, just like flash. We should come clean here. flash is a session in disguise (you can think of it as a specialized session due to its auto-expiring properties). Not surprisingly, then, the flash and session interfaces are identical. You store values in the session according to a key:

```
session[:account_id] = @account.id
session[:account_id] # => 1

session['message'] = "Hello world!"
session['message'] # => "Hello world!"
```

Session as a Resource

Now that you understand sessions, youcan go back to your main task: allowing users to log in and log out. You create a session when the user logs in and clear (destroy) it when they're done. Of course, you do that in a RESTfull way, by treating the session as a resource:

Start by generating a sessions controller:

```
$ rails generate controller Sessions
```

create	app/controllers/sessions_controller.rb	
invoke	erb	
create	app/views/sessions	
invoke	test_unit	
create	test/functional/sessions_controller_test.rb	
invoke	helper	
create	app/helpers/sessions_helper.rb	
invoke	test_unit	
create	test/unit/helpers/sessions_helper_test.rb	

Now, define this as a resource in your routes file in config/routes.rb, as shown in Listing 7-16.

Listing 7-16. Adding session to routes.rb in config/routes.rb: http://gist.github.com/338904

```
Blog::Application.routes.draw do
  root :to => "articles#index"
```

```
  resources :articles do
    resources :comments
  end
  resources :users
  resource :session
end
```

Notice that you define `session` as a resource and not `resources`, because you never deal with a set of sessions at once. You never list sessions in an index or anything like that—you just need to create or destroy a *single* session at a time.

Let's step back and try to understand the difference between `resource` and `resources` definitions. The main benefit you get from defining resources in your routes file is the named routes that are generated for you. In case of a single resource definition, you get different named routes: none of them are pluralized, all are singular, and there's no index action. Rails maps six actions instead of the seven in a `resources` definition. Table 7-2 provides a quick comparison between `resources` named routes and `resource` named routes.

Table 7-2. *Named Routes:* resources *vs.* resource

Request Method	resources Named Routes	resource Named Routes	Controller Action
GET	articles_path	Not available	index
POST	articles_path	session_path	create
GET	article_path	session_path	show
PUT	article_path	session_path	update
DELETE	article_path	session_path	destroy
GET	edit_article_path	edit_session_path	edit
GET	new_article_path	new_session_path	new

■ **NOTE** Although a singular name is used for the resource, the controller name is still taken from the plural name, so `sessions_controller` is the controller for the `session` resource in this case.

To avoid confusion, let's map this in your mind; to log in, you need to create a session; to log out, you clear that session. You use `new_session_path` as your login path, and the new template is your login page. POSTing the form in the new session page to `session_path` creates the session. Finally, submitting a DELETE request to `session_path` clears that session, performing a logout. Now, let's map it in the routes file; see Listing 7-17.

Listing 7-17. Adding session to routes.rb in config/routes.rb: http://gist.github.com/338912

```
Blog::Application.routes.draw do
  root :to => "articles#index"
  resources :articles do
    resources :comments
  end
  resources :users
  resource :session
  match '/login' => "sessions#new", :as => "login"
  match '/logout' => "sessions#destroy", :as => "logout"
end
```

You basically define two named routes, login_path and logout_path, which are more meaningful than new_session_path and session_path when referring to those actions.

Logging In a User

As you did for Active Record resources, in the create action, you first check the validity of the resource—in this case through authentication—and you save the state if all is good. If the validity check fails, you return the user to the login page with an error message. In this controller, you never save a record to the database—you save a session object. Listing 7-18 shows the create action.

Listing 7-18. create Method in app/controllers/sessions_controller.rb:

http://gist.github.com/338919

```
class SessionsController < ApplicationController
  def create
    if user = User.authenticate(params[:email], params[:password])
      session[:user_id] = user.id
      redirect_to root_path, :notice => "Logged in successfully"
    else
      flash.now[:alert] = "Invalid login/password combination"
      render :action => 'new'
    end
  end
end
```

First, you use the authenticate class method from the User model to attempt a login (see Listing 5-37 in Chapter 5). Remember that authenticate returns a User object if the authentication succeeds; otherwise, it returns nil. Therefore, you can perform your conditional and your assignment in one shot using if user = User.authenticate(params[:email], params[:password]). If the assignment takes place, you want to store a reference to this user so you can keep the user logged in—a perfect job for the session:

```
session[:user_id] = user.id
```

Notice that you don't need to store the entire User object in session. You store just a reference to the user's id. Why not store the entire User object? Well, think about this for a minute: what if the user is stored in session and later changes their login? The old login would remain in the session and would therefore be *stale*. This can cause problems if the underlying User model changes. Your entire object could become stale, potentially causing a NoMethodError when accessing attributes that didn't exist on the model at the time it was placed in session. The best bet is to just store the id.

With a reference to the logged-in user safely stored in session, you can redirect to the root path, corresponding to the articles controller.

If the assignment doesn't take place and the User.authenticate method returns nil, you know the provided login and password are invalid, and you return to the login page with an alert message using flash.now. RESTfully speaking, the login page is where you enter the *new* session information, so it's basically the new action.

■ **NOTE** flash.now differs from the regular flash call by setting a flash message that is only available to the current action. If you remember, regular flash makes messages available after a redirect.

But wait: you don't have a new action yet. Don't you need to define it first? The truth is, you don't need to initialize anything there—all you need is its template. By having the template, Rails automatically renders that template when it doesn't find the action definition. Let's create the new template, as shown in Listing 7-19.

Listing 7-19. new Session Template in app/views/sessions/new.html.erb: http://gist.github.com/338925

```
<h1>Login</h1>

<%= form_tag session_path do %>
  <div class="field">
    <%= label_tag :email %><br />
    <%= text_field_tag :email %>
  </div>
  <div class="field">
    <%= label_tag :password %><br />
    <%= password_field_tag :password %>
  </div>
  <div class="actions">
    <%= submit_tag 'Login' %>
  </div>
<% end %>
```

Notice that you use form_tag instead of form_for, which you used earlier with Active Record objects; that's because session isn't an Active Record object. You also submit to session_path because it's a resource, not resources, as explained earlier. Again, because you aren't dealing with an Active Record object, you use label_tag, text_field_tag, and password_field_tag helpers.

Logging Out a User

The user is logged in when a session is created, so in order to log out the user, you need to clear that session. You do so in the destroy action. The destroy action is fairly straightforward. You clear the session by using the reset_session method that comes with Rails, which does exactly as it says: it resets the session by clearing all the values in it. After you clear the session, you redirect back to the login_path, which is your login screen.

Another way to do this is to specifically clear the user_id key from the session hash, but it's safer for the logout in particular to clear all the session values. Listing 7-20 shows how the sessions controller looks after you add the destroy method.

Listing 7-20. Updated Sessions Controller in app/controllers/sessions_controller.rb:

http://gist.github.com/338944

```ruby
class SessionsController < ApplicationController
  def create
    if user = User.authenticate(params[:email], params[:password])
      session[:user_id] = user.id
      redirect_to root_path, :notice => "Logged in successfully"
    else
      flash.now[:alert] = "Invalid login/password combination"
      render :action => 'new'
    end
  end

  def destroy
    reset_session
    redirect_to root_path, :notice => "You successfully logged out"
  end
end
```

Go ahead and try it. Create a user by going to http://localhost:3000/users/new. Then, log in by visiting the login path at http://localhost:3000/login; see Figure 7-4. Finally, if you want to log out, go to http://localhost:3000/logout.

Figure 7-4. Login page

Don't worry about remembering all the URLs. You link to them when you update your application layout.

Improving Controllers and Templates

Chapter 6 and earlier parts of this chapter covered generating controllers, creating templates and layouts, and DRYing up with partials. Let's take this a step forward: first you update article views, and then you add filters to some of your controllers, making sure some actions require authorization.

Cleaning Up the Articles Index Page

The current articles index page uses a table markup to list articles. If you've ever visited a blog, you've never seen one like that; so, let's change the table markup and loop to a more friendly markup that uses the article's partial in app/views/articles/_article.html.erb. Listing 7-21 shows the updated articles index.

Listing 7-21. Updated Articles Index in app/views/articles/index.html.erb:

http://gist.github.com/338960

```
<h1>Listing articles</h1>

<div id="articles">
  <%= render @articles %>
</div>

<br />

<%= link_to 'New article', new_article_path %>
```

■ **CAUTION** Be careful with reusing partials. In some cases, you may prefer to keep separate files. You reuse the article partial here just to simplify things.

Visit your root path at http://localhost:3000. If all goes right, you should see something similar to Figure 7-5. That looks like a real blog!

Figure 7-5. *Blog-like home page*

Adding Categories to the Article Form

In Chapter 5, you added categories to the Article model, but neither your controller nor your templates know about this yet. Let's remedy that now, starting with the article form. Add the code shown in bold in Listing 7-22 to the form partial in app/views/articles/_form.html.erb.

Listing 7-22. Modified app/views/articles/_form.html.erb: http://gist.github.com/341499

```
<%= form_for(@article) do |f| %>
  <% if @article.errors.any? %>
  <div id="errorExplanation">
    <h2><%= pluralize(@article.errors.count, "error") %>
prohibited this article from being saved:</h2>
    <ul>
    <% @article.errors.full_messages.each do |msg| %>
      <li><%= msg %></li>
    <% end %>
    </ul>
  </div>
  <% end %>
```

```
<div class="field">
  <%= f.label :title %><br />
  <%= f.text_field :title %>
</div>
<div class="field">
  <%= f.label :location %><br />
  <%= f.text_field :location %>
</div>
<div class="field">
  <%= f.label "Categories" %><br />
  <% for category in Category.all %>
    <%= check_box_tag 'article[category_ids][]', category.id,
@article.category_ids.include?(category.id), :id => dom_id(category) %>
      <%= label_tag dom_id(category), category.name, :class => "check_box_label" %>
  <% end %>
</div>
<div class="field">
  <%= f.label :excerpt %><br />
  <%= f.text_field :excerpt %>
</div>
<div class="field">
  <%= f.label :body %><br />
  <%= f.text_area :body %>
</div>
<div class="field">
  <%= f.label :published_at %><br />
  <%= f.datetime_select :published_at %>
</div>
<div class="actions">
  <%= f.submit %>
</div>
<% end %>
```

To offer articles the chance to be part of one or more categories, you show all the categories as check boxes. But how do you associate those check boxes with the article?

Remember that Chapter 5 talked about the methods that each association adds to your model when you use them. In the case of the Article model, the has_and_belong_to_many :categories association adds the category_ids method, which returns an array of the associated category ids; it also adds the category_ids=(category_ids) method, which replaces the current associated categories with the ones supplied.

Knowing that, look back at the new code added to the form: you loop through all the categories and draw a check box for each one. The check_box_tag call deserves a closer look:

```
check_box_tag 'article[category_ids][]', category.id,
@article.category_ids.include?(category.id), :id => dom_id(category)
```

Notice how you use a form tag helper check_box_tag instead of an Active Record form helper check_box. You do that to be able to customize the name of the generated check-box form elements.

The check_box_tag method is an Action View form helper that generates a check box. The check_box_tag method takes four arguments: the first defines the name of the check box, the second specifies the value of the check box, and the third defines whether the check box is checked. Finally, an optional fourth argument can be passed; it's a hash of HTML options. In this case, you pass `:id =>` `dom_id(category)` as the last parameter to give the check box an id you refer to later.

The name you use is `article[category_ids][]`. The `article[category_ids]` part associates this field with the `params[:article]` hash of attributes; the `[]` at the end of the name makes sure all the check-box values are passed as an array. For example, if categories 5 and 2 are selected, `params[:article][:category_ids]` is `[5, 2]` when the form is submitted.

When Rails generates the HTML markup from a form tag helper, it autogenerates the element's id from the element's name. For example, the HTML id of `check_box_tag('article[category_ids]')` is `article_category_ids`. If you loop over all the categories and depend on Rails to generate the ids of the check boxes, all the rendered check boxes have the same HTML id. Not only is it standards incompliant to have multiple elements with the same id, but it also makes your life harder if you want to refer to any of those elements later. You solve this problem by setting the id of every check box by passing the id to `check_box_tag` as the last argument.

The `dom_id(category)` method is a helper method that generates an HTML-friendly id for your object. For example, if a category's id is 3, the `dom_id` of this category is `category_3`.

That's about it. Now that you have category integration for articles, try adding a new article; you should see a form similar to Figure 7-6.

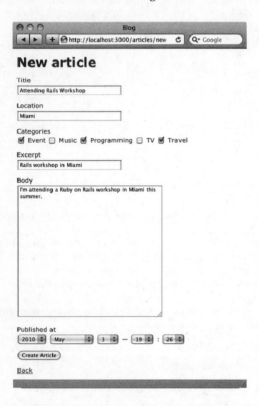

Figure 7-6. Updated article form with category check boxes

Fill the mandatory fields, select a couple of categories, and submit the form. Check the parameters output in your rails server window. You should see something similar to the following output, depending on the values you entered—pay attention to the category array):

```
Parameters: {"authenticity_token"=>"FqpxvxGqPzlQ/biDC+muT2KGyFHp1OCIbm+4KjBi1jI=",

"article"=>{"title"=>"Attending Rails Workshop", "location"=>"Miami",

"category_ids"=>["2", "1", "3"], "excerpt"=>"Rails workshop in Miami",

"body"=>"I'm attending a Ruby on Rails workshop in Miami this summer.",

"published_at(1i)"=>"2010", "published_at(2i)"=>"5", "published_at(3i)"=>"3",

"published_at(4i)"=>"19", "published_at(5i)"=>"26"}, "commit"=>"Create Article"}
```

If you try to edit the article you just created, you see that your categories are selected, and you can modify them like any other article attribute. The category_ids= method that the has_and_belong_to_many association added for you does all the magic behind the scenes.

Using Controller Filters

Filters provide a way for you to perform operations either before or after an action is invoked. There's even an around filter that can wrap the execution of an action. Of the three, the before filter is the most commonly used, so this section focuses on it.

All the code you place in before_filter is run before the action in question is called. Pretty simple, really. But there's a catch: if before_filter returns false, the action isn't executed. We often use this to protect certain actions that require a login. If you have an events controller, and you want the new and create actions to remain open (anyone can access them), but you want to restrict all other actions to logged-in users, you can do so using filters:

```
class EventsController < ApplicationController
  before_filter :authenticate, :except => [:new, :create]
end
```

This causes the authenticate method to be run before every action except those listed. Assume the authenticate method is defined in the application_controller controller and is therefore available to every other controller in the system. If the authenticate method returns false, the requested action isn't executed, thereby protecting it from unauthorized visitors.

You can also use the :only modifier to specify that the filter is to run for *only* the given actions. You can write the preceding example more concisely as follows:

```
before_filter :authenticate, :only => :destroy
```

Without the :only or :except modifier, the filter runs for all actions.

Controller inheritance hierarchies share filters downward, but subclasses can also add or skip filters without affecting the superclass. Let's say you apply a global filter to the application_controller, but

you have a particular controller that you want to be exempt from filtration. You can use
skip_before_filter, like this:

```
class ApplicationController < ActionController::Base
  before_filter :authenticate_with_token
end

class PublicController < ApplicationController
  # We don't want to check for a token on this controller
  skip_before_filter :authenticate_with_token
end
```

Filters are a fairly involved topic, and we've only scratched the surface. Still, you've seen the most
common usage pattern: protecting actions. For more information about filters, including usage
examples, check out the Rails API documentation at
http://api.rubyonrails.org/classes/ActionController/Filters/ClassMethods.html.

Requiring Authentication with Filters

In your blog application, you want to protect blog creation and modification, restricting access to
registered users. To do this, you use filters that call specific methods and check for the user_id session
you set on user login. Recall that any methods you add to the application_controller are available to all
other controllers (because it's the superclass of all controllers).

Open the application_controller in app/controllers/application_controller.rb, and add the
protected methods that enforce your authentication requirement, as shown in Listing 7-23.

Listing 7-23. Modified app/controllers/application_controller.rb: http://gist.github.com/341622

```
class ApplicationController < ActionController::Base
  protect_from_forgery

  protected
    # Returns the currently logged in user or nil if there isn't one
    def current_user
      return unless session[:user_id]
      @current_user ||= User.find_by_id(session[:user_id])
    end

    # Make current_user available in templates as a helper
    helper_method :current_user

    # Filter method to enforce a login requirement
    # Apply as a before_filter on any controller you want to protect
    def authenticate
      logged_in? ? true : access_denied
    end

    # Predicate method to test for a logged in user
    def logged_in?
      current_user.is_a? User
```

```
      end

      # Make logged_in? available in templates as a helper
      helper_method :logged_in?

      def access_denied
        redirect_to login_path, :notice => "Please log in to continue"
and return false
      end
end
```

The current_user method acts like an *accessor* for the currently logged-in user. Because it returns a User object, you can call instance methods of User on it, such as current_user.email. The authenticate method is your filter method (the one you call from individual controllers). It checks whether there is a currently logged-in user via logged_in? (which, in turn, checks that there is actually a User returned by current_user) and calls access_denied if there isn't. access_denied redirects to the login_path in the sessions controller with a notice message in the flash.

You want two of these methods available in templates as well: logged_in? and current_user. Having logged_in? available allows you to make dynamic decisions about whether a user is logged in. You can use this to show or hide administrative controls (such as adding or editing a given article). Having current_user around also proves useful in templates, allowing you to access information about users, such as their email address. Rails provides a handy way to extend the visibility of methods to templates by declaring them as helpers. You can use helper_method followed by a symbolic reference to the method in question, as you do in helper_method :logged_in?. You can also pass an array of method references to helper_method if you want to declare them all at once.

Let's apply the filter to the articles controller now. You also apply a filter to the users controller to restrict who can edit user profiles.

Applying Filters to Controllers

You apply filters using a declarative syntax. In this case, you want to check that a user is authenticated *before* you process a protected action, so you use before_filter. Add the filter to the articles controller, just inside the class body, as shown in Listing 7-24.

Listing 7-24. Before Filter Added in app/controllers/articles_controller.rb:

http://gist.github.com/341628

```
class ArticlesController < ApplicationController
  before_filter :authenticate, :except => [:index, :show]

  #...
end
```

Notice how you're able to selectively apply the filter to specific actions. Here, you want every action to be protected *except* index and show. The :except modifier accepts either a single value or an array. You use an array here. If you want to protect only a few actions, you can use the :only modifier, which, as you would expect, behaves the opposite of :except.

You also want to use a filter in the users controller. Right now, anyone can edit a user as long as they know the user id. This would be risky in the real world. Ideally, you want the edit and update actions to respond only to the currently logged-in user, allowing that user to edit their profile. To do this, instead of retrieving User.find(params[:id]), you retrieve current_user and apply a filter to protect the edit and update actions. Listing 7-25 shows the latest version of the users controller; the updated code is highlighted in bold.

Listing 7-25. Before Filter Added in app/controllers/users_controller.rb:

http://gist.github.com/341632

```
class UsersController < ApplicationController
  before_filter :authenticate, :only => [:edit, :update]

  def new
    @user = User.new
  end

  def create
    @user = User.new(params[:user])
    if @user.save
      redirect_to articles_path, :notice => 'User successfully added.'
    else
      render :action => 'new'
    end
  end

  def edit
    @user = current_user
  end

  def update
    @user = current_user
    if @user.update_attributes(params[:user])
      redirect_to articles_path,
:notice => 'Updated user information successfully.'
    else
      render :action => 'edit'
    end
  end
end
```

Try it. If you attempt to add, edit, or delete an article, you're asked to log in (see Figure 7-7).

Figure 7-7. Authentication required

You don't want to keep deleting a comment as a public task; therefore, authorization code is required in the comments controller. First, you add a before_filter to authorize users before calling the destroy action. Next, in the destroy action, you find the article, making sure it belongs to the current user by using current_user.articles.find. Then, you find the comment on that article; and finally, you destroy it. Listing 7-26 shows the updated code for the comments controller.

Listing 7-26. Authorization Before Deleting a Comment in app/controllers/comments_controller.rb:

http://gist.github.com/388584

```
class CommentsController < ApplicationController
  before_filter :load_article, :except => :destroy
  before_filter :authenticate, :only => :destroy

  def create
    @comment = @article.comments.new(params[:comment])
    if @comment.save
      redirect_to @article, :notice => 'Thanks for your comment'
    else
      redirect_to @article, :alert => 'Unable to add comment'
    end
  end
```

```
def destroy
  @article = current_user.articles.find(params[:article_id])
  @comment = @article.comments.find(params[:id])
  @comment.destroy
  redirect_to @article, :notice => 'Comment deleted'
end

private
  def load_article
    @article = Article.find(params[:article_id])
  end
end
```

Adding Finishing Touches

You're almost finished with your work in this chapter. Only a few tasks remain. You need to spruce up your templates a bit and make them a little cleaner. You also need to make it possible for article owners to edit and delete their articles. Finally, you want to update the layout and apply some CSS styles to make things look pretty. Ready? Let's get started!

Using Action View Helpers

One of the ways you can clean up your templates is with helpers. Rails ships with a bevy of formatting helpers to assist in displaying numbers, dates, tags, and text in your templates. Here's a quick summary:

- *Number helpers:* The NumberHelper module provides methods for converting numbers into formatted strings. Methods are provided for phone numbers, currency, percentage, precision, positional notation, and file size. See http://api.rubyonrails.org/classes/ActionView/Helpers/NumberHelper.html for more information.

- *Text helpers:* The TextHelper module provides a set of methods for filtering, formatting, and transforming strings that can reduce the amount of in-line Ruby code in your views. See http://api.rubyonrails.org/classes/ActionView/Helpers/TextHelper.html for more information.

- *URL helpers:* Rails provides a set of URL helpers that make constructing links that depend on the controller and action (or other parameters) ridiculously easy. For more information, see http://api.rubyonrails.org/classes/ActionView/Helpers/UrlHelper.html and http://api.rubyonrails.org/classes/ActionController/Base.html.

A very handy URL helper is link_to, which you've used several times already. It creates a hyperlink tag of the given name using a URL constructed according to the options hash given. It's possible to pass a string instead of an options hash to get a link tag that points to any URL. Additionally, if nil is passed as a name, the link itself becomes the name. Here's the fine print:

```
link_to(name, options={}, html_options={})
```

This generates an HTML anchor tag using the following parameters:

- The first argument is the link's name.

- The second argument is the URL to link to, given as a string, a named route, or a hash of options used to generate the URL. It can also be an object, in which case Rails replaces it with its show action named route.

- The third argument is a hash of HTML options for the resulting tag.

In Ruby, if the last argument to a method is a hash, the curly braces are optional. Most link_to helpers therefore look like this:

```
link_to 'New', new_article_path, :id => 'new_article_link'
```

If you use all three arguments and pass in options for HTML (like a class or id attribute), you need to disambiguate them. Consider the following example, which uses two hashes: one for the URL generation and another for the HTML options:

```
link_to 'New', {:controller => 'articles', :action => 'new'}, :class => 'large'
```

Notice that you need to use the curly braces for at least the first hash to inform Ruby that there are three arguments. Using braces on the last hash of options is still optional, and you can just as easily include them:

```
link_to 'New', {:controller => 'articles', :action => 'new'}, {:class => 'large'}
```

Escaping HTML in Templates

You should always escape any HTML before displaying it in your views to prevent malicious users from injecting arbitrary HTML into your pages (which is how cross-site scripting attacks are often carried out). The rule of thumb is that whenever you have data that is provided by the user, you can't trust it blindly. You need to escape it. This includes model attributes as well as parameters. Fortunately, Rails escapes all rendered strings for you.

Try adding a new article with some HTML markup in the body, saving, and visiting the show page. If you enter an anchor HTML tag for example, you see something like Figure 7-8. As you can see, Rails escapes the HTML entered in the body field.

Figure 7-8. Escaped HTML in the article page

If you check the source code, you see that the characters you entered have been escaped:

```
&lt;a href=&quot;#&quot;&gt;No link for you&lt;/a&gt;
```

Sometimes, you may want to display the strings entered by users without escaping them. To do that, Rails provides a helper method called raw that skips the HTML escaping process. To display the article's body in its raw format, which you do shortly, you can call raw(article.body) instead of article.body in the article partial in app/views/articles/_article.html.erb.

Formatting the Body Field

Let's improve the display of the body field. One of the aforementioned text helpers is `simple_format`. This helper converts text to HTML using simple formatting rules. Two or more consecutive newlines are considered a paragraph and wrapped in <p> tags. One newline is considered a line break, and a <br /> tag is appended. Listing 7-27 shows the additions.

Listing 7-27. Formatting Helpers Added in app/views/articles/_article.html.erb:

http://gist.github.com/341839

```
<%= div_for article do %>
  <h3>
    <%= link_to article.title, article %>
    <span class='actions'>
      <%= link_to "Edit", edit_article_path(article) %>
      <%= link_to "Delete", article, :confirm => "Are you sure?",
:method => :delete %>
    </span>
  </h3>
  <%= simple_format article.body %>
<% end %>
```

Adding Edit Controls

You've applied authentication filters, but you still don't have a way to prevent users from editing or deleting articles that belong to other users. To do this, you add a method to the `Article` model that can tell you whether the article in question is owned by the user you pass in. Open the `Article` model, and add the `owned_by?` method, as highlighted in bold in Listing 7-28.

Listing 7-28. Updated app/models/article.rb: http://gist.github.com/388527

```
class Article < ActiveRecord::Base
  validates :title, :presence => true
  validates :body, :presence => true

  belongs_to :user
  has_and_belongs_to_many :categories
  has_many :comments

  scope :published, where("articles.published_at IS NOT NULL")
  scope :draft, where("articles.published_at IS NULL")
  scope :recent, lambda { published.where("articles.published_at > ?",
1.week.ago.to_date)}
  scope :where_title, lambda { |term| where("articles.title LIKE ?", "%#{term}%") }

  def long_title
    "#{title} - #{published_at}"
  end

  def published?
```

```
      published_at.present?
   end

   def owned_by?(owner)
     return false unless owner.is_a? User
     user == owner
   end
end
```

Now, let's use this method in the article and comment partials in app/views/articles/_article.html.erb and app/views/comments/_comment.html.erb respectively, by adding links to edit or delete *only* if the article is owned by the currently logged-in user. See Listings 7-29 and 7-30.

Listing 7-29. Edit Controls for Article in app/views/articles/_article.html.erb:

http://gist.github.com/341845

```
<%= div_for article do %>
  <h3>
    <%= link_to article.title, article %>
    <% if article.owned_by? current_user %>
      <span class='actions'>
        <%= link_to "Edit", edit_article_path(article) %>
        <%= link_to "Delete", article, :confirm => "Are you sure?",
:method => :delete %>
      </span>
    <% end %>
  </h3>
  <%= simple_format article.body %>
<% end %>
```

Listing 7-30. Edit Controls for Comment in app/views/comments/_comment.html.erb:

http://gist.github.com/388593

```
<%= div_for comment do %>
  <h3>
    <%= comment.name %> &lt;<%= comment.email %>&gt; said:
    <% if @article.owned_by? current_user %>
      <span class='actions'>
        <%= link_to 'Delete', [@article, comment],
:confirm => 'Are you sure?', :method => :delete %>
      </span>
    <% end %>
  </h3>
  <%= comment.body %>
<% end %>
```

■ **NOTE** When you try this in your browser, you may not see the edit and delete links for any of the articles because their user_id field is nil. This is great console practice for you. Start your console with rails console, find your own user using user = User.find_by_email('email@example.com'), and update all articles in the system using Article.update_all(["user_id = ?", user.id]).

Making Sure Articles Have Owners

You need to make sure that when you add an article, a user is assigned. To do that, you update the create method in the articles controller to use the association between User and Article. When creating the @article variable, instead of using Article.new, you use current_user.articles.new: it instantiates an article object with the user_id field set to the id of current_user. That's exactly what you need.

Applying the same logic, you change the edit, update, and destroy actions to retrieve only articles belonging to the logged-in user. In code parlance, you use current_user.articles.find wherever you were using Article.find. Listing 7-31 shows the changes to make in app/controllers/articles_controller.rb.

Listing 7-31. Updated app/controllers/articles_controller.rb: http://gist.github.com/341925

```ruby
class ArticlesController < ApplicationController
  before_filter :authenticate, :except => [:index, :show]

  # GET /articles
  # GET /articles.xml
  def index
    @articles = Article.all

    respond_to do |format|
      format.html # index.html.erb
      format.xml  { render :xml => @articles }
    end
  end

  # GET /articles/1
  # GET /articles/1.xml
  def show
    @article = Article.find(params[:id])

    respond_to do |format|
      format.html # show.html.erb
      format.xml  { render :xml => @article }
    end
  end

  # GET /articles/new
  # GET /articles/new.xml
  def new
    @article = Article.new
```

```ruby
    respond_to do |format|
      format.html # new.html.erb
      format.xml  { render :xml => @article }
    end
  end

  # GET /articles/1/edit
  def edit
    @article = current_user.articles.find(params[:id])
  end

  # POST /articles
  # POST /articles.xml
  def create
    @article = current_user.articles.new(params[:article])

    respond_to do |format|
      if @article.save
        format.html { redirect_to(@article,
:notice => 'Article was successfully created.') }
        format.xml  { render :xml => @article, :status => :created,
:location => @article }
      else
        format.html { render :action => "new" }
        format.xml  { render :xml => @article.errors,
:status => :unprocessable_entity }
      end
    end
  end

  # PUT /articles/1
  # PUT /articles/1.xml
  def update
    @article = current_user.articles.find(params[:id])

    respond_to do |format|
      if @article.update_attributes(params[:article])
        format.html { redirect_to(@article,
:notice => 'Article was successfully updated.') }
        format.xml  { head :ok }
      else
        format.html { render :action => "edit" }
        format.xml  { render :xml => @article.errors,
:status => :unprocessable_entity }
      end
    end
  end

  # DELETE /articles/1
  # DELETE /articles/1.xml
  def destroy
    @article = current_user.articles.find(params[:id])
```

```
        @article.destroy

      respond_to do |format|
        format.html { redirect_to(articles_url) }
        format.xml  { head :ok }
      end
    end
  end
end
```

Adding Custom Helpers

Your blog application is looking pretty good, but let's make it a bit more user-friendly. One thing you can do is add a helpful cancel link beside each submit button on the forms, so users can back out of editing. You could do this by adding a link_to helper beside each button, but you'd need to do this for every form. Because you probably want to repeat this pattern throughout the application, this could end up being a lot of duplication. Why not create a custom helper to do this for you? Listing 7-32 shows the method submit_or_cancel added to the application_helper.

Listing 7-32. The submit_or_cancel Method in app/helpers/application_helper.rb:

http://gist.github.com/341856

```
module ApplicationHelper
  # Creates a submit button with the given name with a cancel link
  # Accepts two arguments: Form object and the cancel link name
  def submit_or_cancel(form, name='Cancel')
    form.submit + " or " +
        link_to(name, 'javascript:history.go(-1);', :class => 'cancel')
  end
end
```

Now, let's use this helper on your forms. Open both the user and the article form partials in app/views/users/_form.html.erb and app/views/articles/_form.html.erb, and update them so they look like Listings 7-33 and 7-34.

Listing 7-33. Updated app/views/users/_form.html.erb: http://gist.github.com/341857

```
<%= form_for(@user) do |f| %>
  <% if @user.errors.any? %>
  <div id="errorExplanation">
    <h2><%= pluralize(@user.errors.count, "error") %>
prohibited this user from being saved:</h2>
    <ul>
    <% @user.errors.full_messages.each do |msg| %>
      <li><%= msg %></li>
    <% end %>
    </ul>
  </div>
  <% end %>

  <div class="field">
```

```
    <%= f.label :email %><br />
    <%= f.text_field :email %>
  </div>
  <div class="field">
    <%= f.label :password %><br />
    <%= f.password_field :password %>
  </div>
  <div class="field">
    <%= f.label :password_confirmation %><br />
    <%= f.password_field :password_confirmation %>
  </div>
  <div class="actions">
    <%= submit_or_cancel(f) %>
  </div>
<% end %>
```

Listing 7-34. Updated app/views/articles/_form.html.erb: http://gist.github.com/341858

```
<%= form_for(@article) do |f| %>
  <% if @article.errors.any? %>
  <div id="errorExplanation">
    <h2><%= pluralize(@article.errors.count, "error") %>
prohibited this article from being saved:</h2>
    <ul>
    <% @article.errors.full_messages.each do |msg| %>
      <li><%= msg %></li>
    <% end %>
    </ul>
  </div>
  <% end %>

  <div class="field">
    <%= f.label :title %><br />
    <%= f.text_field :title %>
  </div>
  <div class="field">
    <%= f.label :location %><br />
    <%= f.text_field :location %>
  </div>
  <div class="field">
    <%= f.label "Categories" %><br />
    <% for category in Category.all %>
      <%= check_box_tag 'article[category_ids][]', category.id,
@article.category_ids.include?(category.id), :id => dom_id(category) %>
      <%= label_tag dom_id(category), category.name, :class => "check_box_label" %>
    <% end %>
  </div>
  <div class="field">
    <%= f.label :excerpt %><br />
    <%= f.text_field :excerpt %>
  </div>
  <div class="field">
```

```
    <%= f.label :body %><br />
    <%= f.text_area :body %>
  </div>
  <div class="field">
    <%= f.label :published_at %><br />
    <%= f.datetime_select :published_at %>
  </div>
  <div class="actions">
    <%= submit_or_cancel(f) %>
  </div>
<% end >
```

As in the earlier examples, every time you copy and paste view-code in more than one template, it means that you very likely can extract it into a helper method.

Giving It Some Style

Your blog application could use a little varnish. Let's update the layout and apply a style sheet.

Updating the Layout

Let's update the main layout and add some style hooks that you can target via CSS. You also add some pieces to allow the user to log in, log out, edit their password, and add a new article. The final result looks like Listing 7-35.

Listing 7-35. Updated app/views/layouts/application.html.erb: http://gist.github.com/341867

```
<!DOCTYPE html>
<html>
<head>
  <title>Blog</title>
  <%= stylesheet_link_tag :all %>
  <%= javascript_include_tag :defaults %>
  <%= csrf_meta_tag %>
</head>
<body>
  <div id="header">
    <h1><%= link_to "Blog", root_path %></h1>
    <div id="user_bar">
      <% if logged_in? %>
        <%= link_to "New Article", new_article_path %> |
        <%= link_to "Edit Password", edit_user_path(current_user) %> |
        <%= link_to "Logout", logout_path %>
      <% else %>
        <%= link_to "Login", login_path %>
      <% end %>
    </div>
  </div>
  <div id="main">
```

```
    <%= content_tag(:p, notice, :class => 'notice') if notice.present? %>
    <%= content_tag(:p, alert, :class => 'alert') if alert.present? %>
    <%= yield %>
  </div>
  <div id="footer">
    A simple blog built for the book
<a href="http://beginningrails.com">Beginning Rails 3</a>
  </div>
</body>
</html>
```

You add a link to add a new article in the application layout; therefore, you no longer need that link on the articles index page. Update the app/views/articles/index.html.erb file to remove the new article link. It should look like Listing 7-36.

Listing 7-36. Remove New Article Link from app/views/articles/index.html.erb:

http://gist.github.com/341893

```
<h1>Listing articles</h1>

<div id="articles">
  <%= render @articles %>
</div>
```

Applying a Style Sheet

We've prepared a simple CSS style sheet that you can apply to make the application look pretty. Listing 7-37 shows the application.css file, which you should create in public/stylesheets/application.css. You're no longer using the public/stylesheets/scaffold.css file; remove it to avoid any styling conflicts.

Listing 7-37. The public/stylesheets/application.css File: http://gist.github.com/341881

```
* {
  margin: 0 auto;
}

body {
  background-color: #fff;
  color: #333;
}

body, p, ol, ul, td {
  font-family: verdana, arial, helvetica, sans-serif;
  font-size:   13px;
  line-height: 18px;
}

pre {
  background-color: #eee;
```

```
  padding: 10px;
  font-size: 11px;
}

p {
  padding: 5px;
}

a {
  color:#D95E16;
  padding:0 2px;
  text-decoration:none;
}

a:hover {
  background-color:#FF813C;
  color:#FFFFFF;
}

.notice { color: green; }
.alert  { color: red; }

#header, #main, #footer {
  width: 800px;
}

#header {
  font-family:"Myriad Web Pro",Helvetica,Arial,sans-serif;
  letter-spacing: 1px;
  border-bottom: 5px solid #333333;
  color:#333333;
  padding: 15px 0;
  height: 35px;
}

#header #user_bar {
  float: right;
  font-size: 10px;
}

#footer {
  border-top: 5px solid #C1C1C1;
  margin-top: 10px;
  clear:both;
  padding: 10px 0;
  text-align: center;
  font-size: 11px;
}

#header h1 {
  padding-top: 14px;
  float: left;
```

```
    font-size: 30px;
}

#header h1 a{
    color: black;
}

#header h1 a:hover {
    background-color: white;
    color: black;
    border-bottom: 4px solid #ccc;
}

#header p {
    float: right;
}

#main h1 {
    font-size: 16px;
    padding: 10px 0;
    border-bottom: 1px solid #bbb;
    margin-bottom: 10px;
}

#main table{
    margin: 0;
}

#main form{
    text-align: left;
}

#main form br{
    display: none;
    float: left;
}

#main form label {
    width: 150px;
    display: block;
    text-align: right;
    padding-right: 10px;
    float: left;
    line-height: 21px;
    vertical-align: center;
    background-color: #F0F0F0;
    border: 2px solid #ccc;
    margin-right: 10px;
}

#main form label.check_box_label {
    width: auto;
```

```
    display: inline;
    text-align: right;
    padding-right: 10px;
    line-height: 21px;
    vertical-align: center;
    background-color: #FFF;
    border: none;
}

#main form .field, #main form .actions {
    padding-top: 10px;
    clear: both;
}

#main form input[type=text], #main form input[type=password], #main form textarea {
    float: left;
    font-size: 14px;
    width: 250px;
    padding: 2px;
    border: 2px solid #ccc;
}

#main form input[type=checkbox] {
    margin: 4px;
    float: left;
}

#main form textarea {
    height: 150px;
}

#main form input[type=submit] {
    margin-left: 175px;
    float:left;
    margin-right: 10px;
    margin-bottom: 10px;
}

#main h3 {
    padding-top: 10px;
    height: 20px;
}

#main h3 .actions{
    display:none;
    font-weight: normal;
    font-size: 10px;
}

#main h3:hover .actions{
    display: inline;
}
```

```css
.fieldWithErrors {
  display:table;
  float:left;
  margin:0;
  width:100px;
  margin-right: 10px;
}

#main form .fieldWithErrors label{
  border: 2px solid red;
  margin-right: 0px;
}

#main form .fieldWithErrors input, #main form .fieldWithErrors  textarea{
  width: 250px;
  border: 2px solid red;
}

#errorExplanation {
  width: 413px;
  border: 2px solid red;
  padding: 7px;
  padding-bottom: 12px;
  margin-bottom: 20px;
  background-color: #f0f0f0;
  margin: 0;
}

#errorExplanation h2 {
  text-align: left;
  font-weight: bold;
  padding: 5px 5px 5px 15px;
  font-size: 12px;
  margin: -7px;
  background-color: #c00;
  color: #fff;
}

#errorExplanation p {
  color: #333;
  margin-bottom: 0;
  padding: 5px;
  margin: 0;
}

#errorExplanation ul li {
  font-size: 12px;
  list-style: square;
}
```

Yikes! That's a lot of CSS! Don't worry, though. Like all the other listings in the book, you can get the code from the Gist URL in the listing caption. The code is also available on the book's web site (http://beginningrails.com) so you can download it and copy it into your project. We certainly don't expect you to copy it by hand.

With the CSS in place, your application is starting to look nice. If you've done everything correctly, it should look a lot like Figure 7-9.

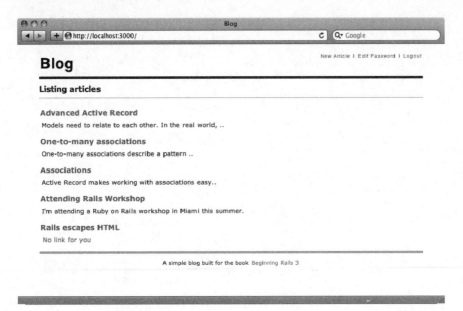

Figure 7-9. *Final layout with CSS*

Summary

This chapter discussed a fair number of advanced topics, including nested resources, sessions and state, the philosophy of the shared-nothing architecture, and how to protect actions using filters. But you didn't stop there. You also learned how to sanitize HTML to protect your application from defacement by malicious users, and how to create your own helpers to improve your interface. You even took the time to make your application look pretty, sprucing up the layout and adding some CSS.

The next chapters build on this knowledge, starting with techniques to improve user interaction by way of a technology known as Ajax.

## CHAPTER 8

Improving Interaction with Ajax

Ajax represents a fundamental shift in what the Web is capable of and is one of the defining characteristics of the Web 2.0 movement. First coined by Jesse James Garrett in his 2005 essay "Ajax: A New Approach to Web Applications" (http://adaptivepath.com/ideas/essays/archives/000385.php), Ajax stands for Asynchronous JavaScript and XML. By enabling web applications to make requests to the server behind the scenes without refreshing the browser, Ajax can dramatically improve the responsiveness and usability of the user interface. It enables live searching, in-place editing, autocompletion, drag-and-drop reordering, and a host of interface techniques that were previously only available to desktop applications. Although the acronym may be relatively recent, Ajax isn't exactly new. In fact, it has been around for several years. The problem was that it was prohibitively difficult to implement successfully. Times have changed, though; and with modern web frameworks like Rails, Ajax is accessible to the masses.

This chapter focuses on Ajax. It starts by introducing Rails' Ajax support, facilitated by two default JavaScript libraries that come bundled with Rails: Prototype and script.aculo.us; then, you utilize Rails' modularity to switch to a more commonly used JavaScript library called jQuery. With that out of the way, you learn how to use these libraries to implement Ajax techniques in your blog application to enhance the comments behaviour.

■ **NOTE** If you need to get the code at the exact point where you finished Chapter 7, download the zip file from http://github.com/downloads/ccjr/blog/chapter08.zip and extract it on your computer.

Ajax and Rails

Ajax is a combination of technologies centered around the XMLHttpRequest object, a JavaScript API originally developed by Microsoft but now supported in all modern browsers. Of course, you could interface with the XMLHttpRequest API directly, but it wouldn't be fun. A far better idea is to use one of several libraries that abstract the low-level details and make cross-browser support possible.

One of Rails' main features is the promise to make Ajax easier for web developers to use. Toward that end, it implements a set of conventions that enable you to implement even the most advanced techniques with relative ease.

Most of the Ajaxy features you implement in Rails applications are coded using JavaScript; so, familiarity with JavaScript code always helps and is pretty important for today's web developers.

Prototype and jQuery

The default JavaScript library that ships with Rails is Prototype (`http://prototypejs.org`). Although Prototype is a separate library, it's maintained and distributed as part of the Rails source code and was copied to your Rails project when you created your application using the `rails` command. This well-thought-out library handles most of the work associated with creating the rich, highly interactive applications that characterize Web 2.0. Even if JavaScript isn't your main strength, using third-party JavaScript libraries like Prototype and jQuery makes working with JavaScript much easier.

Previous chapters talked about Rails' modularity and how you can use your object-relational mapping (ORM) or templating language of choice if you didn't want to stick to Rails' defaults (Active Record and ERb, respectively). The same modularity concept applies to JavaScript libraries; you put it in practice by using the jQuery JavaScript library instead of Prototype in your blog application.

jQuery is similar to Prototype in making working with JavaScript easier. It's widely used due to its stability, beautiful syntax, and extensibility. jQuery has a large set of plug-ins for different tasks; you can check them out by visiting the jQuery plug-in directory at `http://plugins.jquery.com`.

Installing jQuery

To use jQuery in your application, you must first install the jQuery JavaScript adapter. Rails integrates with JavaScript libraries using adapters; the adapter is a JavaScript file that's available in `public/javascripts/rails.js`. The current `rails.js` adapter in your application is the default adapter for Prototype; you replace it with the jQuery adapter that's available to download from `http://github.com/rails/jquery-ujs/raw/master/src/rails.js`. Download the file, and replace your existing JavaScript adapter in `public/javascripts/rails.js`.

After replacing the adapter, you need to get rid of the Prototype library files and include the jQuery ones. Remove the Prototype library by deleting its four files: `controls.js`, `dragdrop.js`, `effects.js`, and `prototype.js` from `public/javascripts/`. Then, download the jQuery library from `http://code.jquery.com/jquery-1.4.2.min.js`, and place it in the same directory in `public/javascripts/jquery-1.4.2.min.js`.

The last thing you need to do is to make sure your application layout includes the JavaScript files you just added to the project. Open your application layout template from `app/views/layouts/application.html.erb`, and update the `javascript_include_tag` call so the file looks like Listing 8-1.

Listing 8-1. Importing the jQuery JavaScript File in app/views/layouts/application.html.erb:

http://gist.github.com/352367

```
<!DOCTYPE html>
<html>
<head>
  <title>Blog</title>
  <%= stylesheet_link_tag :all %>
  <%= javascript_include_tag 'jquery-1.4.2.min', 'rails', 'application' %>
  <%= csrf_meta_tag %>
</head>
<body>
  <div id="header">
    <h1><%= link_to "Blog", root_path %></h1>
    <div id="user_bar">
```

```
    <% if logged_in? %>
      <%= link_to "New Article", new_article_path %> |
      <%= link_to "Edit Password", edit_user_path(current_user) %> |
      <%= link_to "Logout", logout_path %>
    <% else %>
      <%= link_to "Login", login_path %>
    <% end %>
    </div>
  </div>
  <div id="main">
    <%= content_tag(:p, notice, :class => 'notice') if notice.present? %>
    <%= content_tag(:p, alert, :class => 'alert') if alert.present? %>
    <%= yield %>
  </div>
  <div id="footer">
    A simple blog built for the book
<a href="http://beginningrails.com">Beginning Rails 3</a>
  </div>
</body>
</html>
```

jQuery and DOM

jQuery provides several utility functions that make working with JavaScript better. Perhaps the most important of these is the $() function, which is a selector function to access one or more elements in a web page. Truth be told, $() is far more than a simple selector wrapper. The real magic stems from the fact that any element accessed using it is automatically extended by jQuery.

The biggest part of the jQuery framework is its Document Object Model (DOM) extensions. These DOM extensions allow you to write things like: $('.comment').removeClass('active').hide();, which gets all the elements with the CSS class name comment, removes the active class name, and hides all elements from the view. The elements with the class name comment wouldn't have these methods natively. Because they were fetched using $(), jQuery makes those functions available.

■ **TIP** Wikipedia defines DOM as follows: "The Document Object Model (DOM) is a cross-platform and language-independent convention for representing and interacting with objects in HTML, XHTML and XML documents."

The $() function finds elements in a web page by matching them to a CSS selector. Table 8-1 lists some examples of the most commonly used CSS selectors. For a complete list, see http://www.w3.org/TR/CSS2/selector.html.

Table 8-1. *CSS Selectors*

Function	Description
$('#article_123')	Returns the element matching the given ID article_123
$('.comment')	Returns a list of elements with the class name comment
$('div.article')	Returns a list of div elements with the class name article

Moving to Practice

Now that you know what Ajax is, how it works, and the reasons behind using a JavaScript framework such as jQuery, you can apply some of this knowledge to enhance the usability of your application. Mainly, you use Ajax in your pages when you think a snappier interaction is possible and recommended. Let's begin Ajax-ifying the blog application in the article page.

Not All Users Comment

If you look at the article page, you quickly notice that every time users read a post, they're presented with a form for entering comments. Although reader participation is paramount, most users are only interested in reading the content. You can modify the article page to not load the comment form automatically; instead, it will load the form only after a user clicks the "new comment" link.

Loading a Template via Ajax

One of the rules of good interface design is to make things snappy. That is to say, the interface should be responsive and quick to load. A good way to achieve this is to load elements (like forms or content areas) onto the page whenever the user requests them. Modify the article's show template as shown in Listing 8-2.

Listing 8-2. The Article Partial in app/views/articles/show.html.erb: http://gist.github.com/353475

```
<%= render @article %>

<h3>Comments</h3>
<div id="comments">
  <%= render @article.comments %>
</div>

<%= link_to "new comment", new_article_comment_path(@article, :format => :js),
:remote => true, :id => 'new_comment_link' %>
```

The template hasn't changed a lot: you no longer directly render the comment form, and you add a link called "new comment". The new link still uses the well-known link_to helper to generate a link; however, you pass in the :remote => true option, which tells Rails that you want the request triggered by this link to hit the server using Ajax.

There are a couple of things to note in the use of link_to in Listing 8-2. First, you send the request to a URL that already exists; the new_article_comment_path route identifies a path to a new comment. However, you pass in the :format => :js argument, which tells Rails that you're requesting a JavaScript representation of your page, fitting your intention. Second, you use the :id => 'new_comment_link' option to give the rendered HTML element an ID that you can refer to later.

On the server side, you don't need to make any changes to the comments controller. As currently implemented, you don't explicitly implement a new action; the default behavior in this case is to render the new template in app/views/comments/new.html.erb. That isn't really what you want—this template shouldn't be the result of this JavaScript call. Instead, you want a separate JavaScript template to be used as response for this action.

Responding to Requests with :format => :js

Your controller reads the format parameter passed in from the browser. To make sure you send a response that includes JavaScript code, you must create a template with the .js.erb template extension. Create the app/views/comments/new.js.erb template as per Listing 8-3. The following text explains all the lines in the template to make sure you know what's happening.

Listing 8-3. The .js.erb New Comment Template in app/views/comments/new.js.erb:

http://gist.github.com/353484

```
$("<%= escape_javascript
render(:file => 'comments/new.html.erb') %>").insertAfter('#comments');
$('#new_comment_link').hide();
```

The first line renders the existing app/views/comments/new.html.erb template into a string variable that you dynamically insert into the HTML page, right after the comments div—that's achieved by using jQuery's insertAfter method, which, as its name implies, inserts a block of HTML after an existing HTML element. Table 8-2 lists similar jQuery methods that you can use in place of insertAfter.

Table 8-2. jQuery Methods for Inserting HTML into a Page

Method	Description
insertAfter(target)	Inserts the preceding element after the target element passed as a parameter
insertBefore(target)	Inserts the preceding element before the target element passed as a parameter
append(content)	Appends the preceding element with the passed content element
prepend(content)	Prepends the preceding element with the passed content element

Going back to Listing 8-3, the second and last line hides the new_comment_element, which contains the link to add a new comment. Because you already have the comment form in your page, it makes little sense to keep that link around. Hiding an element is achieved by calling jQuery's hide method on the element you want to hide.

■ **NOTE** In a similar fashion, you can call jQuery's show method to display a hidden element. As you can see, it's very important that you know your way around jQuery to be able to build complex user interfaces.

Let's see what you built in practice. Open your browser to any existing article, such as http://localhost:3000/articles/2, and notice that the comments form is no longer there (see Figure 8-1). As soon as you click the "new comment" link, the comment form pops up into place, and you can add comments (see Figure 8-2). You achieved your goal of keeping the user interface cleaner, while allowing users to quickly access functionality without having to move to a new page. That's a good start.

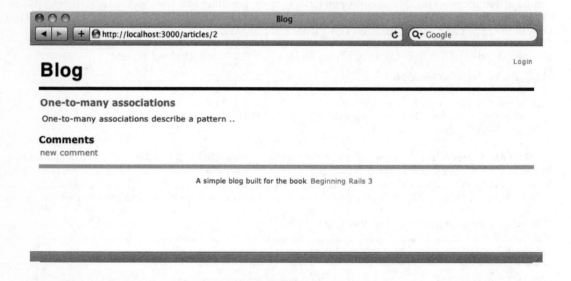

Figure 8-1. The article page without the comment form

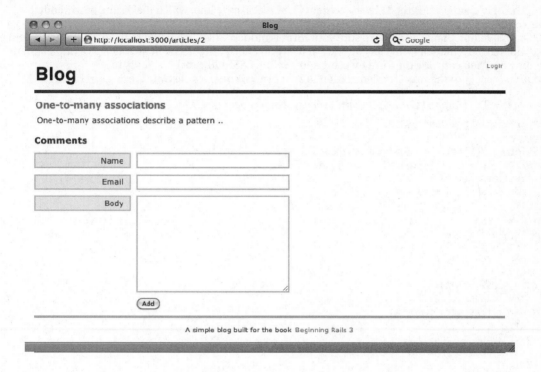

Figure 8-2. The article page with the comment form and without the "new comment" link

Making a Grand Entrance

In the previous section, you added an element to the screen via Ajax—the comment form. It's a pretty big form, it's a very obvious inclusion on the page, and your users won't miss it; however, sometimes you may want to add just an extra link or highlight some text on a page. jQuery is so awesome that it provides a set of methods for adding animation to a web page.

You use a simple one-line command to make sure users understand that something is being added to the page. Be sure the template at apps/views/comments/new.js.erb looks like Listing 8-4.

Listing 8-4. The Updated New Comment Template in app/views/comments/new.js.erb:

http://gist.github.com/353497

```
$("<%= escape_javascript
render(:file => 'comments/new.html.erb') %>").insertAfter('#comments');
$('#new_comment').slideDown();
$('#new_comment_link').hide();
```

The only change adds the $('#new_comment').slideDown(); line, which makes the newly added new_comment element appear in the page with a sliding motion.

A final minor change is to make sure your form is hidden when you add it to the page. It may sound odd, but having a hidden form lets you show it using an effect, after it's been included as a new element on the page. You can hide the form by using some inline CSS: add :html => {:style => 'display:none'} to the form_for declaration in apps/views/comments/new.html.erb, as in Listing 8-5.

Listing 8-5. The Updated Comment Form in app/views/comments/new.html.erb:

http://gist.github.com/353502

```
<%= form_for([@article, @article.comments.new],
:html => {:style => 'display: none;'}) do |f| %>
  <div class="field">
    <%= f.label :name %><br />
    <%= f.text_field :name %>
  </div>
  <div class="field">
    <%= f.label :email %><br />
    <%= f.text_field :email %>
  </div>
  <div class="field">
    <%= f.label :body %><br />
    <%= f.text_area :body %>
  </div>
  <div class="actions">
    <%= f.submit 'Add' %>
  </div>
<% end %>
```

Open your browser at any article page, and look at the shiny effect that is being applied.

■ **NOTE** You very likely want to learn more about all the available effects in jQuery. To do so, head over to http://api.jquery.com/category/effects/.

Using Ajax for Forms

Another user-interaction improvement is to not refresh the page after a user adds a new record. In quite a few applications, users may be required to enter a considerable amount of data in forms; so, this technique is important to grasp.

In the same way you made a link submit data via Ajax, you add the :remote => true option to the form_for helper you're using; this tells Rails you want the form data to be submitted via Ajax (see Listing 8-6). By sticking with the form_for helper, you don't have to change the way you read parameters in controllers. The :remote => true option is definitely one you'll use frequently.

Listing 8-6. The Updated Comment Form in app/views/comments/new.html.erb:

http://gist.github.com/353505

```erb
<%= form_for([@article, @article.comments.new], :remote => true,
:html => {:style => 'display: none;'}) do |f| %>
  <div class="field">
    <%= f.label :name %><br />
    <%= f.text_field :name %>
  </div>
  <div class="field">
    <%= f.label :email %><br />
    <%= f.text_field :email %>
  </div>
  <div class="field">
    <%= f.label :body %><br />
    <%= f.text_area :body %>
  </div>
  <div class="actions">
    <%= f.submit 'Add' %>
  </div>
<% end %>
```

Although the changes in the view are minimal, you have to make a few more changes in your controller layer. You want to respond to JavaScript and HTML requests in different ways. Change the create method in your comments controller to look like Listing 8-7.

Listing 8-7. The Updated Comments Controller in app/controllers/comments_controller.rb:

http://gist.github.com/353507

```ruby
class CommentsController < ApplicationController
  before_filter :load_article, :except => :destroy
  before_filter :authenticate, :only => :destroy

  def create
    @comment = @article.comments.new(params[:comment])
    if @comment.save
      respond_to do |format|
        format.html { redirect_to @article, :notice => 'Thanks for your comment' }
        format.js
      end
    else
      respond_to do |format|
        format.html { redirect_to @article, :alert => 'Unable to add comment' }
        format.js { render 'fail_create.js.erb' }
      end
    end
  end

  def destroy
    @article = current_user.articles.find(params[:article_id])
```

```
      @comment = @article.comments.find(params[:id])
      @comment.destroy
      redirect_to @article, :notice => 'Comment deleted'
    end

  private
    def load_article
      @article = Article.find(params[:article_id])
    end
end
```

The main method in this code is the respond_to helper. By using respond_to, you can have some code in the format.html block that's called when you receive a regular request and some code in the format.js block that's called when a JavaScript request is received. Hang on! There is no code in format.js! When no code is added to a format block, Rails looks for a template named after the view, just like regular views, which means it looks for create.js.erb. When a submitted comment fails validation, you also want to warn the user by displaying error messages; for that, you use format.js { render 'fail_create.js.erb' } to explicitly render a specific template.

The new apps/views/comments/create.js.erb and app/views/comments/fail_create.js.erb templates are shown in Listings 8-8 and 8-9.

Listing 8-8. The Template in app/views/comments/create.js.erb: http://gist.github.com/353510

```
$('#comments').append("<%= escape_javascript(render(@comment)) %>");
$('#new_comment')[0].reset();
```

Listing 8-9. The Template in app/views/comments/fail_create.js.erb: http://gist.github.com/354866

```
alert("<%= @comment.errors.full_messages.to_sentence %>");
```

In the create.js.erb template, you run a couple of simple JavaScript commands. First, you render the template for a new comment—using render(@comment)—and append that HTML to the end of the comments div, achieved by using jQuery's append method. The $('#new_comment')[0].reset() line is a simple call to reset all the elements of the new comment form, which is blank and ready to accept another comment from your user.

In the fail_create.js.erb template, you use the alert JavaScript function to display a dialog box with the validation error message, as shown in Figure 8-3.

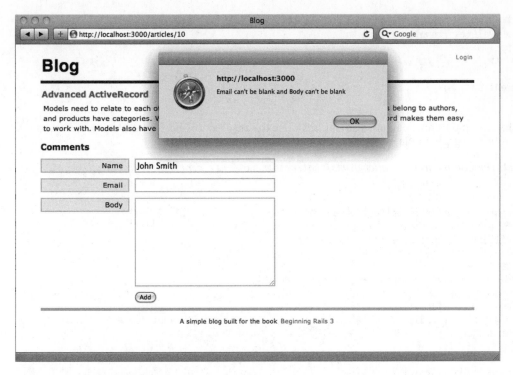

Figure 8-3. Displaying an error message

Give it a try: point your browser to an existing article, for example at
http://localhost:3000/articles/2, and enter a few—or lots of—comments. As you can see, you can
interact with the page in a much more efficient way: there's no need to wait until a full page-reload
happens.

Deleting Records with Ajax

To complete the "making things snappy" section, you may want to delete some of the comments that are
added by users. You can combine the techniques you've learned in this chapter to let users delete
comments without delay.

You already have a link to delete comments in the comment template at
app/views/comments/_comment.html.erb. To use Ajax with that link, you again need to add the :remote =>
true option to the method call (see Listing 8-10).

Listing 8-10. The Template in app/views/comments/_comment.html.erb: http://gist.github.com/354807

```
<%= div_for comment do %>
  <h3>
    <%= comment.name %> &lt;<%= comment.email %>&gt; said:
    <% if @article.owned_by? current_user %>
      <span class='actions'>
```

```erb
        <%= link_to 'Delete', [@article, comment], :confirm => 'Are you sure?',
:method => :delete, :remote => true %>
      </span>
    <% end %>
  </h3>
  <%= comment.body %>
<% end %>
```

The changes in the controller are also minimal. Use the respond_to and format block to make sure you support both regular and JavaScript requests, as shown in Listing 8-11.

Listing 8-11. The Comments Controller in app/controllers/comments_controller.rb:

http://gist.github.com/354809

```ruby
class CommentsController < ApplicationController
  before_filter :load_article, :except => :destroy
  before_filter :authenticate, :only => :destroy

  def create
    @comment = @article.comments.new(params[:comment])
    if @comment.save
      respond_to do |format|
        format.html { redirect_to @article, :notice => 'Thanks for your comment' }
        format.js
      end
    else
      respond_to do |format|
        format.html { redirect_to @article, :alert => 'Unable to add comment' }
        format.js { render 'fail_create.js.erb' }
      end
    end
  end

  def destroy
    @article = current_user.articles.find(params[:article_id])
    @comment = @article.comments.find(params[:id])
    @comment.destroy
    respond_to do |format|
      format.html { redirect_to @article, :notice => 'Comment deleted' }
      format.js
    end
  end

  private
    def load_article
      @article = Article.find(params[:article_id])
    end
end
```

You wire up the "delete" link in the comment partial to send an Ajax request to the controller. The controller responds to those Ajax requests with the default action, which is to render the app/views/comments/destroy.js.erb file (see Listing 8-12).

Listing 8-12. The app/views/comment/destroy.js.erb File: http://gist.github.com/354811

```
$("#<%= dom_id(@comment) %>").remove()
```

Open your browser to an article page—make sure you are logged in as the article owner—with some comments you want to delete—or add lots of spam-like comments. See how quickly you can get rid of comments now? It's a lot better that waiting for page reloads.

Summary

To be sure, Ajax is a large topic. Entire books and conferences are devoted to this subset of technology, so it goes without saying that this chapter only scratches the surface. Still, in short order, you've learned the basics of implementing Ajax in Rails applications, and you know where to go when you need to dig deeper.

The chapter started by mentioning the Prototype library that is bundled with Rails. You learned about the jQuery JavaScript library and saw how to use it with Rails in place of Prototype.

You learned how to make remote Ajax calls using the remote => true option for links and forms. You also used a simple visual effect to show new elements on the page, thanks to the jQuery library.

Finally, you learned about using JavaScript templates—which have the .js.erb extension—to produce responses to Ajax requests using JavaScript code.

At this stage, you have a solid grasp of the Action Pack side of web development with Rails. Next, you look at how to conquer another common component of web application development: sending mail.

CHAPTER 9

■ ■ ■

Sending and Receiving E-Mail

It's a rare web application that doesn't need to send e-mail from time to time. For example, you may want to send messages to welcome users who sign up to your site, relay passwords, or confirm orders placed with an online store. Rails ships with a library called Action Mailer, which provides developers with an easy-to-use yet powerful tool to handle e-mail.

This chapter explains how Action Mailer works and how to use it in your applications. You first learn how to configure it, and then you see a few examples of how to send e-mail in various formats. In addition to sending e-mail, Action Mailer can also *receive* e-mail, an advanced topic that the chapter touches on briefly.

■ **NOTE** If you need to get the code at the exact point where you finished Chapter 8, download the zip file from `http://github.com/downloads/ccjr/blog/chapter09.zip` and extract it on your computer.

Setting Up Action Mailer

Like Active Record and Action Pack, Action Mailer is one of the components that make up the Rails framework. It works much like the other components of Rails: mailers are implemented to behave like controllers, and mailer templates are implemented as views. Because it's integrated into the framework, it's easy to set up and use, and it requires very little configuration to get going.

When you send e-mail using an e-mail client such as Outlook or a web-based e-mail application like Gmail or Yahoo Mail, your messages are sent via a mail server. Unlike a web server, Rails doesn't provide a built-in mail server. You need to tell Action Mailer where your e-mail server is located and how to connect to it. This sounds a bit complicated, but it's really quite easy. Depending on the kind of computer you're using, you may have a mail server built in (this is true of most UNIX systems). If not, you can use the same server that you use to process your regular e-mail. If this is the case, you can find your server information in your e-mail client settings, as provided by your Internet service provider (ISP), or in the settings section of your web-based e-mail application, like Gmail.

Configuring Mail Server Settings

Before you can send e-mail from your Rails application, you need to tell Action Mailer how to communicate with your mail server. Action Mailer can be configured to send mail using either sendmail or a Simple Mail Transfer Protocol (SMTP) server. SMTP is the core Internet protocol for relaying mail messages between servers. If you're on Linux, OS X, or any other UNIX-based system, you're in luck: you can use sendmail, and as long as it's in the standard location (/usr/bin/sendmail), you don't need to configure anything. If you're on Windows, or if you want to use SMTP, you have some work to do.

Action Mailer options are set at the class level on ActionMailer::Base. The best place to set these options is in your environment files, located in the config directory of your application. You can also add your configuration in an initializer file in config/initializers; doing so ensures that your settings apply for all environments. In most cases, though, you have different setting for the development and production environments; it may be wiser to add settings in any of the environment-specific configuration files (config/environments/*.rb), because it takes precedence over the global configuration.

This section describes how to set up Action Mailer to use SMTP, because it works on all systems and is the default delivery method. To do this, you supply the SMTP settings via the smtp_settings option. The smtp_settings method expects a hash of options, most of which are shown in Table 9-1.

Table 9-1. *Server Connection Settings*

Setting	Description
address	The address of your mail server. The default is localhost.
port	The port number of your mail server. The default is port 25.
domain	If your e-mail server responds to different domain names, you may need to specify your domain name here.
authentication	If your mail server requires authentication, you need to specify the authentication type here. This can be one of :plain, :login, or :cram_md5.
user_name	The username you use to authenticate when you connect to the mail server, if your server requires authentication.
password	The password you use to authenticate when you connect to the mail server, if your server requires authentication.

Listing 9-1 shows a typical configuration for a server that requires authentication, in this case Gmail. You can use this sample configuration as a starting point to configure your connection. Change each of the settings (authentication, username, password, and address) to connect to your own SMTP server. If you're using sendmail as the delivery method, add ActionMailer::Base.delivery_method = :sendmail; then, everything should "just work."

Listing 9-1. Sample Action Mailer Configuration Using SMTP, in config/environments/development.rb:
http://gist.github.com/354995

```
Blog::Application.configure do
  # Settings specified here will take precedence over those in config/environment.rb

  # In the development environment your application's code is reloaded on
  # every request.  This slows down response time but is perfect for development
  # since you don't have to restart the webserver when you make code changes.
  config.cache_classes = false

  # Log error messages when you accidentally call methods on nil.
  config.whiny_nils = true

  # Show full error reports and disable caching
  config.consider_all_requests_local       = true
  config.action_view.debug_rjs             = true
  config.action_controller.perform_caching = false

  # Email configuration
  config.action_mailer.raise_delivery_errors = true

  # Gmail SMTP server setup
  ActionMailer::Base.smtp_settings = {
    :address => "smtp.gmail.com",
    :enable_starttls_auto => true,
    :port => 587,
    :authentication => :plain,
    :user_name => "beginningrails@gmail.com",
    :password => 'pleasechange'
  }

  # Print deprecation notices to the Rails logger
  config.active_support.deprecation = :log
end
```

Make sure you modify the options to your own credentials. Restart your server if it's running, and your application is ready to send mail.

■ **NOTE** If you need to use any advanced Action Mailer settings, the Rails API has a good chunk of information at http://api.rubyonrails.org/classes/ActionMailer/Base.html.

Configuring Application Settings

In addition to the mail server settings, Action Mailer has a set of configuration parameters you can tweak to make the library behave in specific ways according to the application or the environment. You stick with the defaults here, so you don't need to set up any special application settings. For reference, Table 9-2 lists the most common configuration options. Just like the server settings, these can be specified in an initializer file or in the environment-specific configuration files (`config/environments/*.rb`).

Table 9-2. Common Action Mailer Application Settings

Option	Description
template_root	Indicates the base folder from which template references will be made. The default is app/views.
raise_delivery_errors	Allows you to indicate whether you want errors to be raised when an error occurs while trying to deliver e-mail.
perform_deliveries	Indicates whether messages should really be delivered to the mail server.
deliveries	Keeps an array of all delivered e-mail when the delivery method is set to :test. This is useful when you're in testing mode.
default_charset	Specifies the default character set to be used when sending messages. The default is UTF-8.
default_content_type	Specifies the default content type that will be used for outbound mail. The default is text/plain.

■ **NOTE** When you create a new Rails application, the configuration files automatically use sensible defaults for each of the development, test, and production environments. Take a quick look in `config/environments` to see how Action Mailer behaves in development, production, and test mode to make sure you understand your application's behavior.

Sending E-Mail

Now that you have Action Mailer configured, it's time to see it in action. This section explores all the possibilities in the Action Mailer world, starting with basic text-only e-mail and then adding extra e-mail options such as attachments.

To demonstrate Action Mailer, let's enhance the blog application by allowing users to send e-mail to their friends, so they can share information about a specific article. This is a common feature in today's web applications, affectionately referred to as "send to friend."

By now, you know that Rails provides helpful generators to get started writing your own code. You saw generators in action when you created models and controllers in previous chapters. The mailer generator works just like the other generators.

Enter the following command to generate the Notifier class with one method named email_friend:

```
$ rails generate mailer Notifier email_friend
```

create	app/mailers/notifier.rb	
invoke	erb	
create	app/views/notifier	
create	app/views/notifier/email_friend.text.erb	
invoke	test_unit	
create	test/functional/notifier_test.rb	

The generator creates a mailer class named Notifier, containing the email_friend method you specified on the command line. Notice that the generated Action Mailer class is created in the app/mailers directory; Notifier and any Action Mailer class are subclasses of the ActionMailer::Base class. The generator also creates a template file in the views directory (app/views/notifier/email_friend.text.erb) that corresponds to the email_friend method (action) you use to set up the mailer message.

Just like controllers, Action Mailer classes contain methods that, when triggered, execute some code and render a related view of the same name, unless otherwise specified.

Listing 9-2 shows the Notifier class located in app/mailers/notifier.rb. The email_friend method has some code that will be the starting point for most of the methods you write using Action Mailer.

Listing 9-2. Notifier Class, in app/mailers/notifier.rb

```ruby
class Notifier < ActionMailer::Base
  default :from => "from@example.com"

  # Subject can be set in your I18n file at config/locales/en.yml
  # with the following lookup:
  #
  #   en.actionmailer.notifier.email_friend.subject
  #
  def email_friend
    @greeting = "Hi"

    mail :to => "to@example.org"
  end
end
```

Action Mailer classes have a class-wide configuration hash that you can modify using the `default` method. Notice the first line in the `Notifier` class definition: it sets the sender address (using `:from`) for all e-mails sent from this class to from@example.com.

In the `email_friend` method body, the first line defines an instance variable named `@greeting`; just like in controllers, those variables are available in your views. Also in the `email_friend` method body, the `mail` method is called with a parameter of `:to => "to@example.org"`, specifying the e-mail address that will receive this message. The `mail` method accepts an options hash that specifies the various headers of the message. Table 9-3 lists the available methods you use to configure an individual message.

Table 9-3. *Mailer Instance Variables*

Method name	Description	Example
subject	The subject of the e-mail message to be sent.	`:subject => "Action Mailer is powerful"`
to	A string or array of e-mail addresses to which the message will be sent.	`:to => "friend@example.com"`
from	A string specifying the sender of the e-mail message.	`:from => "sender@example.com"`
reply_to	A string specifying the reply-to e-mail address.	`:reply => "sender@example.com"`
date	The date header. The default is the current date.	`:date => Time.now`
cc	A string or array of e-mail addresses to carbon-copy with the message.	`:cc => "admin@example.com"`
bcc	A string or array of e-mail addresses to blind-carbon-copy with the message.	`:bcc => ["support@example.com", "sales@example.com"]`

The mailer generator creates a template named after the action in the `Notifier` class in the /app/views/notifier folder: `email_friend.text.erb`. This is the template that generates the body of the e-mail sent when using the `email_friend` method. This template works similarly to the templates used for regular views in Action Pack. It's an ERb file, which can contain text and markup mixed with some Ruby code. It also has the same one-to-one relationship between action and view exhibited by Action Pack—each action in your mailer class expects one template in the app/views directory.

Handling Basic E-Mail

Let's start enhancing the blog application by adding "notify a friend" functionality to the article page. The first iteration is a very basic example that sends a text e-mail message containing a brief message.

The first piece of the puzzle is to make a change to the routes file, to include a route for the action that will be called after the user submits the form. You add a member route to `articles` using the `member` method, to give a notify_friend_article route. Make sure your config/routes.rb file looks like Listing 9-3.

Listing 9-3. Added a notify_friend Action to config/routes.rb: http://gist.github.com/355014

```
Blog::Application.routes.draw do
  root :to => "articles#index"
  resources :articles do
    member do
      post :notify_friend
    end
    resources :comments
  end
  resources :users
  resource :session
  match '/login' => "sessions#new", :as => "login"
  match '/logout' => "sessions#destroy", :as => "logout"
end
```

■ **NOTE** Using the member method inside your resources block helps define a route that requires the id of the resource. Custom member routes are similar to the default member routes, such as edit_article_path and article_path. Following the same convention, you can define collection routes using the collection method. Custom collection routes are similar to the default collection routes, such as articles_path, which don't require an id.

You want to show users a link that slides down a form where they can enter the e-mail address of the friend to whom they want to send a message. Let's update the article's show view to include the new link directly after rendering the article's partial. Add the code shown in Listing 9-4 in app/views/articles/show..html.erb.

Listing 9-4. "Notify a Friend" Functionality Added to app/views/articles/show.html.erb:
http://gist.github.com/355029

```
 <%= render @article %>

<%= link_to 'Email a friend', '#',
:onclick => "$('#notify_friend_form').slideDown()" %>
<%= render 'notify_friend' %>

<h3>Comments</h3>
<div id="comments">
  <%= render @article.comments %>
</div>

<%= link_to "new comment", new_article_comment_path(@article, :format => :js),
:remote => true, :id => 'new_comment_link' %>
```

Notice that you also render a partial named notify_friend. Create the partial in app/views/articles/_notify_friend.html.erb so it looks like Listing 9-5.

Listing 9-5. "Notify a Friend" Partial in app/views/articles/_notify_friend.html.erb:

http://gist.github.com/355030

```
<%= form_tag(notify_friend_article_path(@article), :id => 'notify_friend_form',
:style => 'display:none') do %>
  <div class="field">
    <%= label_tag :name, 'Your name' %><br />
    <%= text_field_tag :name %>
  </div>
  <div class="field">
    <%= label_tag :email, "Your friend's email" %><br />
    <%= text_field_tag :email %>
  </div>
  <div class="actions">
    <%= submit_tag 'Send' %> or
    <%= link_to 'Cancel', '#', :onclick => "$('#notify_friend_form').slideUp()" %>
  </div>
<% end %>
```

Now, when you go to any article page, you see a link to e-mail a friend. Because you don't want to show the form all the time, you made the form hidden. If users are interested in recommending the article by sending an e-mail to a friend, they can click the link, and the form will be revealed through the help of some clever JavaScript. The end result is shown in Figures 9-1 and 9-2.

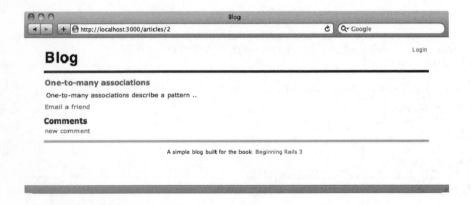

Figure 9-1. Article page without "notify a friend" form

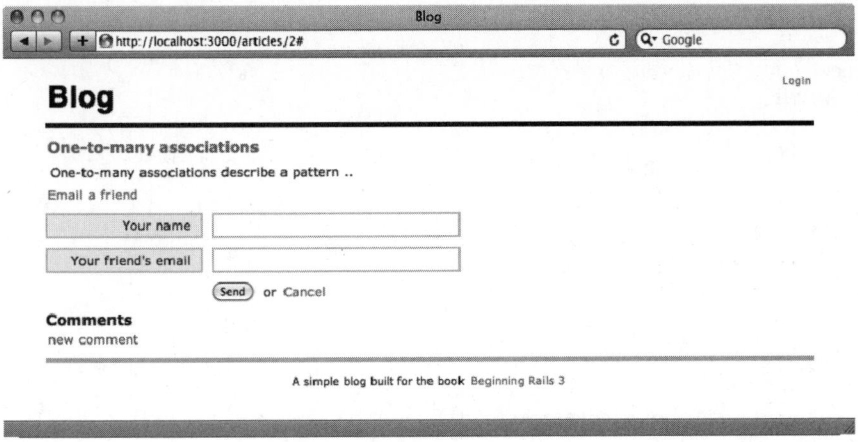

Figure 9-2. Article page with visible "notify a friend" form

The interface is ready to go, but the articles controller doesn't know how to handle this request yet. Your form is configured to submit to an action called notify_friend, but that action doesn't exist. Update the articles controller and add the notify_friend method shown in Listing 9-6.

Listing 9-6. notify_friend Action Added to app/controllers/articles_controller.rb:

http://gist.github.com/355036

```ruby
class ArticlesController < ApplicationController
  before_filter :authenticate, :except => [:index, :show, :notify_friend]

  # GET /articles
  # GET /articles.xml
  def index
    @articles = Article.all

    respond_to do |format|
      format.html # index.html.erb
      format.xml  { render :xml => @articles }
    end
  end

  # GET /articles/1
  # GET /articles/1.xml
  def show
    @article = Article.find(params[:id])

    respond_to do |format|
      format.html # show.html.erb
      format.xml  { render :xml => @article }
```

```ruby
      end
    end

    # GET /articles/new
    # GET /articles/new.xml
    def new
      @article = Article.new

      respond_to do |format|
        format.html # new.html.erb
        format.xml  { render :xml => @article }
      end
    end

    # GET /articles/1/edit
    def edit
      @article = current_user.articles.find(params[:id])
    end

    # POST /articles
    # POST /articles.xml
    def create
      @article = current_user.articles.new(params[:article])

      respond_to do |format|
        if @article.save
          format.html { redirect_to(@article,
:notice => 'Article was successfully created.') }
          format.xml  { render :xml => @article, :status => :created,
:location => @article }
        else
          format.html { render :action => "new" }
          format.xml  { render :xml => @article.errors,
:status => :unprocessable_entity }
        end
      end
    end

  # PUT /articles/1
  # PUT /articles/1.xml
  def update
    @article = current_user.articles.find(params[:id])

    respond_to do |format|
      if @article.update_attributes(params[:article])
        format.html { redirect_to(@article,
:notice => 'Article was successfully updated.') }
        format.xml  { head :ok }
      else
        format.html { render :action => "edit" }
        format.xml  { render :xml => @article.errors,
:status => :unprocessable_entity }
```

```
      end
    end
  end

  # DELETE /articles/1
  # DELETE /articles/1.xml
  def destroy
    @article = current_user.articles.find(params[:id])
    @article.destroy

    respond_to do |format|
      format.html { redirect_to(articles_url) }
      format.xml  { head :ok }
    end
  end

  def notify_friend
    @article = Article.find(params[:id])
    Notifier.email_friend(@article, params[:name], params[:email]).deliver
    redirect_to @article, :notice => "Successfully sent a message to your friend"
  end
end
```

The action you just added is short and concise, but there's something that deserves a closer look. To perform the delivery, you call a class method on the Notifier class called email_friend; by calling deliver after email_friend, Action Mailer executes the email_friend method in the Notifier class and generates an e-mail message as per that method. After the e-mail message is created, it's passed to the deliver method, which performs the actual delivery.

This is important. Every time you create a mail action, you call it directly from the mailer class (in this case, Notifier), and then you call deliver. If you had a mailer class called BlogMailer and a mail action called invitation, you'd call it using BlogMailer.invitation.deliver.

Before you try this, the email_friend method still needs a bit of work. You need to augment it so that it sets a meaningful title and uses the name and email parameters you collect from the form and pass into the method. Listing 9-7 shows the changes.

Listing 9-7. Updated Notifier Mailer in app/mailers/notifier.rb: http://gist.github.com/390971

```
class Notifier < ActionMailer::Base
  default :from => "from@example.com"

  def email_friend(article, sender_name, receiver_email)
    @article = article
    @sender_name = sender_name

    mail :to => receiver_email, :subject => "Interesting Article"
  end
end
```

Notice how you add three arguments: article, sender_name, and receiver_email. You start by defining two instance variables @article and @sender_name to make them available in your view template. Then, you modify the mail method call to send the e-mail to the receiver_email address with the subject "Interesting Article".

Next, you want your e-mail message to have some sort of formatting and include the URL of your application. Change the template file located in app/views/notifier/email_friend.text.erb and make it look like Listing 9-8.

Listing 9-8. Notifier Template, in app/views/notifier/email_friend.text.erb:

http://gist.github.com/355053

```
Your friend <%= @sender_name %> thinks you may like the following article:

<%= @article.title %>: <%= article_url(@article, :host => "localhost:3000") %>
```

Finally, you can give this a try in a browser. Fill out the e-mail form using your own e-mail address, so you can see what the e-mail message looks like. If all goes according to plan, you should receive a message that looks something like Figure 9-3.

Figure 9-3. Message delivered to user's inbox

This is a plain text message, the default content type. The next section shows how to send e-mail messages that use rich, HTML formatting.

Sending HTML E-Mail

So far, your e-mail message is pretty plain. To make it more interesting and informative, you can add a link to the specific article being recommended. You can also make it more visually appealing for users with rich e-mail clients (like Gmail) by adding some HTML formatting.

Making another analogy to controllers, whenever you want to render an e-mail template with HTML content, you need to change the template extension from .text.erb to .html.erb; Rails takes care of setting the appropriate e-mail headers.

In this case, if you keep the .text.erb file and add a template with a .html.erb extension, Rails sends both templates, representing the same e-mail, know as a *multipart* message. The e-mail client that receives a multipart message recognizes that there are alternatives for the same message and chooses the most appropriate part based on the environment or the user's preferences.

Let's put together an HTML template for the message in app/views/notifier/email_friend.html.erb. The file should look like Listing 9-9.

Listing 9-9. HTML email_friend Template in app/views/notifier/email_friend.html.erb:

http://gist.github.com/355076

```
<html>
<body>
<p>
  One of your friends, <%= @sender_name %>,
  thinks you like an article we have written.
</p>

<p>
  Come check all the information about <strong><%= @article.title %></strong> at
  <%= article_url @article, :host => 'localhost:3000' %>
</p>
</body>
</html>
```

Use the application to send yourself another e-mail. It looks pretty good, as shown in Figure 9-4. If your users don't have a rich e-mail client and can't read HTML mail, they get the plain text version.

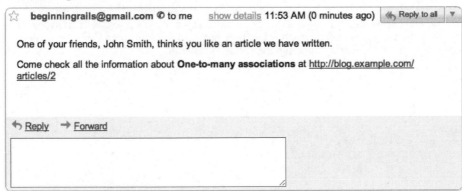

Figure 9-4. HTML message delivered to a user's inbox

■ **NOTE** If you think maintaining both text and HTML versions of an e-mail message is a lot of work, it may be safe to stick with the HTML message.

Adding Attachments

In some cases, you may want to add attachments to an e-mail message. Action Mailer makes this a straightforward task by providing the attachment helper. You tell attachment which file you want to attach to the e-mail, and it does its magic.

Let's walk through an example of attaching a file to an e-mail message. Assume that you want to send a photo related to one of the articles in the blog application every time a user sends an e-mail about that article to a friend. Just for demonstration, use the default Rails logo, which should be in the public/images directory (a vestige of the "Welcome to Rails" index.html file you deleted back in Chapter 6). To attach this image file to the e-mail you created in the previous section, add a call to the attachments method in the email_friend method in the Notifier class, as shown in Listing 9-10.

Listing 9-10. Adding an Attachment to the Mailer in app/models/notifier.rb:

http://gist.github.com/355081

```
class Notifier < ActionMailer::Base
  default :from => "from@example.com"

  def email_friend(article, sender_name, receiver_email)
    @article = article
    @sender_name = sender_name

    attachments["rails.png"] = File.read(Rails.root.join("public/images/rails.png"))
    mail :to => receiver_email, :subject => "Interesting Article"
  end
end
```

When you call the attachments method, first you identify the name of the file the e-mail receiver sees; in this case, the receiver sees a file named rails.png because you call attachments["rails.png"]. Next, you tell Rails where the file you want to attach is located: you load the Rails logo from the project using the Rails.root method. The resulting message looks like Figure 9-5.

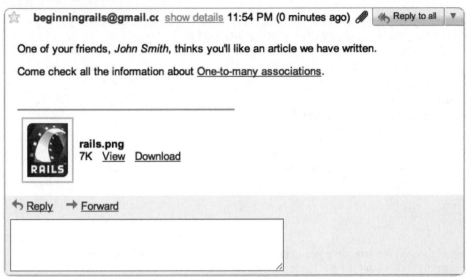

Figure 9-5. *Message with an attachment delivered to a user's inbox*

■ **TIP** You can specify the body of an attachment by using the `File.read` method if the file you're sending exists on disk. Alternatively, you can generate the file on the fly if it's a dynamic file, like a personalized PDF or Word document.

Letting Authors Know About Comments

Just to make sure you've grasped how to send e-mail from your Rails applications, this section quickly goes over the complete flow to add another mailer action. If you remember, in Chapter 5, you added an observer to be invoked every time a new comment is added.

In total, you change three files. First, you add a new action to the `Notifier` mailer class; second, you add a new template with the contents of the e-mail to send; last, you change the observer to invoke the mailer when new comments are added. Listings 9-11 to 9-13 show the code.

Listing 9-11. Adding the `comment_added` Method to app/models/notifier.rb:

http://gist.github.com/358011

```
class Notifier < ActionMailer::Base
  default :from => "from@example.com"

  def email_friend(article, sender_name, receiver_email)
```

```
    @article = article
    @sender_name = sender_name

    attachments["rails.png"] = File.read(Rails.root.join("public/images/rails.png"))
    mail :to => receiver_email, :subject => "Interesting Article"
  end

  def comment_added(comment)
    @article = comment.article
    mail :to => @article.user.email,
:subject => "New comment for '#{@article.title}'"
  end
end
```

Listing 9-12. The comment_added *Mailer Template in* app/views/notifier/comment_added.html.erb*:*

http://gist.github.com/358023

```
<html>
<body>
  <p>
    Someone added a comment to one of your articles <i><%= @article.title %></i>.
    Go read the comment: <%= link_to @article.title,
article_url(@article, :host => 'localhost:3000') %>.
  </p>
</body>
</html>
```

Listing 9-13. Updates to app/model/comment_observer.rb: *http://gist.github.com/358027*

```
class CommentObserver < ActiveRecord::Observer
  def after_create(comment)
    Notifier.comment_added(comment).deliver
  end
end
```

Now that those changes have been made, create an article with your user account, and add some comments. You should receive one e-mail message per comment. If you wanted, you could add the comment text to the e-mail; that way, you wouldn't need to go the article page to read the comment. You could easily implement that by changing the mailer view.

Receiving E-Mail

So far, you've seen that Action Mailer has extensive support for sending all types of mail messages. But what if your application needs to receive e-mail? You can handle incoming e-mail in a Rails application a few different ways. This section explains how to use a Rails process and how to read e-mail from your mail server. The approach you choose depends a lot on your operating system and e-mail server.

Using a Rails Process

In an Action Mailer class, you can write a `receive` method that receives a `Mail::Message` object as a parameter, which corresponds to an incoming e-mail message your code can process. Inside the `receive` method, it's easy to extract details about the incoming e-mail, such as header, subject, body text, and/or attachments.

For example, the blog application can have a special e-mail address (such as new@blog.example.com) that can be monitored to create a new article whenever an e-mail arrives. This way, users can send an e-mail to new@blog.example.com and create a new article without needing to open their browsers. The implementation of this feature looks something like Listing 9-14.

Listing 9-14. Example Mailer Class with `receive` Method

```
class ExampleMailer < ActionMailer::Base
  def receive(email)
    article = Article.new
    article.title = email.subject
    article.body = email.body
    article.save
  end
end
```

This code is pretty simple and takes care of receiving mail; however, this is just the first part of the solution. The remaining part is tricky and may demand some research and system administration skills. You need to tell your mail server that it should redirect messages sent to a specific address to a special process. In this case, the process is the Rails runner script, which executes the Ruby code passed as parameter as if it were running from within a Rails application. You can see this technique in action by saving an e-mail message to any location on disk and invoking the `receive` method using the following command (POSIX only):

```
rails runner ExampleMailer.receive(STDIN.read) < email.txt
```

This chapter doesn't go into the implementation details of configuring a script to route incoming mail to your Rails process because it's impossible to cover all setups. Visit the Rails wiki at http://oldwiki.rubyonrails.com/rails/pages/HowToReceiveEmailsWithActionMailer to look up information about your particular setup.

Reading E-Mail Using POP or IMAP

If you don't have control over the e-mail server being used and can't write a server-side script, you can still read e-mail from your mail server as your regular e-mail client does. To do this, you can create a separate Ruby script that fetches e-mail, and run it as a background process that polls for new messages.

The code in Listing 9-15 connects to a mail server through POP3 and checks a specific mailbox to see if any new e-mail has arrived. If so, the script reads that message and passes it to the `ExampleMailer.receive` method for processing. This example uses a POP3 server, but it could just as easily use an IMAP server. The only difference would be that you would use the `Net::IMAP` class instead of the `Net::POP3` class to connect to the mail server. Both classes are part of the Ruby Standard Library.

Listing 9-15. Sample Ruby Script for Reading E-Mail Messages

```
Net::POP3.start("mail.example.com", nil, "username", "password") do |pop|
  if pop.mails.empty?
    logger.info "NO MAIL"
  else
    pop.mails.each do |email|
      begin
        logger.info "receiving mail..."
        ExampleMailer.receive(email.pop)
        email.delete
      rescue Exception => e
        logger.error "Error receiving email: #{Time.now.to_s} - #{e.message}"
      end
    end
  end
end
```

This script starts by trying to connect to the POP3 server with the credentials indicated on the first line. As soon as the connection is established, it checks to see if there are any new e-mail messages by using the pop.mails.empty? method. If there are new e-mail messages, it iterates through each of them, calling ExampleMailer.receive(email.pop). After a message is processed, it's deleted from the server to avoid reprocessing the same message the next time the script is called.

Summary

In this chapter, you learned how to send e-mail from your web applications using Action Mailer. You configured Action Mailer to talk to your mail server and learned the most common configuration parameters you can use to fine-tune how Action Mailer works with your application.

You learned that Action Mailer allows you to send e-mail messages based on templates, and how to use implicit parts for text and HTML messages, as well as how to use the attachment helper to add attachments to your messages.

You also touched briefly on receiving mail using Action Mailer. The chapter only scratched the surface, this being a rather advanced technique. Still, you have a good starting point, should your application ever need to perform this task, and you know where to look when you need more information.

This chapter brings is the end of your tour of the main Rails libraries: Active Record, Action Pack, and Action Mailer. The next chapter covers one of the most important techniques to improve the quality of your code: testing.

CHAPTER 10

■ ■ ■

Testing Your Application

Smart developers test their code. Take a minute to read that sentence again, and let it sink in: smart developers test their code. The fact is, testing is one of the most important things you can do to improve the quality of your code, reduce the cost of change, and keep your software bug-free. Rails (and the Ruby community at large) takes testing seriously. Not surprisingly, Rails goes out of its way to make testing hassle-free.

The basic idea of testing is simple: you write code that exercises your program and tests your assumptions. Instead of just opening a browser and adding a new user manually to check whether the process works, you write a test that automates the process—something repeatable. With a test in place, every time you modify the code that adds a new user, you can run the test to see if your change worked—and, more important, whether your seemingly innocuous change broke something else.

If you stop and think about it, you're already testing your software. The problem is that you're doing it manually, often in an ad hoc fashion. You may make a change to the way users log in, and then you try it in your browser. You make a change to the sign-up procedure, and then you take it for a spin. As your application grows in size, it becomes more and more difficult to manually test like this, and eventually you miss something important. Even if you're not testing, you can be sure that your users are. After all, they're the ones using the application in the wild, and they'll find bugs you never knew existed. The best solution is to replace this sort of visual, ad hoc inspection with automatic checking.

Testing becomes increasingly important when you're refactoring existing code. *Refactoring* is the process of improving the design of code without changing its behavior. The best way to refactor is with a test in place acting as a safety net. Because refactoring shouldn't result in an observable change in behavior, it shouldn't break your tests either. It's easy, therefore, to see why many programmers won't refactor without tests.

Given the importance placed on testing, it may seem odd that this book leaves it to the tenth chapter. Ideally, you should be writing tests as you go, never getting too far ahead without testing what you've written. But we decided that explaining how to test would be overwhelming while you were still learning the basics of Ruby and the Rails framework. Now that you have a good deal of knowledge under your belt, it's time to tackle testing.

■ **NOTE** If you need to get the code at the exact point where you finished Chapter 9, download the zip file from `http://github.com/downloads/ccjr/blog/chapter10.zip` and extract it on your computer.

How Rails Handles Testing

Rails defines three different kinds of tests, each designed to test a specific piece of your application:

- *Unit testing* tests your models.

- *Functional testing* tests your controllers.

- *Integration testing* tests at a high level through multiple controllers.

Because Rails is an integrated environment, it can make assumptions about the best ways to structure and organize your tests. Rails provides the following:

- Test directories for unit, functional, and integration tests

- Fixtures for easily working with database data

- An environment explicitly created for testing

The default Rails skeleton generated by the `rails` command creates a directory just for testing. If you open it, you see subdirectories for each of the aforementioned test types:

```
test
|-- unit              <-- model tests
|-- functional      <-- controller tests
|-- performance <-- profiling testing through integration tests
`-- fixtures          <-- test data
```

In addition to the `unit` and `functional` directories, Rails creates the `integration` directory when you generate your first integration test. There is also a `performance` directory and a `fixtures` directory. What are these for?

Fixtures are textual representations of table data written in YAML—a data-serialization format. Fixtures are loaded into the database before your tests run; you use them to populate your database with data to test against. Look at the users fixtures file in `test/fixtures/users.yml`, shown in Listing 10-1.

Listing 10-1. Users Fixture, `test/fixtures/users.yml`

```
# Read about fixtures at http://ar.rubyonrails.org/classes/Fixtures.html

one:
  email: MyString
  password: MyString

two:
  email: MyString
  password: MyString
```

Rails generates the users fixtures file for you when you generate the user model. As you can see, the file has two fixtures: one and two. Each fixture has both attributes `email` and `password` set to `MyString`; but, if you remember, you renamed the `password` column `hashed_password` back in Chapter 5. Let's update the users fixtures file to reflect the new column name and use meaningful data. Listing 10-2 shows the updated fixture.

Listing 10-2. Updated Users Fixtures in `test/fixtures/users.yml`: http://gist.github.com/358067

```
eugene:
  email: 'eugene@example.com'
```

```
  hashed_password: 'e5e9fa1ba31ecd1ae84f75caaa474f3a663f05f4' # => secret

lauren:
  email: 'lauren@example.com'
  hashed_password: 'e5e9fa1ba31ecd1ae84f75caaa474f3a663f05f4' # => secret
```

The performances directory is used to store performance tests. They're basically integration tests that run a code profiler on your tests; the results of those tests are outputted to the `tmp/performance` directory.

Remember that every time you generated a model or a controller while building the blog application, Rails automatically generated test files for you. This is another example of its opinionated nature—Rails thinks you should test, so it goes out of its way to remind you.

You may also remember that Rails created three SQLite databases for the blog application: one for development (which is all you've been using thus far), one for production, and one for testing. Not surprisingly, Rails uses the testing database just for testing.

Rails drops and re-creates this test database on every run of the test suite. Make sure you don't list your development or production database in its place, or all your data will be gone.

Unit Testing Your Rails Application

You know that Rails generated some tests automatically. Let's open one of them now and take a look. Start with the Article test, located in `test/unit/article_test.rb`, as shown in Listing 10-3.

Listing 10-3. Generated Article Unit Test, in test/unit/artilce_test.rb

```
require 'test_helper'

class ArticleTest < ActiveSupport::TestCase
  # Replace this with your real tests.
  test "the truth" do
    assert true
  end
end
```

Although there's not much to it (all it does is test that `true` is, in fact, true), this test gives you a template from which to build your real tests. It has the following elements:

- The test class is a subclass of Rails' enhanced version of Ruby's built-in testing framework, `Test::Unit`. It's called `ActiveSupport::TestCase`.

- Tests are implemented as blocks using the `test` method, with the first parameter as the description of that test—`"the truth"` in this case.

- Within a test case, *assertions* are used to test expectations. The "Testing with Assertions" section explains how these work.

If you peek inside the `test/unit` directory, you see a similar test case for every model you've generated so far: `Article`, `Comment`, `Category`, `User`, and `Profile`. You also see a test for `CommentObserver`. Each looks almost exactly the same as the Article test. Let's run the unit tests now using the `rake test:units` command from your command prompt, and see what happens:

```
$ rake test:units
```

```
Loaded suite

Started

......

Finished in 0.115422 seconds.



6 tests, 6 assertions, 0 failures, 0 errors, 0 skips
```

Take a closer look at the output. If a test case passes, as each did this time, you see a . (dot) character. When the test case produces an error, you see an E. If any assertion fails to return true, you see an F. Finally, when the test suite is finished, it prints a summary.

Testing the Article Model

Let's test the Article model. If you recall from Chapter 4, one of the first things you did with your Article model was basic CRUD operations. Well, testing that you can create, read, update, and delete articles is a great place to start. Here's a quick summary of the specific things you test in this chapter:

- Creating a new article

- Finding an article

- Updating an article

- Destroying an article

Before you begin, you need to create a few fixtures (remember that a fixture is a textual representation of test data).

Creating Fixtures

You create fixtures for articles. Open the test/fixtures/articles.yml file, and replace its content with the code as shown in Listing 10-4.

Listing 10-4. Articles Fixtures in test/fixtures/articles.yml: http://gist.github.com/358400

```
welcome_to_rails:
  user: eugene
  title: "Welcome to Rails"
  body: "Rails is such a nice web framework written in Ruby"
  published_at: <%= 3.days.ago %>
```

That's all you need to do. The data in the fixtures is inserted automatically into your test database before your tests run. With fixtures in place, you're ready to start creating test cases.

■ **TIP** Fixtures are parsed by ERb before they're loaded, so you can use ERb in them just as you can in view templates. This is useful for creating dynamic dates, as you so in published_at: <%= 3.days.ago %>.

The following sections present the test cases one at a time, beginning with *create*.

Adding a Create Test

Open the test/unit/article_test.rb file, and create the first test case by deleting the test "the truth" method and replacing it with a test called test "should create article". Your file should look like Listing 10-5.

Listing 10-5. The Create Article Test in test/unit/article_test.rb: http://gist.github.com/358401

```
require 'test_helper'

class ArticleTest < ActiveSupport::TestCase
  test "should create article" do
    article = Article.new

    article.user  = users(:eugene)
    article.title = "Test article"
    article.body  = "Test body"

    assert article.save
  end
end
```

The test "should create article" case is standard article-creation fare. You create a new article in the same way you'd create one from the console. The only real difference is on the last line of the test case:

```
assert article.save
```

■ **NOTE** Fixtures can be accessed in your test cases by name. Use fixture(:name), where fixture is the plural name of the model and :name is the symbolized name of the fixture you're after. This returns an Active Record object on which you can call methods. Here, you get at the eugene user fixture using users(:eugene).

Before you go any further, let's take a deeper look at assertions as they pertain to Test::Unit and ActiveSupport::TestCase.

Testing with Assertions

Assertions are statements of expected outcome. As the README for Test::Unit states, assertions are like saying "I assert that x should be equal to y." If the assertion turns out to be correct, the assertion passes. If the assertion turns out to be false, the assertion fails, and Test::Unit reports a failure.

Test::Unit ships with a bevy of built-in assertions, and Rails adds a bunch of its own. You see the Rails-added assertions as you look at each test case; but first, here's the standard set of Test::Unit assertions for reference:

```
assert(boolean, message=nil)
assert_block(message="assert_block failed.") do ... end
assert_equal(expected, actual, message=nil)
assert_in_delta(expected_float, actual_float, delta, message="")
assert_instance_of(klass, object, message="")
assert_kind_of(klass, object, message="")
assert_match(pattern, string, message="")
assert_nil(object, message="")
assert_no_match(regexp, string, message="")
assert_not_equal(expected, actual, message="")
assert_not_nil(object, message="")
assert_not_same(expected, actual, message="")
assert_nothing_raised(*args) do ... end
assert_nothing_thrown(message="") do ... end
assert_operator(object1, operator, object2, message="")
assert_raise(expected_exception_klass, message="") do ... end
assert_respond_to(object, method, message="")
assert_same(expected, actual, message="")
assert_send(send_array, message="")
assert_throws(expected_symbol, message="") do ... end
```

The assert method is perhaps the most basic of the lot. It asserts that the return value of its first argument is true. And you know that article.save returns true if the article saves and returns false otherwise. So, by asserting article.save, you successfully test that the article was saved. Pretty easy, isn't it?

■ **TIP** Geoffrey Grosenbach (a.k.a. topfunky) has a useful cheat sheet that summarizes all available assertions. You can download it from http://nubyonrails.com/articles/ruby-rails-test-rails-cheat-sheet.

Let's run the test. This time, run only the article test, invoking Ruby directly:

```
$ ruby -Itest test/unit/article_test.rb
```

```
Loaded suite test/unit/article_test

Started

.

Finished in 0.168879 seconds.


1 tests, 1 assertions, 0 failures, 0 errors, 0 skips
```

Just as the output from the test says, you ran one test (test "should create article"), which included one assertion (assert article.save), and everything passed. Life is good!

Notice the -Itest parameter that you pass to the ruby command. You add that to make sure Ruby includes the test directory while running the article_test file; that is required because Rails provides a file called test/test_helper.rb to be included in all your tests. When you run tests using the rake command, rake takes care of adding test/test_helper.rb for you.

Adding a Find Test

Next on the list is testing that you can successfully find an article. You use the data in the fixture you created to help you. Add the method shown in Listing 10-6 after test "should create article".

Listing 10-6. Test Case for Finding an Article in test/unit/article_test.rb:

http://gist.github.com/358402

```ruby
require 'test_helper'

class ArticleTest < ActiveSupport::TestCase
  test "should create article" do
    article = Article.new

    article.user  = users(:eugene)
    article.title = "Test article"
    article.body  = "Test body"

    assert article.save
  end

  test "should find article" do
    article_id = articles(:welcome_to_rails).id
    assert_nothing_raised { Article.find(article_id) }
  end
end
```

Here, you test that you can find an article of the given id. First, you grab the id attribute from the fixture, and then you test that you can use `Article.find` to retrieve it. You use the assertion `assert_nothing_raised` because you know that `find` raises an exception if the record can't be found. If no exception is raised, you know that finding works. Again, run the test and see what happens:

```
$ ruby -Itest test/unit/article_test.rb
```

```
Loaded suite test/unit/article_test

Started

..

Finished in 0.133271 seconds.


2 tests, 2 assertions, 0 failures, 0 errors, 0 skips
```

Sure enough, finding works! So far, so good.

Adding an Update Test

Your next move is to test updating. Add the test `"should update article"` case, as shown in Listing 10-7.

Listing 10-7. Test Case for Updating an Article in test/unit/article_test.rb:

http://gist.github.com/358403

```ruby
require 'test_helper'

class ArticleTest < ActiveSupport::TestCase
  test "should create article" do
    article = Article.new

    article.user  = users(:eugene)
    article.title = "Test article"
    article.body  = "Test body"

    assert article.save
  end

  test "should find article" do
    article_id = articles(:welcome_to_rails).id
    assert_nothing_raised { Article.find(article_id) }
  end
```

```
  test "should update article" do
    article = articles(:welcome_to_rails)
    assert article.update_attributes(:title => 'New title')
  end
end
```

First, you find the "Welcome to Rails" article from your fixture, and then you assert that changing the title via update_attributes returns true. Once again, run the test and see what happens:

```
$ ruby -Itest test/unit/article_test.rb
```

```
Loaded suite test/unit/article_test

Started

...

Finished in 0.226404 seconds.




3 tests, 3 assertions, 0 failures, 0 errors, 0 skips
```

Adding a Destroy Test

Only one more test to go: destroy. You find an article, destroy it, and assert that Active Record raises an exception when you try to find it again. Listing 10-8 shows the test.

Listing 10-8. Test Case for Destroying an Article in test/unit/article_test.rb:

http://gist.github.com/358404

```
require 'test_helper'

class ArticleTest < ActiveSupport::TestCase
  test "should create article" do
    article = Article.new

    article.user  = users(:eugene)
    article.title = "Test article"
    article.body  = "Test body"

    assert article.save
  end

  test "should find article" do
    article_id = articles(:welcome_to_rails).id
    assert_nothing_raised { Article.find(article_id) }
```

```
  end

  test "should update article" do
    article = articles(:welcome_to_rails)
    assert article.update_attributes(:title => 'New title')
  end

  test "should destroy article" do
    article = articles(:welcome_to_rails)
    article.destroy
    assert_raise(ActiveRecord::RecordNotFound) { Article.find(article.id) }
  end
end
```

The assert_raise assertion takes as an argument the class of the exception you expect to be raised for whatever you do inside the given block. Because you've deleted the article, you expect Active Record to respond with a RecordNotFound exception when you try to find the article you just deleted by id. Run the test, and see what happens:

```
$ ruby -Itest test/unit/article_test.rb
```

```
Loaded suite test/unit/article_test

Started

....

Finished in 0.215428 seconds.



4 tests, 4 assertions, 0 failures, 0 errors, 0 skips
```

And there you have it. You've successfully tested article CRUD.

Testing Validations

You have a few validations on your Article model, specifically for the presence of a title and body. Because you want to make sure these are working as expected, you need to test them. Add the method shown in Listing 10-9 to test that you can't create invalid articles.

Listing 10-9. Test Case for Validations in test/unit/article_test.rb: http://gist.github.com/358405

```
require 'test_helper'

class ArticleTest < ActiveSupport::TestCase
  test "should create article" do
    article = Article.new
```

```
    article.user  = users(:eugene)
    article.title = "Test article"
    article.body  = "Test body"

    assert article.save
  end

  test "should find article" do
    article_id = articles(:welcome_to_rails).id
    assert_nothing_raised { Article.find(article_id) }
  end

  test "should update article" do
    article = articles(:welcome_to_rails)
    assert article.update_attributes(:title => 'New title')
  end

  test "should destroy article" do
    article = articles(:welcome_to_rails)
    article.destroy
    assert_raise(ActiveRecord::RecordNotFound) { Article.find(article.id) }
  end

  test "should not create an article without title nor body" do
    article = Article.new
    assert !article.valid?
    assert article.errors[:title].any?
    assert article.errors[:body].any?
    assert_equal ["can't be blank"], article.errors[:title]
    assert_equal ["can't be blank"], article.errors[:body]
    assert !article.save
  end
end
```

This is pretty straightforward, although you may have to read it a few times before it clicks. First, you instantiate a new Article object in the local variable article. Without having given it any attributes, you expect it to be invalid. So, you assert that it's not valid using assert !article.valid? (notice the !, which negates truth). Next, you access the errors hash to explicitly check for the attributes you expect to be invalid:

```
assert article.errors[:title].any?
assert article.errors[:body].any?
```

You also want to check that the validation responses are what you expect. To do this, you use the assert_equal assertion. Here's its basic syntax:

```
assert_equal(expected, actual)
```

To check the error messages, you again access the errors hash, but this time you ask for the specific messages associated with the given attribute:

```
assert_equal ["can't be blank"], article.errors[:title]
assert_equal ["can't be blank"], article.errors[:body]
```

Finally, you assert that `article.save` returns `false` using `!article.save`. Run the test one more time:

```
$ ruby -Itest test/unit/article_test.rb
```

```
Loaded suite test/unit/article_test

Started

.....

Finished in 0.304773 seconds.

5 tests, 10 assertions, 0 failures, 0 errors, 0 skips
```

Feels good, doesn't it? Life isn't all roses, though, and requirements change. What if one day you decide to make a change to the `Article` model and remove the validation requirements for the `title` attribute? If that were to happen, your test would fail. If you want to try it, open the `Article` model in `app/models/article.rb`, and remove `validates :title, :presence => true`, and then run the tests again.

When your requirements change, you often need to update your tests. We recommend updating the tests *first* (which should make them fail) and then updating your code (which makes them pass). This is also knows as Test Driven Development (TDD).

Functional Testing Your Controllers

Tests to check your controllers are called *functional* tests. When you tested your models, you didn't test them in the context of the web application—there were no web requests and responses, nor were there any URLs to contend with. This focused approach lets you home in on the specific functionality of the model and test it in isolation. Alas, Rails is for building web applications; and although unit-testing models is important, it's equally important to test the full request/response cycle.

Testing the Articles Controller

Functional tests aren't that much different from unit tests. The main difference is that Rails sets up request and response objects for you; those objects act just like the live requests and responses you get when running the application via a web server. If you open the articles controller test in `test/functional/articles_controller_test.rb` and examine the first few lines, as shown in Listing 10-10, you can see how this is done.

Listing 10-10. Setup of a Functional Test in `test/functional/articles_controller_test.rb`

```
require 'test_helper'
```

```
class ArticlesControllerTest < ActionController::TestCase
  # ...
end
```

Just as in the unit test, the first thing you do is require the `test_helper`. The `test_helper.rb` file sets up some common environment variables and generally endows `Test::Unit` with specific methods that make testing Rails applications easier.

■ **NOTE** You can think of `test_helper` as being akin to `application_helper`. Any methods you define here are available to all your tests.

Notice that `ArticlesControllerTest` is actually a subclass of `ActionController::TestCase`, which performs some magic for you behind the scenes. It prepares three instance variables for you to use in your tests: the first is `@controller` as an instance variable of `ArticlesController`, after which it instantiates both `@request` and `@response` variables, which are instances of `ActionController::TestRequest` and `ActionController::TestResponse`, respectively. As you can no doubt tell by their names, these objects are made specifically for testing, and they're designed to simulate the Action Controller environment as closely as possible.

Most of the time, you don't need to worry about all this. Still, it's important to know what's going on. Because the test you're looking at was created by the scaffold generator, it has quite a bit more code than you would get from the standard controller generator. There's a problem with this code, though: not all the test cases will pass—at least, not without some modification. Warts and all, this gives you a good start and serves well as a template.

As you look over the `articles` controller functional test file, notice that each test case tests a specific request for an action on the controller. There's a test for every action: `index`, `show`, `new`, `create`, `edit`, `update`, and `destroy`. Let's walk through each test case, making adjustments as you go.

Creating a Test Helper

Before you test your actions, a little foresight tells you that in order to create an article, your application expects a logged-in user. So, you need to simulate a logged-in user for your tests. This is a perfect job for a test helper. You can create a helper method called `login_as` that accepts the name of the user to log in as. This method sets up the `session` object, just as your controller expects. You can use this method for any test case that requires a login.

To begin, open the `test_helper` file in your editor, and add the `login_as` method as shown in Listing 10-11. You can find the test helper file in `test/test_helper.rb`; the method you're adding is highlighted in bold.

Listing 10-11. The `login_as` Test Helper in `test/test_helper.rb`: http://gist.github.com/358406

```
ENV["RAILS_ENV"] = "test"
require File.expand_path(File.dirname(__FILE__) + "/../config/environment")
require 'rails/test_help'

class ActiveSupport::TestCase
  # Setup all fixtures in test/fixtures/*.(yml|csv)
```

```
    # for all tests in alphabetical order.
    #
    # Note: You currently still have to declare fixtures
    # explicitly in integration tests
    # -- they do not yet inherit this setting
    fixtures :all

    # Add more helper methods to be used by all tests here...
    def login_as(user)
      @request.session[:user_id] = users(user).id
    end
end
```

The login_as method is simple. All it does is manually set user_id in the @request.session object (just like your login action does) to the id of the given user, as obtained from the fixture. If you give it the name of one of your users fixtures, say, :eugene, it sets session[:user_id] to users(:eugene).id.

Now that you've created a way to simulate a logged-in user, you're ready to proceed with your tests, beginning with the index action.

Testing the Index Action

The updated setup method and test "should get index" are shown in Listing 10-12. Make sure yours looks like this before you proceed.

Listing 10-12. Updated Test Case for the Index Action in test/functional/articles_controller_test.rb:

http://gist.github.com/358409

```
require 'test_helper'

class ArticlesControllerTest < ActionController::TestCase
  setup do
    @article = articles(:welcome_to_rails)
  end

  test "should get index" do
    get :index
    assert_response :success
    assert_template 'index'
    assert_not_nil assigns(:articles)
  end

  test "should get new" do
    get :new
    assert_response :success
  end

  test "should create article" do
    assert_difference('Article.count') do
      post :create, :article => @article.attributes
    end
```

```
    assert_redirected_to article_path(assigns(:article))
  end

  test "should show article" do
    get :show, :id => @article.to_param
    assert_response :success
  end

  test "should get edit" do
    get :edit, :id => @article.to_param
    assert_response :success
  end

  test "should update article" do
    put :update, :id => @article.to_param, :article => @article.attributes
    assert_redirected_to article_path(assigns(:article))
  end

  test "should destroy article" do
    assert_difference('Article.count', -1) do
      delete :destroy, :id => @article.to_param
    end

    assert_redirected_to articles_path
  end
end
```

The setup method is executed before every test case. In this case, the setup method assigns the :welcome_to_rails record from the fixtures to an instance variable @article; the @article variable is available to all test cases in the ArticlesControllerTest class.

Functional tests define methods that correspond to HTTP verbs (GET, POST, PUT, and DELETE), which you use to make requests. The first line of the test "should get index" method makes a GET request for the index action using get :index. Here's the full syntax you use for these requests:

```
http_method(action, parameters, session, flash)
```

In the case of test "should get index", you have no parameters to submit along with the request, so your call is simple. It makes a GET request to the index action just as if you had done so with a browser. After the request has been made, you need to assert your expectations:

```
assert_response :success
```

The assert_response assertion is a custom assertion defined by Rails (that is, it's not part of the standard Test::Unit library), and it does exactly what its name implies: it asserts that there was a successful response to the request.

Every time you make an HTTP request, the server responds with a status code. When the response is successful, the server returns a status code of 200. When an error occurs, it returns 500. And when the browser can't find the resource being requested, it returns 404. In your assertion, you use the shortcut :success, which is the same as 200. You could have used assert_response(200), but it's easier to remember words like *success* or *error* than HTTP status codes, which is why we avoid using the latter whenever possible. Table 10-1 lists the shortcuts available when using assert_response.

Table 10-1. Status-Code Shortcuts Known to `assert_response`

Symbol	Meaning
`:success`	Status code was 200
`:redirect`	Status code was in the 300–399 range
`:missing`	Status code was 404
`:error`	Status code was in the 500–599 range

■ **TIP** You can pass an explicit status-code number to `assert_response`, such as `assert_response(501)` or its symbolic equivalent `assert_response(:not_implemented)`. See `http://iana.org/assignments/http-status-codes` for the full list of codes and default messages you can use.

You also want to assert that the proper template was rendered in response to the request, for which you use another of Rails' custom assertions: `assert_template`. Here, you expect to see the `index` template (from `app/views/articles/index.html.erb`) to be rendered, so test this expectation:

`assert_template 'index'`

You need to do one more thing: assert that the correct instance variables were assigned. If you look at the `articles` controller, you see that you set an instance variable called `@articles` that contains the articles collection. Rails gives you the ability to test whether this assignment was successful by way of the `assigns` method:

`assert_not_nil assigns(:articles)`

This asserts that `@articles` was, in fact, assigned (by virtue of the fact that it shouldn't be `nil`). You can use this technique to test for the existence of any instance variable set within your controllers. Useful, isn't it? Using `assigns` gives you access to the instance variable, so you can do with it as you please.

Testing the Show Action

Listing 10-13 shows the `test "should show article"` case.

Listing 10-13. Updated Test Case for the show Action in test/functional/articles_controller_test.rb:
http://gist.github.com/358410

```ruby
require 'test_helper'

class ArticlesControllerTest < ActionController::TestCase
  setup do
    @article = articles(:welcome_to_rails)
  end

  test "should get index" do
    get :index
    assert_response :success
    assert_template 'index'
    assert_not_nil assigns(:articles)
  end

  test "should get new" do
    get :new
    assert_response :success
  end

  test "should create article" do
    assert_difference('Article.count') do
      post :create, :article => @article.attributes
    end

    assert_redirected_to article_path(assigns(:article))
  end

  test "should show article" do
    get :show, :id => @article.to_param

    assert_response :success
    assert_template 'show'

    assert_not_nil assigns(:article)
    assert assigns(:article).valid?
  end

  test "should get edit" do
    get :edit, :id => @article.to_param
    assert_response :success
  end

  test "should update article" do
    put :update, :id => @article.to_param, :article => @article.attributes
    assert_redirected_to article_path(assigns(:article))
  end
```

```
    test "should destroy article" do
      assert_difference('Article.count', -1) do
        delete :destroy, :id => @article.to_param
      end

      assert_redirected_to articles_path
    end
  end
end
```

The test "should show article" case is almost the same as test "should get index", but with one notable difference: you need to identify the record you want to show. If you were requesting this in a browser, the URL would look like /articles/1. Therefore, you need to pass in the :id parameter with a value of 1. If you look closely at the test request, you can see how this is done:

```
get :show, :id => @article.to_param
```

@article.to_param by default gets the id attribute of the :welcome_to_rails article you're getting from the fixtures that is assigned to the @article variable. You should always use the to_param method instead of id because it's the method Rails uses to generate URLs internally. You can pass arbitrary parameters in this fashion. You see more of this when you test the create and update actions, both of which require a set of article parameters.

One more thing to notice here: you can treat the result of assigns(:article) as you would any Article object and call methods on it:

```
assert assigns(:article).valid?
```

So, not only can you assert that there is an instance variable named @article, but you can also assert that it contains a valid Article object.

Testing the New Action

Listing 10-14 shows the test "should get new" case.

Listing 10-14. Updated Test Case for the new Action in test/functional/articles_controller_test.rb:
http://gist.github.com/358413

```
require 'test_helper'

class ArticlesControllerTest < ActionController::TestCase
  setup do
    @article = articles(:welcome_to_rails)
  end

  test "should get index" do
    get :index
    assert_response :success
    assert_template 'index'
    assert_not_nil assigns(:articles)
  end
```

```
test "should get new" do
  login_as(:eugene)
  get :new
  assert_response :success
end

test "should create article" do
  assert_difference('Article.count') do
    post :create, :article => @article.attributes
  end

  assert_redirected_to article_path(assigns(:article))
end

test "should show article" do
  get :show, :id => @article.to_param

  assert_response :success
  assert_template 'show'

  assert_not_nil assigns(:article)
  assert assigns(:article).valid?
end

test "should get edit" do
  get :edit, :id => @article.to_param
  assert_response :success
end

test "should update article" do
  put :update, :id => @article.to_param, :article => @article.attributes
  assert_redirected_to article_path(assigns(:article))
end

test "should destroy article" do
  assert_difference('Article.count', -1) do
    delete :destroy, :id => @article.to_param
  end

  assert_redirected_to articles_path
  end
end
```

The test "should get new" case is pretty simple. First, you use the login_as helper method you created earlier to log in as a user; then, you get the new action; and finally, you assert the success of the response.

Testing the Create Action

Listing 10-15 shows the test "should create article" case. Notice how you use login_as helper, because this action expects a logged-in user.

Listing 10-15. Test Case for the create Action in test/functional/articles_controller_test.rb:

http://gist.github.com/358414

```
require 'test_helper'

class ArticlesControllerTest < ActionController::TestCase
  setup do
    @article = articles(:welcome_to_rails)
  end

  test "should get index" do
    get :index
    assert_response :success
    assert_template 'index'
    assert_not_nil assigns(:articles)
  end

  test "should get new" do
    login_as(:eugene)
    get :new
    assert_response :success
  end

  test "should create article" do
    login_as(:eugene)
    assert_difference('Article.count') do
      post :create, :article => { :title => 'Post title',
                                  :body  => 'Lorem ipsum..' }
    end

    assert_response :redirect
    assert_redirected_to article_path(assigns(:article))
  end

  test "should show article" do
    get :show, :id => @article.to_param

    assert_response :success
    assert_template 'show'

    assert_not_nil assigns(:article)
    assert assigns(:article).valid?
  end

  test "should get edit" do
    get :edit, :id => @article.to_param
```

```
    assert_response :success
  end

  test "should update article" do
    put :update, :id => @article.to_param, :article => @article.attributes
    assert_redirected_to article_path(assigns(:article))
  end

  test "should destroy article" do
    assert_difference('Article.count', -1) do
      delete :destroy, :id => @article.to_param
    end

    assert_redirected_to articles_path
  end
end
```

To test the create action, you need to submit some form parameters to create a valid article. Fortunately, this is easy. All you need to do is pass a hash of parameters that contains a valid set of article attributes, just as you would using an HTML form (remember that HTML form parameters are converted into a hash object by Rails). Here's how it's done:

```
post :create, :article => { :title    => 'Post title',
                                        :body  => 'Lorem ipsum..' }
```

Unlike the other test cases you've looked at so far, the test "should create article" case uses a request method other than GET. To create a new article, you need to use the POST method. You formulate a POST request that includes a params hash with a valid article.

Notice how you request the post to create an article inside the assert_difference method block? The assert_difference method does a simple job: it takes a parameter and compares it with itself after running the block content. It expects the difference to be 1 by default. For this case, it expects Article.count to return the same count plus 1 after running the post request to create an article, which is the case in a successful create.

Next, you come across another of Rails' additions to Test::Unit, assert_redirected_to. As you can gather from its name, it lets you assert that a redirect to the expected location took place in response to the request:

```
assert_redirected_to(options, message)
```

You're really rolling now. The test "should get edit" case is straightforward, and test "should update article" is similar to test "should create article". Listing 10-16 shows the updated methods.

Listing 10-16. Test Case for the create Action in test/functional/articles_controller_test.rb:

http://gist.github.com/358416

```
require 'test_helper'

class ArticlesControllerTest < ActionController::TestCase
  setup do
    @article = articles(:welcome_to_rails)
  end
```

```
test "should get index" do
  get :index
  assert_response :success
  assert_template 'index'
  assert_not_nil assigns(:articles)
end

test "should get new" do
  login_as(:eugene)
  get :new
  assert_response :success
end

test "should create article" do
  login_as(:eugene)
  assert_difference('Article.count') do
    post :create, :article => { :title => 'Post title',
                                :body  => 'Lorem ipsum..' }
  end

  assert_response :redirect
  assert_redirected_to article_path(assigns(:article))
end

test "should show article" do
  get :show, :id => @article.to_param

  assert_response :success
  assert_template 'show'

  assert_not_nil assigns(:article)
  assert assigns(:article).valid?
end

test "should get edit" do
  login_as(:eugene)
  get :edit, :id => @article.to_param
  assert_response :success
end

test "should update article" do
  login_as(:eugene)
  put :update, :id => @article.to_param, :article => { :title => 'New Title' }
  assert_redirected_to article_path(assigns(:article))
end

test "should destroy article" do
  assert_difference('Article.count', -1) do
    delete :destroy, :id => @article.to_param
  end

  assert_redirected_to articles_path
```

```
    end
end
```

Testing the Destroy Action

Listing 10-17 shows the test "should destroy article" case. Again, because this action expects a logged-in user, you use the login_as helper to log in as :eugene.

Listing 10-17. Test Case for the destroy Action in test/functional/articles_controller_test.rb: http://gist.github.com/358417

```
require 'test_helper'

class ArticlesControllerTest < ActionController::TestCase
  setup do
    @article = articles(:welcome_to_rails)
  end

  test "should get index" do
    get :index
    assert_response :success
    assert_template 'index'
    assert_not_nil assigns(:articles)
  end

  test "should get new" do
    login_as(:eugene)
    get :new
    assert_response :success
  end

  test "should create article" do
    login_as(:eugene)
    assert_difference('Article.count') do
      post :create, :article => { :title => 'Post title',
                                  :body  => 'Lorem ipsum..' }
    end

    assert_response :redirect
    assert_redirected_to article_path(assigns(:article))
  end

  test "should show article" do
    get :show, :id => @article.to_param

    assert_response :success
    assert_template 'show'

    assert_not_nil assigns(:article)
    assert assigns(:article).valid?
```

```
    end

    test "should get edit" do
      login_as(:eugene)
      get :edit, :id => @article.to_param
      assert_response :success
    end

    test "should update article" do
      login_as(:eugene)
      put :update, :id => @article.to_param, :article => { :title => 'New Title' }
      assert_redirected_to article_path(assigns(:article))
    end

    test "should destroy article" do
      login_as(:eugene)
      assert_nothing_raised { Article.find(@article.to_param) }

      assert_difference('Article.count', -1) do
        delete :destroy, :id => @article.to_param
      end
      assert_response :redirect
      assert_redirected_to articles_path

      assert_raise(ActiveRecord::RecordNotFound) { Article.find(@article.to_param) }
    end
end
```

First, you test that you can find the article in question, knowing full well that find will raise an exception if the article doesn't exist. Then, you formulate a DELETE request to the destroy action, passing in the id of the article to destroy. You assert that the response is a redirect to the index action; and finally, you ensure that the article has been deleted by asserting that Active Record raises a RecordNotFound exception.

Now that you've fixed the articles controller test suite, let's get Ruby to execute all methods, and verify whether you've really fixed everything:

```
$ ruby -Itest test/functional/articles_controller_test.rb
```

```
Loaded suite test/functional/articles_controller_test

Started

.......

Finished in 0.432005 seconds.


7 tests, 18 assertions, 0 failures, 0 errors, 0 skips
```

One Missing Test

Before you can run the complete functional test suite, you still have to fix one test. When you generated the Notifier mailer, Rails added a mailer test file in the test/functional directory, with tests that are now failing because of changes you made in that class. Listing 10-18 shows an updated version of the test.

Listing 10-18. Updated test/functional/notifier_test.rb File: http://gist.github.com/358418

```
require 'test_helper'

class NotifierTest < ActionMailer::TestCase
  test "email_friend" do
    article = articles(:welcome_to_rails)
    message = Notifier.email_friend(article, 'John Smith', 'dude@example.com')

    assert_equal "Interesting Article", message.subject
    assert_equal ["dude@example.com"], message.to
    assert_equal ["from@example.com"], message.from
  end
end
```

In this code, you use the message variable to represent the email message generated by a call to Notifier.email_friend(article, 'John Smith', 'dude@example.com'). You later use the message variable to verify that some properties of the e-mail are as expected, using assert_equal: in this case, subject, sender, and receiver e-mail addresses.

Running the Full Test Suite

Now that your functional testing tour is complete, run the rake test:functionals command, which runs your entire suite of functional tests:

```
$ rake test:functionals
```

```
Loaded suite

Started

...........

Finished in 0.665524 seconds.



11 tests, 24 assertions, 0 failures, 0 errors, 0 skips
```

Not bad—24 assertions all in less than one second! You've got to admit, this is a lot more efficient than manually clicking through your application to test it. Moreover, because this uses the test database, you don't risk polluting your production database with bogus data while you test. Whenever you make a change to your articles controller, you can run this test to see if you've broken any of your expectations.

Now that you have unit and functional tests for articles in place, let's run the entire test suite, which runs both your unit and functional tests. To do this, use the built-in Rake task, test:

```
$ rake test
```

```
Loaded suite

Started

. . . . . . . . . .

Finished in 0.230277 seconds.


10 tests, 15 assertions, 0 failures, 0 errors, 0 skips

Loaded suite

Started

. . . . . . . . . .

Finished in 0.468845 seconds.


11 tests, 24 assertions, 0 failures, 0 errors, 0 skips
```

■ **NOTE** Some of the output is omitted here to cut down on the clutter. Your actual output will look slightly different, but the summary (tests, assertions, failures, and errors) should be the same.

It may interest you to know that the default Rake task is to run all tests. That means running rake with no arguments is the same as running rake test.

Integration Testing

Rails defines one more type of test, and it's the highest level of the bunch. Integration tests go a little further than their functional equivalents. Unlike functional tests, which test a specific controller, integration tests can span multiple controllers and actions with full session support. They're the closest you can get to simulating actual interaction with a web application.

Integration-Testing the Blog Application

Let's get started by generating the integration test. Given that Rails ships with a generator for just about everything, it shouldn't surprise you that it includes one for generating integration tests. It works like the others you've already used:

```
$ rails generate test_unit:integration UserStories
```

```
create  test/integration/user_stories_test.rb
```

Open the newly generated file and take a peek, as shown in Listing 10-19.

Listing 10-19. User Stories Test in test/integration/user_stories_test.rb

```
require 'test_helper'

class UserStoriesTest < ActionDispatch::IntegrationTest
  fixtures :all

  # Replace this with your real tests.
  test "the truth" do
    assert true
  end
end
```

At this stage, it looks a lot like the other test files you've seen so far. Notice, however, that it's a subclass of `ActionController::IntegrationTest`. That's about the only difference, but not for long.

Notice the fixtures call `fixtures :all`, which loads all your fixtures when running this test. You can modify it if you need only one or two fixture files; but in most cases, it's easier to load all of them.

Test cases are added to integration tests in exactly the same way as unit and functional test cases are added: using the `test` method with a description string and a block where you write your assertions. Integration test cases tend to look deceptively like functional tests, but they have a few subtle differences, which we point out as you add them.

Listing 10-20 shows a test case that goes through the process of logging in a user.

Listing 10-20. Login Integration Test in test/integration/user_stories_test.rb:

http://gist.github.com/358420

require 'test_helper'

```ruby
class UserStoriesTest < ActionDispatch::IntegrationTest
  fixtures :all

  test "should login user and redirect" do
    get login_path

    assert_response :success
    assert_template 'new'

    post session_path, :email => 'eugene@example.com', :password => 'secret'

    assert_response :redirect
    assert_redirected_to root_path

    follow_redirect!

    assert_response :success
    assert_template 'index'
    assert session[:user_id]
  end
end
```

When your response is a redirect, you're able to follow it, even when it redirects to another controller. The follow_redirect! method does exactly what you might think: it lets you follow a single redirect response, as long as the last response was, in fact, a redirect. If the last response wasn't a redirect, an exception is raised.

Let's add a test case for the logout action as well, as shown in Listing 10-21.

Listing 10-21. Logout Integration Test in test/integration/user_stories_test.rb:

http://gist.github.com/358421

```ruby
require 'test_helper'

class UserStoriesTest < ActionDispatch::IntegrationTest
  fixtures :all

  test "should login user and redirect" do
    get login_path

    assert_response :success
    assert_template 'new'

    post session_path, :email => 'eugene@example.com', :password => 'secret'
```

```ruby
    assert_response :redirect
    assert_redirected_to root_path

    follow_redirect!

    assert_response :success
    assert_template 'index'
    assert session[:user_id]
  end

  test "should logout user and redirect" do
    get logout_path

    assert_response :redirect
    assert_redirected_to root_path
    assert_nil session[:user]

    follow_redirect!

    assert_template 'index'
  end
end
```

Again, you can follow the redirect and test that the correct template was rendered.

Let's get a little fancier by testing that you can log in, create a new article, and log out, all in a single test. Combine the login and logout tests you've already written and sandwich an article-creation test in the middle, as shown in Listing 10-22.

Listing 10-22. Article Creation Integration Test in test/integration/user_stories_test.rb:

http://gist.github.com/358422

```ruby
require 'test_helper'

class UserStoriesTest < ActionDispatch::IntegrationTest
  fixtures :all

  test "should login create article and logout" do
    # Login
    get login_path

    assert_response :success
    assert_template 'new'

    post session_path, :email => 'eugene@example.com', :password => 'secret'

    assert_response :redirect
    assert_redirected_to root_path

    follow_redirect!

    assert_response :success
```

```ruby
      assert_template 'index'
      assert session[:user_id]

      # Create New Article
      get new_article_path

      assert_response :success
      assert_template 'new'

      post articles_path, :article => {:title => 'Integration Tests',
:body => 'Lorem Ipsum..'}

      assert assigns(:article).valid?
      assert_response :redirect
      assert_redirected_to article_path(assigns(:article))

      follow_redirect!

      assert_response :success
      assert_template 'show'

      # Logout
      get logout_path

      assert_response :redirect
      assert_redirected_to root_path
      assert_nil session[:user]

      follow_redirect!

      assert_template 'index'
    end
end
```

Here's what you get when you run the test:

```
$ ruby -Itest test/integration/user_stories_test.rb
```

```
Loaded suite test/integration/user_stories_test

Started

.

Finished in 0.490546 seconds.


1 tests, 18 assertions, 0 failures, 0 errors, 0 skips
```

Great—and you've just tested the whole stack from dispatcher to database. Not too shabby, is it? If you're thinking that what you've just done looks a lot like you're telling a story (Eugene logs in, Eugene creates article, Eugene logs out), you're right.

Story-Based Testing

Integration tests are great for creating story-based scenarios using a domain-specific language (DSL). They even go so far as to allow you to test multiple users interacting! What are story-based tests? Well, suppose you could do something like this:

```
test "creating an article" do
  eugene = registered_user
  eugene.logs_in 'eugene', 'secret'
  eugene.creates_article
  eugene.logs_out
end
```

Here, you're telling an easy-to-understand story that requires no programming knowledge to follow. Eugene logs in and proceeds to create a new article. When he is finished, he logs out. Behind the scenes, you can test every request, response, and redirect, following Eugene's path through the entire process, just as you did in the `test "should login create article and logout"` case.

Integration tests provide a method called `open_session` that you can use to simulate a distinct user interacting with the application as if from a web browser. Although this lets you simulate multiple connections with ease, you use it to help create an object on which to define your custom story-based methods, like `logs_in` and `creates_article`.

Let's reshape `test "should login create article and logout"` into methods you can add straight onto a new session object. Listing 10-23 shows the updated `user_stories_test.rb` test.

Listing 10-23. Updated User Stories Integration Test in test/integration/user_stories_test.rb:

http://gist.github.com/358423

```
require 'test_helper'

class UserStoriesTest < ActionDispatch::IntegrationTest
  fixtures :all

  test "creating an article" do
    eugene = registered_user
    eugene.logs_in 'eugene@example.com', 'secret'
    eugene.creates_article :title => 'Integration tests', :body => 'Lorem Ipsum...'
    eugene.logs_out
  end

  private
    def registered_user
      open_session do |user|
        def user.logs_in(email, password)
          get login_path

          assert_response :success
```

```
      assert_template 'new'

      post session_path, :email => email, :password => password

      assert_response :redirect
      assert_redirected_to root_path

      follow_redirect!

      assert_response :success
      assert_template 'index'
      assert session[:user_id]
    end

    def user.logs_out
      get logout_path

      assert_response :redirect
      assert_redirected_to root_path
      assert_nil session[:user]

      follow_redirect!

      assert_template 'index'
    end

    def user.creates_article(article_hash)
      get new_article_path

      assert_response :success
      assert_template 'new'

      post articles_path, :article => article_hash

      assert assigns(:article).valid?
      assert_response :redirect
      assert_redirected_to article_path(assigns(:article))

      follow_redirect!

      assert_response :success
      assert_template 'show'
    end
  end
 end
end
```

See how you create a private method called `registered_user` and create a new integration session inside it? The `open_session` method yields a `session` object onto which you attach *singleton* methods (methods that exist only on a particular instance):

```
def registered_user
  open_session do |user|
    def user.logs_in(email, password)
      #...
    end

    def user.logs_out
      #...
    end

    def user.creates_article(article_hash)
      #...
    end
  end
end
```

The return value of `registered_user`, then, is a fresh integration session object that responds to the methods you've created. This means you can create as many user sessions as you want and simulate multiple connections to the application. Listing 10-24 updates the `test "creating an article"` method and renames it `test "multiple users creating an article"`.

Listing 10-24. Updated Article-Creation Story Testing Multiple Users in

test/integration/user_stories_test.rb: http://gist.github.com/358424

```
require 'test_helper'

class UserStoriesTest < ActionDispatch::IntegrationTest
  fixtures :all

  test "multiple users creating an article" do
    eugene = registered_user
    lauren = registered_user

    eugene.logs_in 'eugene@example.com', 'secret'
    lauren.logs_in 'lauren@example.com', 'secret'

    eugene.creates_article :title => 'Integration Tests', :body => 'Lorem Ipsum...'
    lauren.creates_article :title => 'Open Session', :body => 'Lorem Ipsum...'

    eugene.logs_out
    lauren.logs_out
  end

  private
    def registered_user
      open_session do |user|
        def user.logs_in(email, password)
          get login_path

          assert_response :success
          assert_template 'new'
```

```ruby
      post session_path, :email => email, :password => password

      assert_response :redirect
      assert_redirected_to root_path

      follow_redirect!

      assert_response :success
      assert_template 'index'
      assert session[:user_id]
    end

    def user.logs_out
      get logout_path

      assert_response :redirect
      assert_redirected_to root_path
      assert_nil session[:user]

      follow_redirect!

      assert_template 'index'
    end

    def user.creates_article(article_hash)
      get new_article_path

      assert_response :success
      assert_template 'new'

      post articles_path, :article => article_hash

      assert assigns(:article).valid?
      assert_response :redirect
      assert_redirected_to article_path(assigns(:article))

      follow_redirect!

      assert_response :success
      assert_template 'show'
    end
  end
end
end
```

This is only the tip of the iceberg. The sky is the limit for how creative you can get with this style of testing.

Running the Full Test Suite

Now that you have a respectable number of tests for your application, let's use Rake to run the entire suite. Because the default Rake task is test, you can save yourself five keystrokes (a space counts as a keystroke!) and run your tests with just rake:

```
$ rake
```

```
Loaded suite

Started

..........

Finished in 0.237562 seconds.


10 tests, 15 assertions, 0 failures, 0 errors, 0 skips

Loaded suite

Started

...........

Finished in 0.480825 seconds.


11 tests, 24 assertions, 0 failures, 0 errors, 0 skips

Loaded suite

Started

.

Finished in 0.571371 seconds.
```

```
1 tests, 0 assertions, 0 failures, 0 errors, 0 skips
```

Take a moment to bask in the glory of a successful test run.

Rails includes a handy task that generates a formatted display of stats about your program, including the lines of code (LOC). It can show you the ratio between your application and test code. Run it using rake stats:

```
$ rake stats
```

+----------------------+-------+-------+---------+---------+-----+-------+
| Name | Lines | LOC | Classes | Methods | M/C | LOC/M |
+----------------------+-------+-------+---------+---------+-----+-------+
Controllers	202	155	5	21	4	5
Helpers	15	13	0	1	0	11
Models	91	75	6	10	1	5
Libraries	0	0	0	0	0	0
Integration tests	72	51	1	4	4	10
Functional tests	102	81	5	0	0	0
Unit tests	95	74	10	0	0	0
+----------------------+-------+-------+---------+---------+-----+-------+
| Total | 577 | 449 | 27 | 36 | 1 | 10 |
+----------------------+-------+-------+---------+---------+-----+-------+
  Code LOC: 243   Test LOC: 206   Code to Test Ratio: 1:0.8
```

Although the code-to-test ratio is a nice thing to know, it really doesn't tell you much. What matters is how much of the code your tests exercise.

## Summary

This chapter introduced you to the Rails philosophy behind testing and stressed its importance as part of the development cycle. You've now been on a complete tour of the baked-in facilities Rails provides for testing. You learned about testing your models with unit tests, testing your controllers with functional tests, and testing the whole Rails stack with integration tests.

Testing is an important part of the development cycle. Despite the fact that we left it until near the end of this book, it's not something you should treat as an afterthought. Now that you know how to write a Rails application and how to test it, you can combine the steps: write some code, and then test it. As you get into the code/test rhythm, (or better yet, test/code), you'll find that you can write better, more reliable software. And you may sleep a little better at night, too.
```

## CHAPTER 11

Internationalization

Internationalization in Rails was a complex task until Rails version 2.2 came out with internationalization and localization support built in. Since then, launching an application in another language or even multiple languages has become a relatively simple task. According to Wikipedia, "Internationalization is the process of designing a software application so that it can be adapted to various languages and regions without engineering changes. Localization is the process of adapting software for a specific region or language by adding locale-specific components and translating text."

This chapter talks about internationalization and localization support in Rails. You first set up internationalization in the blog application with English as the main language; then, you localize it to another language; and finally, you support both languages and allow the user to pick the language they want.

Internationalization and *localization* are long words, so developers use short names for them. The short name for internationalization is i18n, which is the first and the last letters of the word with the count of how many characters in between. Following the same logic, localization's short name is l10n.

■ **NOTE** If you need to get the code at the exact point where you finished Chapter 10, download the zip file from `http://github.com/downloads/ccjr/blog/chapter11.zip` and extract it on your computer.

Internationalization Logic in Rails

I18n and l10n support in Rails is based on a single module that takes care of all the translation and locale changes for you; this module is called I18n. The I18n module's main method is `translate`, which translates content by looking for a translation text in a locale file, normally located in `config/locales`.

Locales are like languages but are more specific to regions. For example, en represents English in general, whereas en-us represents US English and en-uk represents UK English. In Rails, those differences reflect in the translation files, mainly for localization options like time, date formats, and currency.

If you look in the `config/locales` directory, you see a file called `en.yml`; it's a YAML file that defines the English translations for your application. Open the file, and you see something similar to Listing 11-1.

Listing 11-1. The Default English Locale File in config/locales/en.yml

```
# Sample localization file for English.
# Add more files in this directory for other locales.
# See http://github.com/svenfuchs/rails-i18n/tree/master/rails%2Flocale
# for starting points.
```

```
en:
  hello: "Hello world"
```

A translation file is a YAML file. It starts with the locale symbol, which is also the translation file name; in this case, it's en. Then, the file lists the translations in a key-value pair style: the en.yml example defines the translation of hello as "Hello world".

Now, let's see the translation in action by trying the I18n module in the console. Launch it with rails console:

```
I18n.translate "hello"
=> "Hello world"
I18n.t "hello"
=> "Hello world"
```

You pass the *key* to the translate method, and it returned the corresponding *value* from the English locale file. The I18n module has the t method as an alias for the translate method, which you used in the previous example.

I18n works in Rails by having a set locale. At any time, you can determine the current locale by calling the I18n.locale method. When you don't set the locale yourself, it's set to a default locale, normally en. You can access the default locale by calling I18n.default_locale. Let's check the current locale and the default locale in your application:

```
I18n.locale
=> :en
I18n.default_locale
=> :en
```

To change the locale or the default locale, you can use the I18n.locale= and I18n.default_locale= methods. Change the locale to Brazilian Portuguese, for which locale symbol is pt-br, and try the translate method again:

```
>> I18n.locale = 'pt-br'
=> "pt-br"
>> I18n.translate "hello"
=> "translation missing: pt-br, hello"
```

You don't have a translation for *hello* in Brazilian Portuguese—the translate method returns a string saying "translation missing: pt-br, hello". To define the translation for *hello* in Brazilian Portuguese, you create a new translation file named after the locale symbol pt-br.yml in config/locales as shown in Listing 11-2.

Listing 11-2. The Brazilian Portuguese Locale File in config/locales/pt-br.yml:

http://gist.github.com/360760

```
pt-br:
  hello: "Ola mundo"
```

Rails doesn't reload locale files automatically, unlike other files. So, exit the console, restart it to make sure Rails loads the new translation file, and try again:

```
>> I18n.locale
=> :en
>> I18n.locale = 'pt-br'
=> "pt-br"
>> I18n.t "hello"
=> "Ola mundo"
```

That's how simple it is. All you need are the translation files, each with several translations in key-value pairs. You access those translations by passing the corresponding key to the I18n.translate method or its alias, I18n.t.

Rails manages all its internals using the I18n module. For example, all the Active Record validation messages you saw in Chapters 4 and 5 are called by using the translate method and referring to a translation key. If you change the locale, Rails has no translation for those error messages. Check it out:

```
>> I18n.locale = 'pt-br'
=> "pt-br"
>> article = Article.new
=> #<Article id: nil, title: nil, body: nil, published_at: nil, created_at: nil,
updated_at: nil, excerpt: nil, location: nil, user_id: nil>
>> article.save
=> false
>> article.errors.full_messages
=> ["Title translation missing: pt-br, activerecord, errors, models, article,
attributes, title, blank", "Body translation missing: pt-br, activerecord,
errors, models, article, attributes, body, blank"]
```

Active Record tried to get the translations for the error messages, but it couldn't find them in the Brazilian Portuguese translation file. Let's add them by updating pt-br.yml so it looks like Listing 11-3.

Listing 11-3. Updated Brazilian Portuguese Locale File in config/locales/pt-br.yml:

http://gist.github.com/360764

```
pt-br:
  hello: "Ola mundo"

  activerecord:
    errors:
      models:
        article:
          attributes:
            title:
              blank: "não pode ficar em branco"
            body:
              blank: "não pode ficar em branco"
```

Notice how you nest the keys. The "translation missing" message you saw earlier in the console included a list of names: pt-br, activerecord, errors, models, article, attributes, body, and blank. Those names represent the path inside the pt-br translation file. I18n calls the blank key, for example, by using dots to connect it and its parents; the translate call is I18n.translate('activerecord.errors. models.article.attributes.title.blank'). Now that you've added the translation, try it from the console again (don't forget to restart your console):

```
>> I18n.locale = 'pt-br'
=> "pt-br"
>> article = Article.new
=> #<Article id: nil, title: nil, body: nil, published_at: nil, created_at: nil,
updated_at: nil, excerpt: nil, location: nil, user_id: nil>
>> article.save
=> false
>> I18n.translate('activerecord.errors.models.article.attributes.title.blank')
=> "não pode ficar em branco"
>> article.errors.full_messages
=> ["Title não pode ficar em branco", "Body não pode ficar em branco"]
```

Congratulations! You just translated the validates :title, :presence => true error message for both the title and body attributes of your Article model to Brazilian Portuguese. Now that you understand how I18n works, let's set it up in the blog application.

Setting Up i18n in the Blog Application

Rails at its core uses I18n. You also need to use it. To do so, you must make sure that all hard-coded text and strings are replaced with an I18n.translate method call.

This may sound like a lot of work, but it's fairly simple in this case because your application is still small. We encourage you to use the I18n.translate method in your project as early as possible; that way, you avoid doing the text replacement later—it gets more difficult as your project grows.

Let's begin with your models. The only one that uses strings is the Comment model, which includes a custom validation with an error message. Replace this error message with an I18n.t call to a key, and add that key to your en.yml translation file. Listing 11-4 shows how the comment model should look after you edit it.

Listing 11-4. Updated Comment Model in app/models/comment.rb: http://gist.github.com/360774

```
class Comment < ActiveRecord::Base
  belongs_to :article

  validates :name, :email, :body, :presence => true
  validate :article_should_be_published

  def article_should_be_published
    errors.add(:article_id, I18n.t('comments.errors.not_published_yet'))
if article && !article.published?
  end
end
```

Notice how you use the dots notation in the comments.errors.not_published_yet key. It's good practice to keep the locale file organized; doing so helps you find the translation more easily when your file gets bigger. Because the error message is added to the comment object, you add it under comments; and because it's an error message, you drill a step deeper and place it under errors.

Don't forget to add the translation to your en.yml translation file. It should look like Listing 11-5 after you clean it up and update it with the new translation.

Listing 11-5. Updated English Locale File in config/locales/en.yml: http://gist.github.com/360776

```
en:
  comments:
    errors:
      not_published_yet: is not published yet
```

Now, let's move to controllers. If you check all the controllers, you see that you only need to translate the flash messages. Listing 11-6 shows how ArticlesController should look after you update it. The changes are highlighted in bold.

Listing 11-6. Updated ArticlesController in app/controllers/articles_controller.rb:

http://gist.github.com/360784

```ruby
class ArticlesController < ApplicationController
  before_filter :authenticate, :except => [:index, :show, :notify_friend]

  # GET /articles
  # GET /articles.xml
  def index
    @articles = Article.all

    respond_to do |format|
      format.html # index.html.erb
      format.xml  { render :xml => @articles }
    end
  end

  # GET /articles/1
  # GET /articles/1.xml
  def show
    @article = Article.find(params[:id])

    respond_to do |format|
      format.html # show.html.erb
      format.xml  { render :xml => @article }
    end
  end

  # GET /articles/new
  # GET /articles/new.xml
  def new
    @article = Article.new

    respond_to do |format|
      format.html # new.html.erb
      format.xml  { render :xml => @article }
    end
  end
```

```ruby
  # GET /articles/1/edit
  def edit
    @article = current_user.articles.find(params[:id])
  end

  # POST /articles
  # POST /articles.xml
  def create
    @article = current_user.articles.new(params[:article])

    respond_to do |format|
      if @article.save
        format.html { redirect_to(@article,
:notice => t('articles.create_success')) }
        format.xml  { render :xml => @article,
:status => :created, :location => @article }
      else
        format.html { render :action => "new" }
        format.xml  { render :xml => @article.errors,
:status => :unprocessable_entity }
      end
    end
  end

  # PUT /articles/1
  # PUT /articles/1.xml
  def update
    @article = current_user.articles.find(params[:id])

    respond_to do |format|
      if @article.update_attributes(params[:article])
        format.html { redirect_to(@article,
:notice => t('articles.update_success')) }
        format.xml  { head :ok }
      else
        format.html { render :action => "edit" }
        format.xml  { render :xml => @article.errors,
:status => :unprocessable_entity }
      end
    end
  end

  # DELETE /articles/1
  # DELETE /articles/1.xml
  def destroy
    @article = current_user.articles.find(params[:id])
    @article.destroy

    respond_to do |format|
      format.html { redirect_to(articles_url) }
      format.xml  { head :ok }
    end
```

```
  end

  def notify_friend
    @article = Article.find(params[:id])
    Notifier.email_friend(@article, params[:name], params[:email]).deliver
    redirect_to @article, :notice => t('articles.notify_friend_success')
  end
end
```

There are two things to notice here. First, you call the t method without the I18n module, unlike what you did in the console and the model; that's because the I18n module is integrated with Action Pack to keep things cleaner in the controllers, helpers, and views. Second, you also nest the messages under articles—again, to keep things cleaner. You do the same with the other controllers, also nesting them under their corresponding name: users controller translations go under users, the comments controller goes under comments, the application controller goes under application, and the sessions controller goes under session.

Updating the rest of the controllers is fairly simple. You can do it yourself, or you can download the updated files from the Gist URL http://gist.github.com/360784.

Finally let's look at the views. They're very similar, so you look at a single view here: Listing 11-7 shows the article partial after using translations, with changes in bold. As with controllers, you can apply the rest of the changes yourself using the Gist URLs http://gist.github.com/360814 and http://gist.github.com/360819.

Listing 11-7. Updated article Partial in app/views/articles/_article.html.erb:

http://gist.github.com/360814

```
<%= div_for article do %>
  <h3>
    <%= link_to article.title, article %>
    <% if article.owned_by? current_user %>
      <span class='actions'>
        <%= link_to t('general.edit'), edit_article_path(article) %>
        <%= link_to t('general.delete'), article,
:confirm => t('general.are_you_sure'), :method => :delete %>
      </span>
    <% end %>
  </h3>
  <%= simple_format raw(article.body) %>
<% end %>
```

After updating your code, you're one step away from completing the i18n setup. You still need to add the translations to the default locale file en.yml. Listing 11-8 shows the updated config/locales/en.yml translation file.

Listing 11-8. English Locale File After Implementing i18n Support in config/locales/en.yml:

http://gist.github.com/360824

```
en:
  general:
    are_you_sure: Are you sure?
```

```
    back: Back
    cancel: Cancel
    create: Create
    delete: Delete
    edit: Edit
    editing: Editing
    footer: A simple blog built for the book
    email_a_friend: Email a friend
    search: Search
    send_email: Send email
    show: Show
    title: Blog
    update: Update
    your_name: Your name
    your_friend_email: Your friend's email
    or: or
  application:
    access_denied: Please log in to continue
  articles:
    editing_article: Editing Article
    listing_articles: Listing Articles
    new_article: New Article
    article: article
    create_success: Article was successfully created.
    update_success: Article was successfully updated.
    articles: articles
    notify_friend_success: Successfully sent a message to your friend
  users:
    new_user: New user
    edit_password: Edit Password
    editing_user: Editing user
    create_success: User successfully added.
    update_success: Updated user information successfully.
  sessions:
    email: Email
    password: Password
    login: Login
    logout: Logout
    successful_login: Logged in successfully
    invalid_login: Invalid login/password combination
    logout_success: You successfully logged out
  comments:
    name: Name
    email: Email
    body: Body
    comments: Comments
    new_comment: New comment
    create_success: Thanks for your comment
    create_failure: Unable to add comment
    destroy_success: Comment deleted
    add: Add
```

```
errors:
  not_published_yet: is not published yet
```

That's about it—the blog application has i18n support now.

You must restart your server for Rails to load the translation file. After you do that, browse the site: you don't see any differences yet. Although i18n support is in place, you're still using English as your locale. To see i18n in action, let's change the locale and try Brazilian Portuguese.

Localizing the Blog Application to Brazilian Portuguese

Localizing an i18n-ready Rails application is amazingly simple. All you have to do is add a new translation file and configure your Rails application to use that locale as the default locale, and you're good to go.

Brazilian Portuguese is the locale to which you localize the blog application in this section. The locale symbol for Brazilian Portuguese is pt-br; so, first you change the config/locales/pt-br.yml file, using the same keys as your English translation file, but with Brazilian Portuguese text instead of English.

The separation between the translation files and your application code is very helpful; it gives you the ability to send the translation file to a translator, for example. When you have it back, you plug it into your application and you're all set. Listing 11-9 shows the newly created Brazilian Portuguese translation file.

Listing 11-9. Brazilian Portuguese Locale File in config/locales/pt-br.yml:

http://gist.github.com/391492

```
pt-br:
  general:
    are_you_sure: Tem certeza?
    back: Volta
    cancel: Cancelar
    create: Criar
    delete: Apagar
    edit: Editar
    editing: Editando
    footer: Um blog simples desenvolvido para o livro
    email_a_friend: Avisar um amigo
    search: Pesquisar
    send_email: Mandar email
    show: Mostrar
    title: Blog
    update: Atualizar
    your_name: Seu nome
    your_friend_email: O email do seu amigo
    or: ou
  application:
    access_denied: "Por favor, efetue o login para continuar"
  articles:
    editing_article: Editando Artigo
    listing_articles: Listando Artigos
    new_article: Novo Artigo
    article: artigo
```

```
      create_success: Artigo foi criado com sucesso.
      update_success: Artigo foi atualizado com sucesso.
      articles: artigos
      notify_friend_success: Seu amigo foi avisado a respeito desse artigo
    users:
      new_user: Novo Usuario
      edit_password: Editar senha
      editing_user: Editando usuario
      create_success: Usuario editado com sucesso.
      update_success: Usuario atualizado com sucesso.
    sessions:
      email: Email
      password: Senha
      login: Logar
      logout: Desconectar
      successful_login: Logado com sucesso
      invalid_login: Senha ou Email invalidos
      logout_success: Voce desconectou do sistem com sucesso
    comments:
      name: Nome
      email: Email
      body: Conteudo
      comments: Comentarios
      new_comment: Novo Comentario
      create_success: Obrigado pelo comentario
      create_failure: Nao foi possivel adicionar o comentario
      destroy_success: Comentario deletado
      add: Adicionar
      errors:
        not_published_yet: ainda nao foi publicado

    activerecord:
      errors:
        models:
          article:
            attributes:
              title:
                blank: "não pode ficar em branco"
              body:
                blank: "não pode ficar em branco"

    date:
      formats:
        default: "%d/%m/%Y"
        short: "%d de %B"
        long: "%d de %B de %Y"

      day_names: [Domingo, Segunda, Terça, Quarta, Quinta, Sexta, Sábado]
      abbr_day_names: [Dom, Seg, Ter, Qua, Qui, Sex, Sáb]
      month_names: [~, Janeiro, Fevereiro, Março, Abril, Maio, Junho, Julho,
    Agosto, Setembro, Outubro, Novembro, Dezembro]
      abbr_month_names: [~, Jan, Fev, Mar, Abr, Mai, Jun, Jul, Ago, Set, Out,
```

```
Nov, Dez]
    order: [:day, :month, :year]
```

You still have to tell Rails to use pt-br as the default locale. You do that by adding a configuration to your config/application.rb file. Listing 11-10 shows the updated config/application.rb file with the added line in bold.

Listing 11-10. Setting the Default Locale to Brazilian Portuguese in config/application.rb:

http://gist.github.com/360830

```
require File.expand_path('../boot', __FILE__)

require 'rails/all'

# If you have a Gemfile, require the gems listed there, including any gems
# you've limited to :test, :development, or :production.
Bundler.require(:default, Rails.env) if defined?(Bundler)

module Blog
  class Application < Rails::Application
    # Activate observers that should always be running
    config.active_record.observers = :comment_observer
    # Configure the default encoding used in templates for Ruby 1.9.
    config.encoding = "utf-8"
    # Configure sensitive parameters which will be filtered from the log file.
    config.filter_parameters += [:password]
    # Setting the locale
    config.i18n.default_locale = 'pt-br'
  end
end
```

Restart the server, and check out your Brazilian Portuguese blog application. You've localized the application in two simple steps: adding the translation file and setting up the locale. Figure 11-1 shows the blog application with its Brazilian Portuguese face.

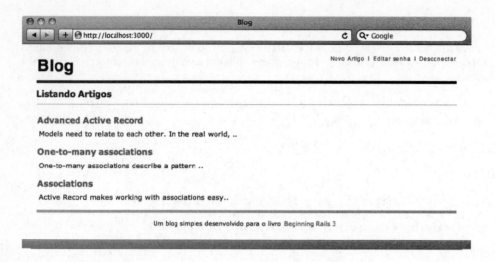

Figure 11-1. Brazilian Portuguese localized interface

Bilingual Blog

You know by now that all it takes to change the locale is to set the I18n.locale configuration to the locale of choice. How about giving users the power to do that themselves? To do so, you implement a controller filter that sets the locale depending on user input and provides the user with a language selector from which to choose the locale.

Let's create a helper in application helper called language_selector that shows the available locales for the user to choose from. Listing 11-11 shows application_helper with the new helper method in bold.

Listing 11-11. language_selector Helper Method in app/helpers/application_helper.rb:

http://gist.github.com/360849

```
module ApplicationHelper
  # Creates a submit button with the given name with a cancel link
  # Accepts two arguments: Form object and the cancel link name
  def submit_or_cancel(form, name=t('general.cancel'))
    form.submit + " #{t('general.or')} " + link_to(name, 'javascript:history.go(-1);', :class
=> 'cancel')
  end

  def language_selector
    if I18n.locale == :en
      link_to "Pt", url_for(:locale => 'pt-br')
    else
      link_to "En", url_for(:locale => 'en')
```

```
      end
    end
end
```

In the language selector method, you show a link to the language that isn't currently selected. You do that by linking to the URL you're at, with an extra :locale parameter using the url_for helper with the :overwrite_params option. The user should always be able to change the language; so, you use this function in the application layout. Listing 11-12 shows the updated application layout with the new helper call in bold.

Listing 11-12. Calling language_selector in app/views/layouts/application.html.erb:

http://gist.github.com/360851

```
<!DOCTYPE html>
<html>
<head>
  <title>Blog</title>
  <%= stylesheet_link_tag :all %>
  <%= javascript_include_tag 'jquery-1.4.2.min', 'rails', 'application' %>
  <%= csrf_meta_tag %>
</head>
<body>
  <div id="header">
    <h1><%= link_to t('general.title'), root_path %></h1>
    <%= language_selector %>
    <div id="user_bar">
      <% if logged_in? %>
        <%= link_to t('articles.new_article'), new_article_path %> |
        <%= link_to t('users.edit_password'), edit_user_path(current_user) %> |
        <%= link_to t('sessions.logout'), logout_path %>
      <% else %>
        <%= link_to t('sessions.login'), login_path %>
      <% end %>
    </div>
  </div>
  <div id="main">
    <%= content_tag(:p, notice, :class => 'notice') if notice.present? %>
    <%= content_tag(:p, alert, :class => 'alert') if alert.present? %>
    <%= yield %>
  </div>
  <div id="footer">
    <%= t('general.footer') %> <a href="http://beginningrails.com">
Beginning Rails 3</a>
  </div>
</body>
</html>
```

Finally let's create a before filter in the application controller that sets the locale to the passed parameter. Listing 11-13 shows the updated application controller with the new additions in bold.

Listing 11-13. Before Filter to Set the Locale in app/controllers/application_controller.rb:

http://gist.github.com/360856

```ruby
class ApplicationController < ActionController::Base
  protect_from_forgery
  before_filter :set_locale

  protected
    # Set the locale from parameters
    def set_locale
      I18n.locale = params[:locale] unless params[:locale].blank?
    end

    # Returns the currently logged in user or nil if there isn't one
    def current_user
      return unless session[:user_id]
      @current_user ||= User.find_by_id(session[:user_id])
    end

    # Make current_user available in templates as a helper
    helper_method :current_user

    # Filter method to enforce a login requirement
    # Apply as a before_filter on any controller you want to protect
    def authenticate
      logged_in? ? true : access_denied
    end

    # Predicate method to test for a logged in user
    def logged_in?
      current_user.is_a? User
    end

    # Make logged_in? available in templates as a helper
    helper_method :logged_in?

    def access_denied
      redirect_to login_path,
:notice => t('application.access_denied') and return false
    end
```

A before filter in an application controller runs before any request reaches any controller action. You call the set_locale method, which checks whether the locale parameter is provided and assigns it to I18n.locale.

Change the application locale configuration back to English—users can select their language of choice now—by removing the config.i18n.default_locale line from config/application.rb (see Listing 11-14).

Listing 11-14. Remove the Locale Configuration in config/application.rb:
http://gist.github.com/391549

```
require File.expand_path('../boot', __FILE__)

require 'rails/all'

# If you have a Gemfile, require the gems listed there, including any gems
# you've limited to :test, :development, or :production.
Bundler.require(:default, Rails.env) if defined?(Bundler)

module Blog
  class Application < Rails::Application
    # Activate observers that should always be running
    config.active_record.observers = :comment_observer
    # Configure the default encoding used in templates for Ruby 1.9.
    config.encoding = "utf-8"
    # Configure sensitive parameters which will be filtered from the log file.
    config.filter_parameters += [:password]
  end
end
```

Restart your server, and try the application, as shown in Figure 11-2.

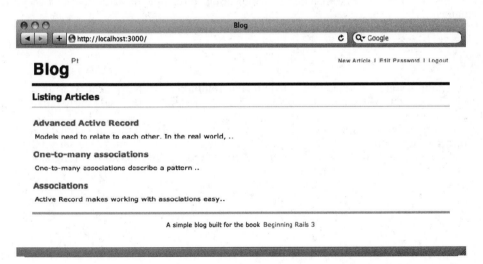

Figure 11-2. Language selector in the English interface

The application loads in English because it's the default locale. Click the Pt link, and see how everything switches to Brazilian Portuguese, as shown in Figure 11-3.

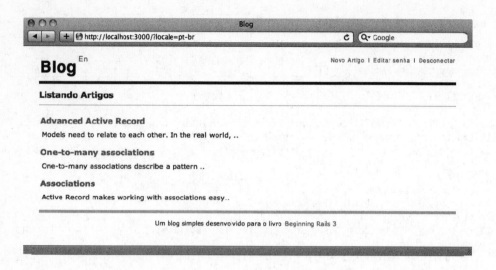

Figure 11-3. Brazilian Portuguese interface with the language selector link

Congratulations! Not only do you have a bilingual blog application, but you also know how easy it is to add more languages.

Summary

After reading this chapter, you have what it takes to launch a multilingual Rails application. You understand the logic behind the I18n module, how the translate method works, and how to create a translation file.

You worked on preparing your application for i18n support; you extracted the hard-coded text and strings into translation keys, and you placed them in a locale translation file. Then, you localized the application to another language. You wrapped up your effort by making the application bilingual application—users can choose the language they want.

CHAPTER 12

■ ■ ■

Extending Rails with Plug-ins

Rails ships with a rich set of features and powerful functionality. It's often said that Rails is designed to solve most problems most of the time. It can't solve all problems or be all things to all people, and it doesn't try to do that. Instead, it provides a mechanism to easily extend and augment the core functionality: *plug-ins*. Plug-ins give developers the freedom to write extensions to Rails without needing to include those additions in the Rails core code.

This chapter shows you how plug-ins extend the functionality of Rails and make it even more comprehensive. You learn how to find and install plug-ins, and how to use plug-ins to add functionality to your blog application. Finally, you create a plug-in from scratch to showcase how you can extract common functionality from an application and share it with other projects and developers.

■ **NOTE** If you need to get the code at the exact point where you finished Chapter 11, download the zip file from `http://github.com/downloads/ccjr/blog/chapter12.zip` and extract it on your computer.

Finding and Installing Plug-ins

To help you manage your plug-ins, Rails ships with a `plugin` command. To see its usage information, run the command with the -h option:

```
$ rails plugin -h
```

```
Usage: plugin [OPTIONS] command

Rails plugin manager.


GENERAL OPTIONS

-r, --root=DIR              Set an explicit rails app directory.

-s, --source=URL1,URL2      Use the specified plugin
```

---

repositories instead of the defaults.

```
-v, --verbose              Turn on verbose output.

-h, --help                 Show this help message.
```

COMMANDS

```
install    Install plugin(s) from known repositories or URLs.

remove     Uninstall plugins.
```

EXAMPLES

```
Install a plugin:

  rails install continuous_builder

Install a plugin from a subversion URL:

  rails install http://dev.rubyonrails.com/svn/rails/plugins/continuous_builder

Install a plugin from a git URL:

  rails install git://github.com/SomeGuy/my_awesome_plugin.git

Install a plugin and add a svn:externals entry to vendor/plugins

  rails install -x continuous_builder
```

As indicated by the output, you need to pass a command as a parameter to the rails plugin command. Table 12-1 shows the plugin command options.

Table 12-1. Plugin Command Options

Command	Description
install	Installs a plug-in from a URL. Here's an example: plugin install git://github.com/rails/continuous_builder.git.
remove	Uninstalls a plug-in. Here's an example: plugin remove continuous_builder.

The plug-in system comes with commands that allow you to install and remove plug-ins from their URLs. Generally, the URL from which a plug-in can be installed is listed from the plug-in's web site documentation.

■ **NOTE** Most Rails developers nowadays use Git as their version control system. They host and manage the development of their plug-ins on GitHub. If you don't have a Git client installed, you can't install plug-ins that are distributed directly from Git repositories. This is yet another good reason to start using Git (http://git-scm.com); check Appendix D for information.

Finding Plug-ins

If you want to find a plug-in to implement a specific feature, try a Google search. Usually, you get results that lead you to the web site of an appropriate plug-in with instructions on how to install it.

If you aren't sure exactly what you want, but you'd like to explore plug-ins by category, such as Controllers, Models, or Testing, you can access sites like the Rails plug-in directory at http://agilewebdevelopment.com/plugins or RailsPlugins at http://railsplugins.org. Both sites contain an extensive categorized list of plug-ins. Each plug-in has a specific page, which includes a description, some information about how to use it, and a link to the plug-in developer's page.

Another option is to go to the Popular Plugins section in the Rails wiki: http://wiki.rubyonrails.org/#popular_plugins. This section has links to different plug-ins categorized by function and purpose. You can also search for Rails plug-ins on GitHub: http://github.com/search?type=Repositories&language=ruby&q=plugin; you can find hundreds of plug-ins that may not be listed in the plug-in directories or in the Rails wiki.

After you install a plug-in, you can usually find instructions for how to use it by reading the README file in the plug-in root folder, located at vendor/plugins/#{plugin_name}.

Installing Plug-ins

Installing a plug-in is a straightforward affair: you invoke the rails script with the plugin install command and the URL of the plug-in you want to install. Plug-ins are installed in the vendor/plugins directory. Using the name *vendor* is common in software projects and generally indicates that the code contained within it is third-party.

Let's install a plug-in using a URL. This works for any plug-in and can use HTTP(S), svn protocol, or git protocol:

```
$ rails plugin install git://github.com/rails/acts_as_list.git
```

```
Initialized empty Git repository in vendor/plugins/acts_as_list/.git/

remote: Counting objects: 13, done.

remote: Compressing objects: 100% (9/9), done.
```

```
remote: Total 13 (delta 2), reused 0 (delta 0)

Unpacking objects: 100% (13/13), done.

From git://github.com/rails/acts_as_list

 * branch            HEAD        -> FETCH_HEAD
```

■ **NOTE** If you're installing a plug-in using the `svn` or `git` protocol, you're expected to have SVN or Git installed. Check Appendix D for more information about how to install Git on your system.

To uninstall a plug-in you no longer want to use, call the remove command:

```
$ rails plugin remove acts_as_list
```

■ **NOTE** Uninstalling plug-ins using the `remove` command only removes the plug-in files from your `vendor/plugins` directory; it doesn't undo any changes in your code. If you used the plug-in by adding code to your application, you have to undo those changes yourself.

Using a Plug-in in Your Application

The `acts_as_taggable_on` Rails plug-in is useful in many web applications. This plug-in implements *tagging*—giving users the ability to add tags to web content. *Tags* are relevant keywords that help identify a piece of content.

In this section, you improve the blog application by adding the ability for users to tag their articles. By installing the `acts_as_taggable_on` plug-in in your application and using it to manage tagging, you can get this feature up and running in no time.

First, use the following command to install the `acts_as_taggable_on` plug-in in the blog application:

```
$ rails plugin install git://github.com/rbarazi/acts-as-taggable-on.git
```

```
Initialized empty Git repository in blog/vendor/plugins/acts-as-taggable-on/.git/

remote: Counting objects: 61, done.

remote: Compressing objects: 100% (50/50), done.

remote: Total 61 (delta 3), reused 5 (delta 0)
```

```
Unpacking objects: 100% (61/61), done.

From git://github.com/rbarazi/acts-as-taggable-on

* branch            HEAD          -> FETCH_HEAD
```

Modifying the Database

The plug-in is installed, but you still have a bit of work to do before you can begin using it. By reading the plug-in's README.rdoc file in vendor/plugins/acts_as_taggable_on, you know that the first thing you need to do is prepare your database by creating the tagging tables required for tag management. Normally, you do that by generating a new migration to create your tables; but instead of manually doing that, acts_as_taggable_on provides a generator that prepares it for you: acts_as_taggable_on:migration.

```
$ rails generate acts_as_taggable_on:migration
```

```
create  db/migrate/20100410172953_acts_as_taggable_on_migration.rb
```

This command creates the db/migrate/20100410172953_acts_as_taggable_on_migration.rb migration, which looks like Listing 12-1.

Listing 12-1. The db/migrate/20100410172953_acts_as_taggable_on_migration.rb Migration File

```ruby
class ActsAsTaggableOnMigration < ActiveRecord::Migration
  def self.up
    create_table :tags do |t|
      t.string :name
    end

    create_table :taggings do |t|
      t.references :tag

      # You should make sure that the column created is
      # long enough to store the required class names.
      t.references :taggable, :polymorphic => true
      t.references :tagger, :polymorphic => true

      t.string :context

      t.datetime :created_at
    end

    add_index :taggings, :tag_id
    add_index :taggings, [:taggable_id, :taggable_type, :context]
  end
```

```
  def self.down
    drop_table :taggings
    drop_table :tags
  end
end
```

The generated migration creates two tables—tags and taggings—that are used to save the tags generated by your application.

Go ahead and execute the migration file by issuing the rake db:migrate command:

```
$ rake db:migrate
```

```
== ActsAsTaggableOnMigration: migrating ========================================

-- create_table(:tags)

   -> 0.0015s

-- create_table(:taggings)

   -> 0.0018s

-- add_index(:taggings, :tag_id)

   -> 0.0005s

-- add_index(:taggings, [:taggable_id, :taggable_type, :context])

   -> 0.0005s

== ActsAsTaggableOnMigration: migrated (0.0046s) ===============================
```

Modifying the Application to Use the Plug-in

With the plug-in successfully installed and the database tables created, all that's left to do is integrate the plug-in into your application.

The first step is to configure the Article model to accept tagging. You can do this by adding the acts_as_taggable call to the Article model declaration, as shown in Listing 12-2.

Listing 12-2. Adding acts_as_taggable in app/models/article.rb: http://gist.github.com/362817

```
class Article < ActiveRecord::Base
  validates :title, :presence => true
  validates :body, :presence => true

  belongs_to :user
  has_and_belongs_to_many :categories
```

```ruby
  has_many :comments

  acts_as_taggable

  scope :published, where("articles.published_at IS NOT NULL")
  scope :draft, where("articles.published_at IS NULL")
  scope :recent, lambda {
published.where("articles.published_at > ?", 1.week.ago.to_date)}
  scope :where_title, lambda { |term|
where("articles.title LIKE ?", "%#{term}%") }

  def long_title
    "#{title} - #{published_at}"
  end

  def published?
    published_at.present?
  end

  def owned_by?(owner)
    return false unless owner.is_a? User
    user == owner
  end
end
```

Just like other class-level model declarations, such as has_many and belongs_to, acts_as_taggable results in the addition of several methods to the class in which it's used. Two instance methods are supplied for adding tags to and listing the tags of a particular object: tag_list= and tag_list. Additionally, a class-level finder is added to enable searching of items by a list of tags: tagged_with. Again, you can find this information in the plug-in's README file.

Let's take this for a quick spin on the console so you can see how it works:

```ruby
>> a = Article.first
=> #<Article id: 1, title: "Advanced Active Record",
body: "Models need to relate to each other. In the real wo...",
published_at: "2010-05-05 04:00:00", created_at: "2010-05-05 15:36:33",
updated_at: "2010-05-05 15:36:33", excerpt: nil, location: nil, user_id: 1>

>> a.tag_list = "development, ruby on rails, plugins"
=> "development, ruby on rails, plugins"

>> a.save
=> true

>> a.tag_list
=> ["development", "ruby on rails", "plugins"]

>> Article.tagged_with("plugins")
=> [#<Article id: 1, title: "Advanced Active Record",
body: "Models need to relate to each other. In the real wo...",
published_at: "2010-05-05 04:00:00", created_at: "2010-05-05 15:36:33",
updated_at: "2010-05-05 15:36:33", excerpt: nil, location: nil, user_id: 1>]
```

```
>> a.tags
=> [#<ActsAsTaggableOn::Tag id: 1, name: "development">,
#<ActsAsTaggableOn::Tag id: 2, name: "ruby on rails">,
#<ActsAsTaggableOn::Tag id: 3, name: "plugins">]
```

In this code, you assign tags to an existing article. To implement the tagging feature in your application's view, you need to be able to assign tags to existing and new articles. This is a simple matter of adding a tag_list field to the article form partial. Modify the partial in app/views/articles/_form.html.erb to include the tag_list field at the very bottom of the form, as shown in Listing 12-3.

Listing 12-3. Adding a Tag Field to the Form in app/views/articles/_form.html.erb:

http://gist.github.com/362819

```
<%= form_for(@article) do |f| %>
  <% if @article.errors.any? %>
  <div id="errorExplanation">
    <h2><%= pluralize(@article.errors.count, "error") %>
prohibited this article from being saved:</h2>
    <ul>
    <% @article.errors.full_messages.each do |msg| %>
      <li><%= msg %></li>
    <% end %>
    </ul>
  </div>
  <% end %>

  <div class="field">
    <%= f.label :title %><br />
    <%= f.text_field :title %>
  </div>
  <div class="field">
    <%= f.label :location %><br />
    <%= f.text_field :location %>
  </div>
  <div class="field">
    <%= f.label "Categories" %><br />
    <% for category in Category.all %>
      <%= check_box_tag 'article[category_ids][]', category.id,
@article.category_ids.include?(category.id), :id => dom_id(category) %>
      <%= label_tag dom_id(category), category.name, :class => "check_box_label" %>
    <% end %>
  </div>
  <div class="field">
    <%= f.label :excerpt %><br />
    <%= f.text_field :excerpt %>
  </div>
  <div class="field">
    <%= f.label :body %><br />
    <%= f.text_area :body %>
```

```
    </div>
    <div class="field">
      <%= f.label :tag_list %><br />
      <%= f.text_field :tag_list %>
    </div>
    <div class="field">
      <%= f.label :published_at %><br />
      <%= f.datetime_select :published_at %>
    </div>
    <div class="actions">
      <%= submit_or_cancel(f) %>
    </div>
<% end %>
```

You treat the `tag_list` attribute like a string attribute of your article object. You can do that because `acts_as_taggable_on` created both the getter `tag_list` and the setter `tag_list=` instance methods for you while magically in the background saving tags in their own records and tables. Figure 12-1 shows the result when rendered in a browser.

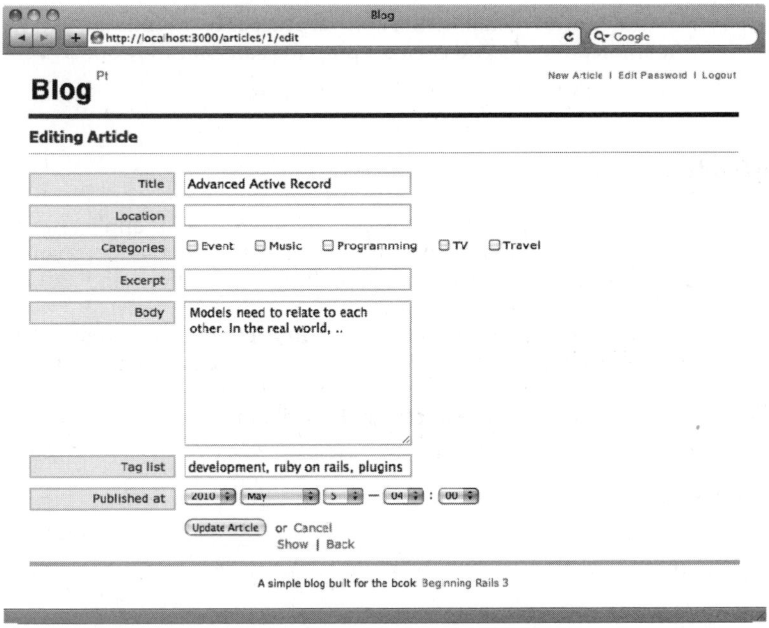

Figure 12-1. *Added "Tag list" field in the article form*

That was a lot of code! Now you can assign tags to articles, but you still need to show those tags in the article page; otherwise, the tags aren't useful. So, open the `article` partial in `app/views/articles/_article.html.erb`, and make sure it looks like Listing 12-4.

Listing 12-4. Showing Tags in the article Partial, app/views/articles/_article.html.erb:

http://gist.github.com/362821

```
<%= div_for article do %>
  <h3>
    <%= link_to article.title, article %>
    <% if article.owned_by? current_user %>
      <span class='actions'>
        <%= link_to t('general.edit'), edit_article_path(article) %>
        <%= link_to t('general.delete'), article, :confirm => t('general.are_you_sure'),
:method => :delete %>
      </span>
    <% end %>
  </h3>
  <% if article.tag_list.present? %>
    <small>Tags: <%= article.tag_list %></small>
  <% end %>
  <%= simple_format raw(article.body) %>
<% end %>
```

That's all there is to it! Just a few minutes after installing the acts_as_taggable_on plug-in, you're finished implementing tagging in your application. As you can see, plug-ins can definitely boost productivity.

Creating Your Own Plug-in

Whenever you find yourself repeatedly writing the same code snippets in different Rails applications, you have a very strong case for extracting this functionality in your own plug-in. Doing so helps you keep the business logic for this functionality in one location instead of in multiple applications and makes it possible to fix bugs in a single place.

To demonstrate how to create your own plug-in, in this section you make one to implement simple text-search functionality for a given model so that the search code can be reused easily. This plug-in is called simple_search.

Rails comes with a plug-in generator that you can use to create the skeleton for a new plug-in. You just need to tell it the name of the plug-in you want to create:

```
$ rails generate plugin simple_search
```

```
      create  vendor/plugins/simple_search

      create  vendor/plugins/simple_search/init.rb

      create  vendor/plugins/simple_search/install.rb

      create  vendor/plugins/simple_search/MIT-LICENSE

      create  vendor/plugins/simple_search/Rakefile
```

```
create      vendor/plugins/simple_search/README

create      vendor/plugins/simple_search/uninstall.rb

create      vendor/plugins/simple_search/lib

create      vendor/plugins/simple_search/lib/simple_search.rb

invoke      test_unit

inside      vendor/plugins/simple_search

create      test

create      test/simple_search_test.rb

create      test/test_helper.rb
```

The generator creates quite a few files. As you can see from the generator's output, they're all in the vendor/plugins/simple_search directory. The structure of a plug-in is specific and follows normal Ruby library conventions. Table 12-2 describes the function of each file and directory.

Table 12-2. Plug-in Directory Structure

File/Directory	Description
lib	Directory where the plug-in code is located.
test	Directory where you can add tests for this plug-in.
README	File that contains a description of the plug-in and instructions for using it.
MIT-LICENSE	License under which this plug-in is released; it's good practice to specify it. Rails assumes the MIT license is used. Feel free to use whatever license best suits your application.
install.rb	Code that is executed when the plug-in is installed.
uninstall.rb	Similar to install.rb, contains code that is executed when the plug-in is uninstalled.
Rakefile	A Rake file with tasks to run the tests for this plug-in and generate documentation.
init.rb	Initialization code that Rails executes automatically to make this plug-in available to your application.

As you saw when you used the acts_as_taggable_on plug-in in the previous section, a plug-in usually adds one or more methods to the class or object on which it's acting. You take a similar path—you add a search method for any Active Record model—in this case to the Article model, to make the search functionality external to your application.

Creating the Plug-in Module

It's time to dive into the plug-in code. Create a module named `SimpleSearch` that contains your plug-in's methods. Listing 12-5 shows the complete plug-in code in vendor/plugins/simple_search/lib/simple_search.rb; an explanation of some of the code follows.

Listing 12-5. Complete SimpleSearch Plug-in in vendor/plugins/simple_search/lib/simple_search.rb:

http://gist.github.com/362822

```ruby
module BeginningRails
  module SimpleSearch
    def simple_search(*fields)
      class_inheritable_accessor :searchable_fields

      raise "Please specify the fields to search on" if fields.empty?
      self.searchable_fields = fields
    end

    def search(value)
      # Initialize the conditions and values arrays
      conditions = []
      # Build the conditions array from the parameters
      self.searchable_fields.each do |field|
        conditions << "#{self.table_name}.#{field.to_s} LIKE '%#{value}%'"
      end
      return self.where(conditions.join(' OR '))
    end
  end
end
```

To prevent namespace clashes, it's always a good idea to give your plug-ins a unique namespace by wrapping them in a uniquely named module. It's possible that someone else may create a plug-in called `SimpleSearch` one day, which would create problems if you had them both installed at the same time. Wrapping your `SimpleSearch` module inside the `BeginningRails` module helps you avoid this (admittedly unlikely) situation.

In the plug-in code, you write the `simple_search` method, which is the class method you use in your models to declare them as searchable. The `simple_search` method accepts an array of field names called `fields`, and includes a list of database fields on which to search; you save the `fields` array into the class-level `searchable_fields` variable for later retrieval. The `fields` parameter is required, so you raise an exception if it's empty.

Next, let's move to the code that performs the actual search—what the user will reach when calling `Article.search` after you add the plug-in to the `Article` model. You require the plug-in user to specify the fields for the search; so, you use those fields to generate a condition string that matches the text you want to search on.

The search method expects a value parameter to search for and returns an array of objects that matches your search. In the search method, you loop through the `searchable_fields` variable that you got earlier from the user in the `simple_search` call, and you cumulatively build your conditions array. Then, you invoke a regular where call using this conditions array joined by an `OR`.

Making the Plug-in Available to Applications

You need to let Rails know what source files it should use when loading your plug-in. You also need to make the simple_search method, which you just created in vendor/plugins/simple_search/lib/simple_search.rb, available to any model that wants to use it, in the same fashion that the acts_as_taggable method was made available to your Article model. You accomplish both tasks by modifying the init.rb file, as shown in Listing 12-6.

Listing 12-6. Updates to vendor/plugins/simply_searchable/init.rb: http://gist.github.com/362823

```
require 'active_record'
require 'simple_search'
ActiveRecord::Base.send(:extend, BeginningRails::SimpleSearch)
```

The require 'active_record' line makes sure the Active Record library is available and loaded. The require 'simple_search' line directs Rails to your plug-in files. By calling ActiveRecord::Base.send(:extend, BeginningRails::SimpleSearch), you extend the ActiveRecord::Base class with the BeginningRails::SimpleSearch module. The extend method makes the plug-in's methods available on a class-level to ActiveRecord::Base, which is the class from which all your models inherit.

■ **NOTE** Unlike most of the components of Rails (models, controllers, and so on), plug-ins don't automatically reload when they're changed. Whenever you modify a plug-in, you need to restart the web server before you see the changes take effect.

Using SimpleSearch

Now that you've written the simple_search plug-in, you add it to the Article model. When searching for information in articles, you want the search functionality to look up values in the title and body fields. Add the line highlighted in Listing 12-7.

Listing 12-7. Adding SimpleSearch to Article in app/models/article.rb: http://gist.github.com/362825

```
class Article < ActiveRecord::Base
  validates :title, :presence => true
  validates :body, :presence => true

  belongs_to :user
  has_and_belongs_to_many :categories
  has_many :comments

  acts_as_taggable
  simple_search :title, :body

  scope :published, where("articles.published_at IS NOT NULL")
  scope :draft, where("articles.published_at IS NULL")
```

```ruby
  scope :recent, lambda {
published.where("articles.published_at > ?", 1.week.ago.to_date)}
  scope :where_title, lambda { |term|
where("articles.title LIKE ?", "%#{term}%") }

  def long_title
    "#{title} - #{published_at}"
  end

  def published?
    published_at.present?
  end

  def owned_by?(owner)
    return false unless owner.is_a? User
    user == owner
  end
end
```

Testing the Plug-in

Before you integrate your plug-in in the blog application, you have to test it and make sure it's
functioning as it's supposed to. Testing plug-ins in Rails 3 is no different from regular tests you write for
your application: you have access to the Rails environment, fixtures, and test database just as in regular
unit, functional and integration tests.

Because you have only the search method defined in your plug-in, you just test that. Open your
vendor/plugins/simple_search/test/simple_search_test.rb file, clean up the test_truth method, and
add the test "should search" method as shown in Listing 12-8.

Listing 12-8. Updating the SimpleSearch Test in

vendor/plugins/simple_search/test/simple_search_test.rb: http://gist.github.com/362826

```ruby
require 'test_helper'

class SimpleSearchTest < ActiveSupport::TestCase
  test "search method is available" do
    assert Article.respond_to?(:search)
  end

  test "should search" do
    assert_equal 1, Article.search("framework").size
    assert_equal 0, Article.search("unknown").size
  end
end
```

You start by testing whether the search method has been added to your Article model in the test "search method is available" method. The test "should search" method asserts that your search method is returning the right number of results when called; as per your fixtures, it returns one result when looking for the keyword *framework* and no results when you look for the keyword *unknown*.

Run this test now. Rails comes with a default task to run plug-in tests, and as you may have guessed, it's called rake test:plugins:

```
$ rake test:plugins
```

```
Started

..

Finished in 0.469858 seconds.



2 tests, 3 assertions, 0 failures, 0 errors, 0 skips
```

Great—your plug-in tests pass. But you have a problem with those tests, because they depend on the Article model, which prevents them from passing when used in any application that doesn't have the Article model.

To fix this issue, you can create a database table and its model just for your plug-in tests; then, make sure you use the table and the model in your plug-in tests instead of the Article model. Let's create a properties table and define the Property model accordingly. Listing 12-9 shows the code to do that.

Listing 12-9. Creating a properties Table and Defining Its Model in

vendor/plugins/simple_search/test/simple_search_test.rb: http://gist.github.com/362827

```ruby
require 'test_helper'

$stdout = StringIO.new

def create_properties_table
  ActiveRecord::Schema.define(:version => 1) do
    create_table :properties do |t|
      t.column :name, :string
      t.column :description, :text
    end
  end
end

class Property < ActiveRecord::Base
  simple_search :name, :description
end

class SimpleSearchTest < ActiveSupport::TestCase
  setup do
```

```
    create_properties_table
    Property.create(:name => 'Some name', :description => 'Some description')
    Property.create(:name => 'another name', :description => 'another description')
  end

  test "search method is available" do
    assert Property.respond_to?(:search)
  end

  test "should search" do
    assert_equal 2, Property.search("name").size
    assert_equal 1, Property.search("another").size
    assert_equal 0, Property.search("swimming").size
  end
end
```

The `create_properties_table` method uses the test database schema to create an extra table for you called `properties` that has `name` and `description` fields. Then, in the `Property` class definition, you call your `simple_search` plug-in method on both the `name` and `description` fields.

Remember from Chapter 10 that Rails creates and drops your test database for every single running test. Now that you need the `properties` table to be part of this, you add it to the setup method in the `SimpleSearchTest` class.

And now that your test creates an independent table and model for itself, you call it instead of `Article`.

To be able to use the `Property` model in your tests, you need some data; you create a couple of records in the setup method. You also add the `$stdout = StringIO.new` line to avoid annoying schema statements from your test results.

You can now install your plug-in and run its tests independently and without any dependency on your blog application models:

```
$ rake test:plugins
```

```
Started

..

Finished in 0.204327 seconds.



2 tests, 4 assertions, 0 failures, 0 errors, 0 skipped
```

Updating the Controller and Views

The plug-in is implemented, and the `Article` model is ready to be searched on. You need to make some changes to the controller and views to use the search functionality. In the `ArticlesController` class, add the search method highlighted in Listing 12-10.

Listing 12-10. Addition to ArticlesController in app/controllers/articles_controller.rb:

http://gist.github.com/362828

```
class ArticlesController < ApplicationController
  before_filter :authenticate, :except => [:index, :show, :notify_friend, :search]

  def search
    @articles = Article.search(params[:keyword])
    render :action => 'index'
  end

  # GET /articles
  # GET /articles.xml
  def index
    @articles = Article.all

    respond_to do |format|
      format.html # index.html.erb
      format.xml  { render :xml => @articles }
    end
  end

  # GET /articles/1
  # GET /articles/1.xml
  def show
    @article = Article.find(params[:id])

    respond_to do |format|
      format.html # show.html.erb
      format.xml  { render :xml => @article }
    end
  end

  # GET /articles/new
  # GET /articles/new.xml
  def new
    @article = Article.new

    respond_to do |format|
      format.html # new.html.erb
      format.xml  { render :xml => @article }
    end
  end

  # GET /articles/1/edit
  def edit
    @article = current_user.articles.find(params[:id])
  end

  # POST /articles
```

```ruby
  # POST /articles.xml
  def create
    @article = current_user.articles.new(params[:article])

    respond_to do |format|
      if @article.save
        format.html { redirect_to(@article,
:notice => t('articles.create_success')) }
        format.xml  { render :xml => @article,
:status => :created, :location => @article }
      else
        format.html { render :action => "new" }
        format.xml  { render :xml => @article.errors,
:status => :unprocessable_entity }
      end
    end
  end

  # PUT /articles/1
  # PUT /articles/1.xml
  def update
    @article = current_user.articles.find(params[:id])

    respond_to do |format|
      if @article.update_attributes(params[:article])
        format.html { redirect_to(@article,
:notice => t('articles.update_success')) }
        format.xml  { head :ok }
      else
        format.html { render :action => "edit" }
        format.xml  { render :xml => @article.errors,
:status => :unprocessable_entity }
      end
    end
  end

  # DELETE /articles/1
  # DELETE /articles/1.xml
  def destroy
    @article = current_user.articles.find(params[:id])
    @article.destroy

    respond_to do |format|
      format.html { redirect_to(articles_url) }
      format.xml  { head :ok }
    end
  end

  def notify_friend
    @article = Article.find(params[:id])
    Notifier.email_friend(@article, params[:name], params[:email]).deliver
```

```
    redirect_to @article, :notice => t('articles.notify_friend_success')
  end
end
```

Because you don't want to require users to be logged in to access the search, you add the search action to the before_filter exception list.

Remember, when you define a new action in your controller, you need to add it to your routes; see Listing 12-11.

Listing 12-11. Updating Routes in config/routes.rb: http://gist.github.com/362829

```
Blog::Application.routes.draw do
  root :to => "articles#index"
  resources :articles do
    member do
      post :notify_friend
    end
    collection do
      get :search
    end
    resources :comments
  end
  resources :users
  resource :session
  match '/login' => "sessions#new", :as => "login"
  match '/logout' => "sessions#destroy", :as => "logout"
end
```

Your controller is ready, and you just need to add a search box in your view to run the search. Add a new partial called app/views/articles/_search.html.erb to contain the search box where users enter keywords to search. This is fairly straightforward—you create a form that submits to the search action as a GET request on the ArticlesController and include a text field for the keyword. Listing 12-12 shows the search partial.

Listing 12-12. The app/views/articles/_search.html.erb File: http://gist.github.com/362830

```
<%= form_tag search_articles_path, :method => :get do %>
  <p>
    Search
    <%= text_field_tag :keyword, params[:keyword] %>
  </p>
<% end %>
```

Now, let's modify the application layout template in app/views/layouts/application.html.erb so that it loads the search partial you just created. Add the line shown in bold in Listing 12-13.

Listing 12-13. Update to app/views/layouts/application.html.erb: http://gist.github.com/362831

```
<!DOCTYPE html>
<html>
<head>
```

```
    <title>Blog</title>
    <%= stylesheet_link_tag :all %>
    <%= javascript_include_tag 'jquery-1.4.2.min', 'rails', 'application' %>
    <%= csrf_meta_tag %>
</head>
<body>
  <div id="header">
    <h1><%= link_to t('general.title'), root_path %></h1>
    <%= language_selector %>
    <div id="user_bar">
      <% if logged_in? %>
        <%= link_to t('articles.new_article'), new_article_path %> |
        <%= link_to t('users.edit_password'), edit_user_path(current_user) %> |
        <%= link_to t('sessions.logout'), logout_path %>
      <% else %>
        <%= link_to t('sessions.login'), login_path %>
      <% end %>
    </div>
    <%= render 'articles/search' %>
  </div>
  <div id="main">
    <%= content_tag(:p, notice, :class => 'notice') if notice.present? %>
    <%= content_tag(:p, alert, :class => 'alert') if alert.present? %>
    <%= yield %>
  </div>
  <div id="footer">
    <%= t('general.footer') %> <a href="http://beginningrails.com">
Beginning Rails 3</a>
  </div>
</body>
</html>
```

That's all there is to it. Restart your web server, and try performing a search. You should see something like the results shown in Figure 12-2.

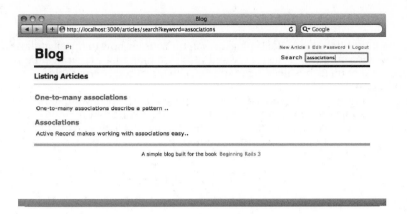

Figure 12-2. Search functionality added to your blog application

You can now use the `simple_search` plug-in in other applications whenever you need simple text-search functionality. And you can come back to it for reference when you build more plug-ins in the future.

WHEN SHOULD YOU USE A PLUG-IN?

Hundreds of plug-ins are available for Rails developers, and you may want to try a few in your applications. However, in some cases, plug-ins may not work to your advantage and may even slow you down. There's no magic formula for knowing when to use a plug-in or when to write your own code, but here are a few tips to help you decide whether to go for a plug-in.

If the functionality you need to create is very common, and your implementation has nothing very specific, you can assume that using a plug-in will be safe and will save you some time. Examples of this type of common functionality are tagging, allowing users to post comments, using external applications like Google Maps, and using a specific API.

If you're implementing a common feature that has a very specific design in your application, you still may save some time by using a plug-in if you feel comfortable adapting the plug-in code to your own needs. This depends not only on your situation but also on how the plug-in has been written. Usually, it's not too complicated to adapt a plug-in to suit your needs.

If you're implementing a feature that is very unique to your application, it's probably a wise move to code the feature directly into the code base of your application. This applies especially if the implementation depends on other parts of your code, such as an authorization and authentication system. If this specific feature is to be shared with other applications under your control, then you may want to extract the functionality into its own plug-in to make the code easy to share among applications.

Summary

In this chapter, you learned about the strengths of Rails' plug-in system. You saw how to install and use a plug-in, which usually takes only a few minutes. You also created your own plug-in. By creating plug-ins, you make your application focus more on its business logic, and you can move code to reusable units outside the scope of your application.

Take the time to read the code of the plug-ins you use in your applications. By reviewing the code behind a plug-in, you'll likely learn some new tricks, and you'll understand how the new methods your code inherits are implemented. You may even be able to help the development of a plug-in by spotting a bug or a better/faster implementation for a specific feature or method.

CHAPTER 13

■ ■ ■

Deploying Your Rails Applications

If you're ready to turn the world on its head by unleashing your million-dollar web application to the public, then let this chapter be your starting point.

The various web-application development platforms in use today have very different deployment methods. If you're using PHP, deployment is usually as simple as dropping the right files into a directory on the remote server (usually via FTP) and then visiting them with your web browser. For PHP applications, there are thousands of hosts, and deployment is simple enough for your parents to accomplish. However, as you all know, with simplicity comes a lack of options. And as anyone who has developed in a language like PHP knows, simplicity can lead to some pretty complicated situations with your development. Luckily, Rails deployment is nothing like PHP deployment.

In the opposite camp, Java/Struts people have some deployment schemes that would make a PhD candidate panic and run away in a cloud of network diagrams. Java deployments can be terribly complex, with lots of little details to worry about and huge amounts of memory required. Fortunately, Rails is much simpler than that.

With Rails, the porridge is just right. Rails takes some setup to get the system purring; but thanks to an ingenious deployment tool known as Capistrano, deploying and updating your application is a simple process.

Deploying with Capistrano

How does Capistrano make Rails deployment easier? The secret is that Capistrano knows a lot about what a typical Rails deployment looks like, so you don't need to tell it much. It makes many assumptions about your application and your deployment setup, but it also provides with myriad ways to override and customize those defaults.

Would you like to see how complicated it is to deploy a new release to the server? Here's an example:

```
$ cap deploy
```

Basically, you tell Capistrano (cap) to deploy, and it remotely grabs a new version of your application from your version control repository (SVN is the default, but Git and other SCMs are also supported), uses it as the current release, and then restarts the servers.

It's that easy to deploy to production. The best part is that this process is repeatable. Every time you make a change to an application and want to deploy the changes, you issue the cap deploy command.

The only difficult part is the server setup. There are a nearly infinite number of ways to configure your Rails stack, and most of the configuration requires a good grasp of *nix (UNIX, Linux, OS X, and so on) system administration. For instance, Capistrano requires that you have Secure Shell (SSH) configured on your deployment box, with associated users and permissions set up for application deployment. Most novice Rails programmers aren't experts in such things, so this chapter doesn't talk about server specifics. Instead, you learn the basics of getting started with Capistrano from the client side.

At the end of this chapter, we recommend a few hosting providers that offer a complete Rails stack for your server. This saves you from installing and setting up the server side yourself, but you still need to know how to operate Capistrano from your end (the client side).

Capistrano Installation

Before you start using Capistrano, you need to install it. Fortunately, Capistrano is incredibly easy to install using the RubyGems package manager:

```
$ gem install capistrano
```

```
Successfully installed net-ssh-2.0.23

Successfully installed net-sftp-2.0.4

Successfully installed net-scp-1.0.2

Successfully installed net-ssh-gateway-1.0.1

Successfully installed highline-1.6.1

Successfully installed capistrano-2.5.19

6 gems installed
```

That's all it takes to install a full working version of Capistrano on your client computer (your development box, most likely). Part of the installation is the addition of a new command-line utility called cap. You can read the help information for most command-line utilities by passing in the --help directive. Do that now:

```
$ cap --help
```

```
Usage: cap [options] action ...

    -d, --debug                 Prompts before each remote command execution.

    -e, --explain TASK          Displays help (if available) for the task.

    -F, --default-config        Always use default config, even with -f.

    -f, --file FILE             A recipe file to load.

May be given more than once.
```

```
    -H, --long-help              Explain these options and
environment variables.

    -h, --help                   Display this help message.

    -l [STDERR|STDOUT|file]      Choose logger method. STDERR used by default.

        --logger

    -n, --dry-run                Prints out commands without running them.

    -p, --password               Immediately prompt for the password.

    -q, --quiet                  Make the output as quiet as possible.

    -r, --preserve-roles         Preserve task roles

    -S, --set-before NAME=VALUE  Set a variable before the recipes are loaded.

    -s, --set NAME=VALUE         Set a variable after the recipes are loaded.

    -T, --tasks [PATTERN]        List all tasks
(matching optional PATTERN) in the loaded recipe files.

    -t, --tool                   Abbreviates the output of -T for
tool integration.

    -V, --version                Display the Capistrano version, and exit.

    -v, --verbose                Be more verbose. May be given more than once.

    -X, --skip-system-config     Don't load the system
config file (capistrano.conf)

    -x, --skip-user-config       Don't load the user config file (.caprc)
```

As you can see, the cap command has a lot of options that you can pass in. Some of these will be useful to you in the future, and it's important to feel comfortable asking for --help when you're working on the command line.

The Capistrano gem adds another command-line utility called capify. You use this command to enable your Rails applications to have their deployment managed by Capistrano. To do that now, execute the following command from your application's root directory:

```
$ capify .
```

```
[add] writing `./Capfile'

[add] writing `./config/deploy.rb'

[done] capified!
```

Capistrano creates two files: config/deploy.rb and Capfile. The deploy.rb file is commonly referred to as the *deployment recipe*. It contains all the basic configuration information for Capistrano. The next section looks at that file. The Capfile file is a collection of basic Rake tasks that allow you to deploy using the rake command instead of cap, if you prefer.

Capistrano Recipes

As mentioned, the config/deploy.rb file contains the recipe that tells Capistrano how you want your application to be deployed. It answers many simple questions, such as these:

- Where do you want to deploy?

- How should you log in to the remote system?

- Where do you want to put the application?

- Where is your source control repository?

Along with this information, the recipe provides many other details vital to any deployment procedure.

The default recipe is shown in Listing 13-1.

Listing 13-1. Default Capistrano Recipe

```
set :application, "set your application name here"
set :repository,  "set your repository location here"

set :scm, :subversion
# Or: `accurev`, `bzr`, `cvs`, `darcs`, `git`, `mercurial`, `perforce`,
# `subversion` or `none`

# Your HTTP server, Apache/etc
role :web, "your web-server here"
# This may be the same as your `Web` server
role :app, "your app-server here"
# This is where Rails migrations will run
role :db,  "your primary db-server here", :primary => true
role :db,  "your slave db-server here"

# If you are using Passenger mod_rails uncomment this:
# if you're still using the script/reapear helper you will need
# these http://github.com/rails/irs_process_scripts
```

```
# namespace :deploy do
#   task :start do ; end
#   task :stop do ; end
#   task :restart, :roles => :app, :except => { :no_release => true } do
#     run "#{try_sudo} touch #{File.join(current_path,'tmp','restart.txt')}"
#   end
# end
```

The first two variables are central to every recipe. The `application` variable gives a name to the application. Capistrano uses the application name to create some directories on the server. The `repository` variable is where you give a URL pointing to your version-control repository. Capistrano requires you to use some type of version-control system and defaults to SVN. Don't worry if you're using Git or any other SCM—you just have to set the `scm` variable to the appropriate value. The next example uses `:git`.

Your repository must be available *from* the deployment server. If it's on your local file system (and your local system isn't accessible remotely), the deployment server has no way to access the code.

■ **NOTE** If you aren't familiar with Git, refer to Appendix D for information about how to get started with this version-control system. Version control is essential for developers, no matter what language or framework you're working with.

The `deploy_to` variable sets the actual location of your application on the production server. Most likely, you use one computer as your web server, application server, and database server. You typically assign a single server to the `:web`, `:app`, and `:db` roles, like this:

```
server "myserver.com", :app, :web, :db, :primary => true
```

However, if your application is a huge success and generates a ton of traffic, you probably need to define many servers with different roles. Capistrano is built to be able to handle very complex deployments as easily as it does single-server architectures. It makes no difference to Capistrano if it's deploying to 15 servers or 1; it repeats the same actions on each server in sequence. Anyone who has ever attempted to synchronize deployment of an application to 15 servers manually has your respect, because it's a Sisyphean task of epic proportions. But with Capistrano, it's easy to control that complexity and ease most of the pain.

Listing 13-2 shows an example recipe for the blog application.

Listing 13-2. Example Recipe

```
set :application, "blog_app"
set :repository,  "git://github.com/ccjr/blog.git"
set :deploy_to, "/vol/www/apps/#{application}"

set :scm, :git

server  "blog.example.com",  :web,  :app, :db, :primary => true
```

Now, let's look at exactly what Capistrano *does* on each application server when you deploy an application.

Capistrano on the Deployment Server

Whenever you set up a Capistrano deployment on the remote deployment server, Capistrano creates a specific folder structure—that is accomplished by running cap deploy:setup, which looks like this:

```
my_app/

|-- current            # A link to the current release

|-- releases

|    |-- 20100424080541    # An older release of the application

|    `-- 20100424082125    # The current (most recent) release

`-- shared

    |-- config         # Symlinked to current/config

    |-- log            # Symlinked to current/log

    `-- tmp            # Symlinked to current/tmp
```

The releases folder contains every version of the application that you've ever deployed. Any time you do a new deployment, Capistrano puts a new version of the application in this folder, named by the timestamp of when it was deployed.

The releases folder can get really big and messy. To clean up this folder, you can either set the :keep_releases variable to the number of releases you want to keep in your recipe file or use the cleanup task offered by Capistrano to delete all old releases and keep only the current one:

```
$ cap deploy:cleanup
```

The current folder uses UNIX's built-in symlink (think *alias*) feature to create a shortcut that always points to the currently deployed release. Keeping older revisions of the application ready to go means that if something goes wrong during a deployment, you can easily roll back to an earlier version of the application with the cap rollback command. All that Capistrano needs to do in that instance is point current toward the previous deployed version in the releases folder.

Because you'll probably frequently swap out your current release, it's important to keep some things common between releases, such as the logs, temporary files, and production configuration. The shared folder is used to house all this information. You must manually tell Capistrano which shared files you want relinked on each deployment.

Custom Capistrano Tasks

You can teach Capistrano to perform many other tasks or change the way it performs any of its current tasks. Suppose you want to clear out a temporary folder every time you deploy. With Capistrano, defining custom tasks like this is easy.

As an example, Listing 13-3 shows a simple custom deployment task that allows you to quickly restart your web server—running Phusion Passenger—on every :web server you have.

Listing 13-3. Sample Custom Task

```
task :restart, :roles => :app, :except => { :no_release => true } do
  run "#{try_sudo} touch #{File.join(current_path,'tmp','restart.txt')}"
end
```

You can run this custom task from the command line on the client by issuing cap restart.

Setting Up Your Server Architecture

First things first. You're probably not a system administrator. If you want to learn how to be one, grab a book on the subject and spend your time getting well versed in the details of administration. Instead of focusing on the details of server administration, this section covers some of the high-level ideas that dominate the server architectures in the Rails world. You'll find these concepts helpful when you're discussing your options with different Rails hosting providers or server administration professionals, so that you understand most of the terminology being used.

There are different schools of thought regarding how to set up the web server architecture for a Rails application. The recommended way is referred to as *modular architecture.*

Modular Architecture

Modular architecture takes a modular approach: the core part of the web server is responsible for servicing requests, and the modules handle those requests accordingly (see Figure 13-1).

Modular architecture is widely used in other programming languages like Python, Perl, and PHP; and since its recent arrival in the Ruby and Rails world, it has become the most dominant and widely used server stack for Rails. This is mostly due to its speed, stability, and ease of use.

The currently available modules for Rails are mod_rails and mod_rack, both packaged under the name *Phusion Passenger.* Passenger is available for both Apache and Nginx web servers.

To use Phusion Passenger with Capistrano, you need to modify Capistrano's start, stop, and restart tasks by adding the code in Listing 13-4 to your deployment recipe.

Listing 13-4. Phusion Passenger Tasks for Capistrano

```
namespace :deploy do
  task :start do ; end
  task :stop do ; end
  task :restart, :roles => :app, :except => { :no_release => true } do
    run "#{try_sudo} touch #{File.join(current_path,'tmp','restart.txt')}"
  end
end
```

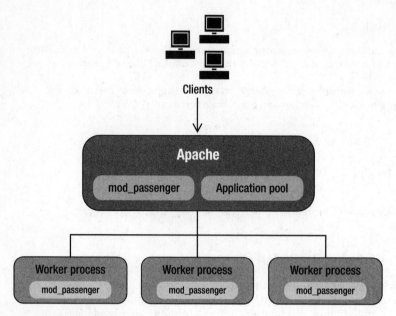

Figure 13-1. *Modular Architecture*

Picking a Web Server

Two popular servers can act as your front-end web server to handle Phusion Passenger:

- *Apache (*`http://apache.org)`*:* The granddaddy of all open source web servers, Apache can do everything. If you want to run SVN, virtual hosts, a chat server, and a proxy, Apache can do all that and more.

- *Nginx (*`http://nginx.net/)`*:* Nginx is a super-fast, high-performance HTTP server that makes a great front end for Phusion Passenger. It boasts a small resource footprint, stands up under heavy load, and is easy to configure.

Becoming an Instant Deployment Expert

As you saw earlier in this chapter, deploying with Capistrano is a piece of cake. However, how you configure your server directly impacts the way your Capistrano scripts are written. If you want to learn about that, you can find literally thousands of sources and books available on the subject. But there's another way: outsource!

It makes sense to find people you can trust to take care of the things that aren't within your area of expertise. For instance, you don't memorize tax codes or build CPUs for your computers. Instead, you hire an accountant and pay Intel for those chips. Knowing how to deploy is very useful; but when you're launching an important product into production mode, you should go with the best.

You can find several relatively cheap Rails hosts. If you're moving toward production with an important project, do *not* use them. The reason they're cheap is because they're cheap. You'll be disappointed. Trust us—we learned the hard way.

If you're going to spend hundreds of hours of your life building something that you hope will make you some money, you want to host it properly. No matter how genius the application is, if people can't access it due to downtime, that application won't get rave reviews.

We recommend two services:

- *Rails Machine* (`http://railsmachine.com`)*:* Rails Machine is a small team of experienced, dedicated, focused people who have a genuine interest in technology and enjoy working with and giving back to the Ruby on Rails community. Rails Machine was founded in 2006 to create the ultimate hosting environment for Rails applications. You drop their Capistrano recipe into your application and fire off a few commands from the terminal, and your application will be ready for the wild.

- *Engine Yard* (`http://engineyard.com`)*:* Like Rails Machine, Engine Yard provides a simple set of Capistrano scripts that make deployment a breeze. Ezra Zygmuntowicz is Engine Yard's primary developer and is a legend in the Rails deployment community. Instead of focusing on dedicated boxes, Engine Yard has a scalable deployment system called Engine Yard Cloud.

Summary

This chapter showed only some of myriad deployment choices. Rails deployment is as new and wild as Rails and is more of an art than a science these days. But with the help of great tools like Capistrano and the new architectures being explored, deployment gets easier with every passing month.

In this chapter, you got an idea of the power that a tool like Capistrano can give you when you're wrestling with something as complicated as application deployment and maintenance. You learned some of the basic concepts and ideas related to building deployments for Rails applications. We also gave you an easy out from dealing with this complexity—sometimes, calling in the experts is the best course of action.

The only thing left for you to do is launch your application and sell it for millions of dollars. That's nearly guaranteed with a good deployment strategy![1]

---

1. No warranty of truthiness. Some limitations apply. See store for details.

APPENDIX A

■ ■ ■

Ruby, a Programmer's Best Friend

Rails is a great framework for the development of web-based applications. One of its greatest advantages over other web frameworks is that it's written in Ruby, a very consistent and elegant object-oriented programming language. In order to increase your productivity as a Rails developer, it's important that you master Ruby. If you're new to programming, don't worry: we explain the concepts in a way you can understand.

This appendix gives you an overview of the features of the Ruby language. It explains how the language is organized and its fundamentals. After reading this appendix, you should better understand how the Ruby language that Rails is built on works, and you should be able to create classes and methods and use control-flow statements in your code.

Ruby has far more features than we can mention in this short introduction. We encourage you to investigate more of the complex features of Ruby as you continue using Rails.

Instant Interaction

A lot of languages require that you write some code, compile, and then run the program to see the results. However, Ruby is *dynamic*, which means you can work with the language live.

Ruby comes with a great little tool: an interactive interpreter called irb (for Interactive Ruby). You can start up an irb session whenever you want by typing **irb** at the command prompt. Using irb, you can play around with code and make sure it works as you expect before you write it into your programs.

You can execute any arbitrary Ruby code in irb and do anything you may otherwise do inside your Ruby programs: set variables, evaluate conditions, and inspect objects. The only essential difference between an interactive session and a regular old Ruby program is that irb echos the return value of everything it executes. This saves you from having to explicitly print the results of an evaluation. Just run the code, and irb prints the result.

You can tell when you're in an irb session by looking for the irb prompt, which looks like irb(main):001:0>, and the arrow symbol (=>), which indicates the response.

To start an irb session, go to the command prompt and type **irb**. You should see the irb prompt waiting for your input:

```
$ irb
irb(main):001:0>
```

Look at that. You're inside Ruby! If you press Enter, Ruby ignores the line and gives you another prompt, but it ends with an asterisk instead of the greater-than sign to indicate that Ruby is expecting something from you to execute. It can only get more exciting from here.

When learning a new programming language, traditionally, the first thing you do is make the language print the string "Hello, World!" In Ruby, you can print something on the screen by using the puts command:

```
irb(main):001:0>  puts "Hello, World!"
Hello, World!
=> nil

irb(main):002:0>  "Hello, World!"
=> "Hello, World!"
```

The first example uses the puts command to print "Hello, World!" to the console and returns nil, Ruby's way of expressing *nothing*. This is because the return value of the puts command is nil. Because Ruby is a pure object-oriented language, everything you're working with is an object, and every operation you perform is a message you send to an object. So, nil is actually an *object* that represent *nothing*,

In the second example, "Hello, World!" is in quotes without the puts. This creates a literal Ruby String object. True to form, irb prints the return value, which in this case is the string itself, "Hello, World!".

Ruby Data Types

A *data type* is a constraint placed on the interpretation of data. Numbers and strings are just two of the data types the Ruby interpreter distinguishes among, and the way Ruby adds numbers is different from the way in which it adds strings. For example, 2 + 3 evaluates to 5, but, "2" + "3" evaluates to "23". The second example may seem surprising at first, but it's simple: numbers surrounded by quotes are interpreted as strings. Read on to find out more.

Strings

A *string* is a sequence of characters that usually represents a word or some other form of text. In Ruby, you can create String objects by putting the characters inside single or double quotation marks:

```
irb(main):001:0>  'Ruby is a great language'
=> "Ruby is a great language"

irb(main):002:0>  "Rails is a great framework"
=> "Rails is a great framework"
```

The main difference between strings delimited by single and double quotes is that the latter are subject to substitutions. Those substitutions are identified by Ruby code inside the #{} construct, which is evaluated and replaced by its result in the final String object:

```
irb(main):003:0>  "Now is #{Time.now}"
=> "Now is 2010-04-05 20:54:31 +0000"

irb(main):004:0>  'Now is #{Time.now}'
=> "Now is \#{Time.now}"
```

■ **NOTE** The time format may be different depending on your locale setting, machine time, and Ruby version.

When you use the hash symbol (#) with the curly braces, Ruby notices and tries to evaluate whatever is between the braces. To *evaluate* means to process it like any other code. So, inside the braces, you say Time.now, which returns the current time. However, when you use single quotes, Ruby doesn't check the string for substitutions before sending it through. Remember that typing a string doesn't mean the user sees it appear—you're just creating the string. If you want the user to see it (outside of irb), you need to add a puts to the front, as you saw in the previous section.

The String class has a large number of methods you need when doing string manipulation, like concatenation and case-changing operations. The following examples list a few of those methods:

```
irb(main):005:0>  "Toronto - Canada".downcase
=> "toronto - canada"

irb(main):006:0>  "New York, USA".upcase
=> "NEW YORK, USA"

irb(main):007:0>  "a " + "few " + "strings " + "together"
=> "a few strings together"

irb(main):008:0>  "HELLO".capitalize
       ⇨  "Hello"
```

■ **TIP** To get a list of methods available for any object, call the methods method using an instance of the object you want to inspect. Type **"a string".methods** in irb to see all the methods you can call on the String object. If you want to find a certain method, try using grep on that method, too. For example, typing **"a string".methods.grep /case/** shows all String methods containing the word *case*.

Numbers

Ruby has a few classes to represent numbers: Fixnum, Bignum, and Float. As the names of the classes suggest, Fixnum and Bignum represent whole numbers and are both subclasses of Integer. Float objects represent real numbers, meaning numbers with a fractional part. As in most programming languages, you can perform basic arithmetic operations in Ruby as you would using a calculator:

```
irb(main):001:0>  1 + 2
=> 3

irb(main):002:0>  2323 + 34545
=> 36868

irb(main):003:0>  9093 - 23236
=> -14143

irb(main):004:0>  343 / 4564
=> 0
```

```
irb(main):005:0>  3434 / 53
=> 64

irb(main):006:0>  99 * 345
=> 34155

irb(main):007:0>  34545.6 / 3434.1
=> 10.059578928977
```

Symbols

Symbols aren't a common feature in most languages. However, as you learn when reading this book, they're extremely useful. Symbol is a data type that starts with a colon, like :controller. You can think of symbols as little named pointers (if you're a C programmer). They're used to point at some data that isn't a traditional String object, in a human-readable format. In fact, they're almost like strings, except you can't modify them:

```
irb(main):001:0>  :my_symbol
=> :my_symbol

irb(main):002:0>  :my_symbol + :second
NoMethodError: undefined method `+' for :my_symbol:Symbol
        from (irb):2
        from /usr/bin/irb:15:in `<main>'
irb(main):003:0>  "my_string" + "second"
=> "my_stringsecond"
```

In computer science, we refer to this condition as being *immutable*, which is a fancy way of saying you can't modify something. Use symbols when you want to name something nicely, and you don't want it changed at all—for example, by having something appended to the end of it.

You can even use symbols in method calls, as Rails does frequently. Because Ruby allows you to omit the braces when passing hashes as method arguments (as long as the hash is either the only argument or the last argument), this has the effect of creating what look like named arguments:

```
has_many :users, :class_name => "Person"
```

Here, you use the :users and :class_name symbols to point at some data. Specifically, you're using them to tell ActiveRecord::Base.has_many what type of relationship it should have with the Person class.

Arrays and Hashes

Sometimes you have a lot of data that you need to keep track of—maybe a list of students, users, or anything that you may keep in a collection. Ruby has two different types of *container* objects for storing collections: arrays and hashes.

Arrays are part of almost every modern language. They keep information in order. You can ask for the first item or the last item, or put items in a certain order. You can think of an Array object as a long series of boxes in which you can put things. You define arrays by using the [ ] notation. Note that in Ruby, you always refer to the first element in an array as 0. Read carefully what happens here:

```
irb(main):001:0>  array = ['Toronto', 'Miami', 'Paris']
=> ["Toronto", "Miami", "Paris"]

irb(main):002:0>  array[0]
=> "Toronto"

irb(main):003:0>  array[1]='New York'
=> "New York"

irb(main):004:0>  array << 'London'
=> ["Toronto", "New York", "Paris", "London"]
```

The Hash object offers another way to keep a collection. Hashes are different from arrays, because they store items using a *key*. Hash objects prior to Ruby 1.9 didn't preserve order; it didn't matter in which order you defined your hash, and you could retrieve it using the key you stored it with. In Ruby 1.9, hash objects preserve order, just like arrays, which enables you to call certain methods on them—for example, hash.first to get the first key, value pair. In Ruby, you often use symbols for hash keys, but in reality, *any* object can function as a key.

You define hashes with curly braces, {}. You can create a Hash object by defining it with {:key => "value", :other_key => "other value" }. Then, you can pull out data by using square brackets on the end of the list. For instance, you retrieve a value by saying @my_hash[:key] from the @my_hash variable. Here are some examples:

```
irb(main):005:0> hash = {:canada => 'Toronto', :france => 'Paris', :uk => 'London'}
=> {:canada=>"Toronto", :france=>"Paris", :uk=>"London"}

irb(main):006:0>  hash[:uk]
=> "London"

irb(main):007:0>  hash[:canada] = 'Calgary'
=> "Calgary"

irb(main):008:0>  hash.first
=> [:canada, "Calgary"]

irb(main):009:0>  hash
=> {:canada=>"Calgary", :france=>"Paris", :uk=>"London"}
```

Notice that on the second line, you redefine what goes into the :canada key. By passing in "Calgary", you override the value of "Toronto" from the preceding command.

Language Basics

Like other programming languages, Ruby includes variables, operators, control-flow statements, and methods. This section shows you how to use them.

Variables

Variables are used to hold values you want to keep for later processing. When you perform a calculation, you probably want to use the result of that calculation somewhere else in your application code, and that's when you need a variable. In Ruby, variables are easily created. You just need to give a variable a name and assign a value to it; there's no need to specify a data type for the variable or define it in your code before you use it.

Let's create a few variables to hold some values you may need later. Notice that you can reuse a variable name by reassigning a value:

```
irb(main):001:0>  test_variable = 'This is a string'
=> "This is a string"

irb(main):002:0>  test_variable = 2010
=> 2010

irb(main):003:0>  test_variable = 232.3
=> 232.3
```

You've created a variable named test_variable and assigned a few different values to it. Because everything in Ruby is an object, the test_variable variable holds a reference to the object you assigned.

Variable names can be any sequence of numbers and letters, as long as they start with a letter or an underscore; however, the first character of a variable indicates the type of the variable. Variables also have a *scope*, which is the context in which the variable is defined. Some variables are used in a small snippet of code and need to exist for only a short period of time; those are called *local variables*. Table A-1 lists the different types of variables supported by Ruby and shows how to recognize them when you're coding. Type some variable names in irb, and you'll get results similar to those shown here.

Table A-1. Ruby Variables

Example	Description
@@count	*Class variables* start with @@. Class variables exist in the scope of a class, so all instances of a specific class have a single value for the class variable.
@name	*Instance variables* start with @. Instance variables are unique to a given instance of a class.
SERVER_IP	You can create a *constant* in Ruby by capitalizing the first letter of a variable, but it's a convention that constants are written in all uppercase characters. Constants are variables that don't change throughout the execution of a program. In Ruby, constants can be reassigned; however, you get a warning from the interpreter if you do so.
var	*Local variables* start with a lowercase letter, and they live for only a short period of time. They usually exist only inside the method or block of code where they're first assigned.

In Ruby, it's considered best practice to use long and descriptive variable names. For example, in Java, you may have a variable named phi; but in Ruby, you write out place_holder_variable for clarity. The basic idea is that code is much more readable if the person looking at it (probably you) doesn't have to guess what phi stands for.

Operators

You can combine Ruby code using operators. Many classes implement operators as methods. Table A-2 lists the most common operators and their functions.

Table A-2. Ruby Operators

Operator	Description
[] []=	Assignment
* / % + **	Arithmetic
<= >= < >	Comparison
.. ...	Range
& ^ |	AND, exclusive OR, regular OR (bitwise)
|| && not or and	Logical operators

Ruby contains a ternary operator that you can use as a short notation for if-else-end. The ternary operator uses the form expression ? value_if_true : value_if_false:

```
a = 10
b = 20
a > b ? a : b
# => 20
```

Blocks and Iterators

Any method in Ruby can accept a *code block*—a fragment of code between curly braces or do..end constructs. Whether the method in question calls the given block is up to it. The block always appears immediately after the method call, with the start of the block coming on the same line as the method invocation.

Here's an example using the times method. times executes the given code block once for each iteration. In this case, "Hello" is printed 5 times:

```ruby
5.times { puts "Hello" }
```

```
Hello

Hello

Hello

Hello

Hello
```

If a method yields arguments to a block, the arguments are named between two pipe characters (|) on the same line as the method call:

```ruby
[1,2,3,4,5].each {|item| puts item }
```

```
1

2

3

4

5
```

Here, each number is yielded to the block in succession. You store the number in the block variable `item` and use `puts` to print it on its own line.

The convention is to use braces for single-line blocks and `do..end` for multiline blocks. Here's an example similar to the previous one; it uses `each_with_index`, which yields the item and its index in the array:

```ruby
["a", "b", "c"].each_with_index do |item, index|
  puts "Item:  #{item}"
  puts "Index: #{index}"
  puts "---"
end
```

```
Item:  a

Index: 0

---
```

```
Item:  b

Index: 1

---

Item:  c

Index: 2

---
```

Control Structures

In all the previous examples, the Ruby interpreter executed the code from top to bottom. However, in the majority of cases, you want to control which methods are to be executed and when they should be executed. The statements you want to be executed may depend on many variables, such as the state of some computation or the user input. For that purpose, programming languages have *control-flow statements*, which allow you to execute code based on conditions. Here are a few examples of how to use if, else, elsif, unless, while, and end. Notice that control structures in Ruby are terminated using the end keyword:

```ruby
now = Time.now
# => 2010-04-05 20:55:03 +0000

if now == Time.now
  puts "now is in the past"
elsif now > Time.now
  puts "nonsense"
else
  puts "time has passed"
end
# => time has passed
```

A trick that makes simple conditionals easy to read is to place if and unless conditional statements at the end of a code line so they act as *modifiers*. Here's how it looks:

```ruby
a = 5
b = 10
puts "b is greater than a" if a < b
```

```
b is greater than a
```

```ruby
puts "a is greater than b" unless a < b
```

```
nil
```

You can also use while statements, as in all major programming languages:

```
a = 5
b = 10

while a < b
  puts "a is #{a}"
  a += 1
end
```

```
a is 5

a is 6

a is 7

a is 8

a is 9
```

Methods

Methods are little programmable actions that you can define to help your development. Let's leave irb for the moment and talk about pure Ruby code. (All of this also works if you type it into irb.)

Suppose that, several times in the application you're writing, you need to get the current time as a string. To save yourself from having to retype Time.now.to_s over and over, you can build a method. Every method starts with def:

```
def time_as_string
  Time.now.to_s
end
```

Anywhere in the application that you want to get the time, you say time_as_string:

```
puts time_as_string
```

```
"2010-04-05 20:55:21 +0000"
```

See how easy that is? Methods can also take in variables:

```
def say_hello_to(name)
  "Hello, #{name}!"
end
```

```
puts say_hello_to("John")
```

```
"Hello, John!"
```

Next, you learn how to put methods together into groups to make them really powerful.

■ **NOTE** You already know that local variables must start with a lowercase letter and can't contain any characters other than letters, numbers, and underscores. Method names are restricted to the same rules, which means they often look like variables. Keywords (like if, or, when, and, and others) share the same set of properties. How does the Ruby interpreter know the difference? When Ruby encounters a word, it sees it as a local variable name, a method invocation, or a keyword. If it's a keyword, then Ruby knows it and responds accordingly. If there's an equals sign (=) to the right of the word, Ruby assumes it's a local variable being assigned. If it's neither a keyword nor an assignment, Ruby assumes it's a method being invoked and sends the method to the implied receiver, self.

Classes and Objects

You've reviewed all the basic types of items in a Ruby application, so let's start using them.

Objects

Ruby is an *object-oriented* (OO) programming language. If you've never worked in an OO language before, the metaphors used can be confusing the first time you hear them. Basically, *objects* are simple ways to separate your code and the data it contains.

Let's say you're writing a program to help track the athletic program at a school. You have a list of all the students who are currently participating on a team, along with their student IDs. This example looks at the rowing team. You could keep an array of arrays representing the students on the team:

```
rowing_team = [[1975, "Smith", "John"], [1964, "Brown", "Dan"], ...]
```

This is an array of [id, first_name, last_name]. You'd probably need to add a comment to explain that. If you wanted multiple teams, you could wrap this in a hash:

```
teams = { :rowing => [[1975, "Smith", "John"], [1964, "Brown", "Dan"], ...],
          :track  => [[1975, "Smith", "John"], [1900, "Mark", "Twain"], ...]
        }
```

That works for now. But it's kind of ugly, and you could easily get confused, especially if you kept adding teams. This style of coding is referred to as *procedural*, and it's not object-oriented. You're keeping track of huge data collections that are made up of simple types. Wouldn't it be nice to keep all this data more organized?

Classes

A *class* is like a blueprint for creating an object. You've been using classes all over the place—Array, String, User, and so on. Now, let's construct a Student class and a Team class.

Here is the basic blueprint for a Student class:

```
class Student
  # Setter method for @first_name
  def first_name=(value)
    @first_name = value
  end

  # Getter method for @first_name
  def first_name
    @first_name
  end

  # Setter method for @last_name
  def last_name=(value)
    @last_name = value
  end

  # Getter method for @last_name
  def last_name
    @last_name
  end

  # Returns full name
  def full_name
    @last_name + ", " + @first_name
  end
end
```

Right now, you're keeping track of the student's first_name and last_name strings. As you can see, you define a method named first_name=(value), and you take value and put it into an instance variable named @first_name. Let's try using this class:

```
# Take the Class, and turn it into a real Object instance
@student = Student.new
@student.first_name = "Bob"
@student.last_name = "Jones"
puts @student.full_name
```

```
"Jones, Bob"
```

Instead of building an stupid array, you've built a smart class. When you call new on the class, it builds a version of itself called an *object*, which is then stored in the @student variable. In the next two lines, you use the = methods to store the student's first and last name. Then, you use the method full_name to give a nicely formatted response.

It turns out that creating reader and writer methods like this is a common practice in OO programming. Fortunately, Ruby saves you the effort of creating them by providing a shortcut called attr_accessor:

```ruby
class Student
  attr_accessor :first_name, :last_name, :id_number

  def full_name
    @last_name + ", " + @first_name
  end
end
```

This behaves in exactly the same as the first version. The attr_accessor bit helps by automatically building the methods you need, such as first_name=. Also, this time you add an @id_number.

Let's build a Team class now:

```ruby
class Team
  attr_accessor :name, :students

  def initialize(name)
    @name = name
    @students = []
  end

  def add_student(id_number, first_name, last_name)
    student = Student.new
    student.id_number  = id_number
    student.first_name = first_name
    student.last_name  = last_name
    @students << student
  end

  def print_students
    @students.each do |student|
      puts student.full_name
    end
  end
end
```

You've added something new to this class: the initialize method. Now, when you call new, you can pass in the name. For example, you can say Team. new('baseball'), and the initialize method is called. Not only does initialize set up the name, but it also sets up an instance variable named @students and turns it into an empty array. The method add_students fills the array with new Student objects.

Let's see how you use this class:

```
team = Team.new("Rowing")
team.add_student(1982, "John", "Smith")
team.add_student(1984, "Bob", "Jones")
team.print_students
```

```
Smith, John

Jones, Bob
```

Containing things in objects cleans up your code. By using classes, you make sure that each object only needs to worry about its own concerns. If you were writing this application without objects, everyone's business would be shared. The variables would all exist around each other, and there would be one *huge* object. Objects let you break things up into small working parts.

By now, you should have a general idea of what's going on with some of the Ruby code you've seen floating around Rails. There is a *lot* more to Ruby that we haven't touched on here. Ruby has some amazing metaprogramming features you can read about in a book that specifically focuses on Ruby, such as *Beginning Ruby: From Novice to Professional,* Second Edition by Peter Cooper (Apress, 2009).

RUBY STYLE

Style is important when you're programming. Ruby programmers tend to be picky about style, and they generally adhere to a few specific guidelines, summarized here:

- Indentation size is two spaces.

- Spaces are preferred to tabs.

- Variables should be lowercase and underscored: `some_variable`, not `someVariable` or `somevariable`.

- Method definitions should include parentheses and no unnecessary spaces: `MyClass.my_method(my_arg)`, not `my_method( my_arg )` or `my_method my_arg`.

Whatever your personal style, the most important thing is to remain consistent. Nothing is worse than looking at code that switches between tabs and spaces, or mixed and lowercase variables.

Ruby Documentation

You can refer to the following documentation for more information about Ruby:

- *Core library:* The Ruby distribution comes with a set of classes known as the Ruby Core library, which includes base classes such as `Object`, `String`, `Array`, and others. In the Ruby Core application programming interface (API) documentation, you can find all the classes and methods included in the Core library. In this short appendix, you've already seen a few classes in action. One of the secrets to effectively using Ruby is to know which classes and methods are available to you. We recommend that you go to the Ruby Core API documentation page at `www.ruby-doc.org/core/` and start to learn more about Ruby classes and methods.

- *Standard library:* In addition to the Core library, the Ruby distribution comes bundled with the Ruby Standard library. It includes a set of classes that extends the functionality of the Ruby language by helping developers perform common programming tasks, such as network programming and threading. Make sure you spend some time reading the Standard library documentation at `www.ruby-doc.org/stdlib/`.

- *Online resources:* The Ruby documentation project home page is located at `www.ruby-doc.org`. There, you can find additional reading resources to help you learn Ruby, such as articles and tutorials, as well as the Core and Standard Ruby API documentation.

Databases 101

Let's begin with a simple definition. A *database* is a piece of software that governs the storage, retrieval, deletion, and integrity of data.

Databases are organized into *tables*. Tables have *columns* (or if you prefer, *fields*), and data is stored in *rows*. If you're familiar with spreadsheets, then the idea is fairly similar. Of course, databases blow spreadsheets out of the water in terms of power and performance.

Structured Query Language (SQL) is the standard way of communicating with databases. Using SQL, you can view column information, fetch a particular row or a set a rows, and search for rows containing certain criteria. You also use SQL to create, drop, and modify tables, as well as insert, update, and destroy the information stored in those tables. SQL is a fairly large topic, so a complete treatment is beyond the scope of this book. That said, you need to know the basics, so consider this a crash course.

■ **NOTE** The output in this appendix assumes you've followed the code in the book up to Chapter 4. If you read this appendix at a different point, you may get different output.

Examining a Database Table

Here's an example definition for a table called `articles`. Note that the examples use SQLite, as they do throughout this book (see Chapter 3). If you're following along using a different piece of database software, the response you see may be slightly different. To start the SQLite utility tool, run the `rails dbconsole` command from the book's project folder on your computer:

```
sqlite> .tables
```

```
articles          schema_migrations
```

You use the SQLite `.tables` command to peek at the tables that exist in the database.

As you can see, the database has two tables: `articles` and `schema_migrations`. You don't get a lot of information about the tables from the `.tables` command, but that can be achieved by querying an internal SQLite table called `sqlite_master`:

```
sqlite> select sql from sqlite_master where name = 'articles';
```

```
CREATE TABLE "articles" ("id" INTEGER PRIMARY KEY AUTOINCREMENT NOT NULL,

"title" varchar(255), "body" text, "published_at" datetime, "created_at" datetime,

"updated_at" datetime, "excerpt" varchar(255), "location" varchar(255))
```

The result of this command is a SQL statement that describes all the fields in the articles table. Each field has a *type*, which defines the kind of data it can store. The id field has a type of *integer*, title has a type of *varchar*, and body is a *text* field. Although it may sound strange, a type of varchar means the field has a variable number of characters up to a defined maximum. In this case, the maximum is 255 characters, which is the typical limit for varchar fields. (If you need to store more than 255 characters, use the *text* field type, like the body field.)

The id column is the one to pay attention to here. It's the *primary key*—a unique identifier for a particular row. Because this key is essential, it absolutely needs to be not null, and it must be unique; you let the database manage its value by automatically incrementing its number each time a new row is created. Notice how this is specified in the articles table column description: PRIMARY KEY AUTOINCREMENT NOT NULL. These are special commands that tell SQLite how to handle this particular field.

Let's look at some data from the articles table:

```
SELECT * FROM articles;
```

```
7|RailsConf|RailsConf is the official gathering for Rails developers..|2010-02-27..

8|RubyConf 2010|The annual RubyConf will take place in..|2010-05-19..
```

Here, you're using the SQL SELECT command to view this table's data. As you can see, you have two records in the table. You probably have different records in your database; the main point here is understanding the commands to see the data, not the data itself.

Working with Tables

The most common use of databases (not only in the context of Rails) is to implement *CRUD* functionality: create, read, update, and delete. Corresponding to the CRUD components are the most commonly used SQL commands: INSERT, SELECT, UPDATE, and DELETE, as shown in Table B-1.

Table B-1. *Common SQL Commands*

Operation	SQL Command
Create	INSERT
Read	SELECT
Update	UPDATE
Delete	DELETE

The following sections use the `articles` table presented in the previous section to show some examples of how these commands work. Remember that it's not necessary to have a complete understanding of SQL to work with Rails. The whole point of Active Record is to alleviate the tedium of needing to construct complex SQL statements to view and otherwise manipulate your data.

Selecting Data

The `SELECT` statement is a powerful and useful SQL command. Using `SELECT`, you can query (or request information from) the database and mine it for information. You can give `SELECT` any number of fields, a set of conditions to be applied to the data to be returned, a limit on the number of rows it returns, and instructions on how to order its results.

Earlier, you used the `SELECT` statement to see the data in the `articles` table:

```
SELECT * FROM articles;
```

The asterisk (*) character is a wildcard that means *every column*. This statement says, "Show me the values in every column for every row." This is the easiest way to look at the contents of a table. But you don't often need to see every single row; and for tables with a lot of data, you could end up with a really large list. So, sometimes it isn't very efficient to select everything. Fortunately, you can also select specific columns by name. For example, to select only the `title` column, do this:

```
sqlite> SELECT title FROM articles;
```

RailsConf

RubyConf 2010

Instead of returning all fields, this command returns only the one requested: `title`. To return both the `title` and the `body` fields, add body to the list of columns to select:

```
sqlite> SELECT title, body FROM articles;
```

```
RailsConf|RailsConf is the official gathering for Rails developers..

RubyConf 2010|The annual RubyConf will take place in..
```

In both cases, the command returns all rows. If there were 100 rows in the table, they would all be returned.

But what if you need to find a particular row? This is where *conditions* come in to play. To supply conditions to a SELECT statement, you use the WHERE clause:

```
SELECT fields FROM table WHERE some_field = some_value;
```

Let's apply this to the articles table by finding a row by its primary key:

```
sqlite> SELECT * FROM articles WHERE id = 7;
```

```
7|RailsConf|RailsConf is the official gathering for Rails developers..|2010-02-27

00:00:00.000000|2010-03-02 22:45:03.777308|2010-03-02 22:45:03.777308||
```

This query returns only the row whose primary key, id, matches the condition. You can use this technique on any field—id, title, or body—or all of them combined. Conditions can be chained together using AND and further modified using OR. For example, the following query returns only records whose titles and authors match the specified criteria:

```
SELECT * FROM articles WHERE title = 'Beginning Rails' AND id = 2;
```

Inserting Data

To insert a row into a table, you use the INSERT command. INSERT requires a table name, a list of fields, and a list of values to insert into those fields. Here's a basic INSERT statement for the articles table:

```
sqlite> INSERT INTO articles (title, body) VALUES ('Intro to SQL',
'This is an introduction to Structured Query Language');
```

SQLite doesn't give any indication that something happened, which means your command was accepted and didn't generate any errors. To see what was inserted, you again use the SELECT command:

```
sqlite> SELECT * FROM articles;
```

```
7|RailsConf|RailsConf is the official gathering for Rails developers..|2010-02-27..

8|RubyConf 2010|The annual RubyConf will take place in..|2010-05-19..

9|Intro to SQL|This is an introduction to Structured Query Language|||||
```

You now have three rows in your table. Notice that in the INSERT statement, you don't specify the id field. That's because, as you recall, it's handled automatically by the database. If you were to insert a value, you wouldn't have a reliable way to guarantee its uniqueness and could cause an error if you attempted to insert a duplicate value. MySQL automatically inserts an id value into the field that's greater than the biggest existing id.

Updating Data

If you want to change the values in a row, you use the UPDATE statement. UPDATE is similar to INSERT, except that like SELECT, it can be modified (or constrained) by *conditions*. If you want to change the title for the "Intro to SQL" article, you can do so like this:

```
sqlite> UPDATE articles SET title = 'Introduction to SQL' WHERE id = 9;
```

Again, SQLite is silent, which means the command has been accepted. The fact that you use the primary key to find and update the row is significant. Although you can match any value in any column, the only surefire way to be sure you're updating the row you want is to use the primary key. You can confirm that the value was updated with another query:

```
sqlite> SELECT title FROM articles WHERE id = 9;
```

```
Introduction to SQL
```

Sure enough, the title field has been updated.

Deleting Data

Of course, not all information in a database will stay there forever. Sometimes you need to delete records, such as when a product goes out of stock or a user cancels their account. That's the purpose of the DELETE statement. It works a lot like the UPDATE statement, in that it accepts conditions and deletes the rows for any records that match the conditions. If you want to delete the article with the id of 9, the DELETE statement is as follows:

```
sqlite> DELETE FROM articles WHERE id = 9;
```

SQLite receives the command and deletes the record identified by the id you specified. And, of course, if you subsequently search for the record, youexists:

```
sqlite> SELECT * FROM articles WHERE id = 9;
```

▪ **CAUTION** When you use either the UPDATE or DELETE command, you're making changes to existing data; so, be careful to use a WHERE clause to limit the records you're updating or deleting. A good practice is to always run a SELECT command first to make sure your query returns the records you're expecting; then, later run the UPDATE or DELETE command.

Understanding Relationships

It's good practice to avoid duplication in your database by creating distinct tables to store certain kinds of information. You relate two tables to one another using an *association*. This makes more sense when you see it in action, so let's look at the articles table again. We added a column named author by running the ALTER TABLE articles ADD COLUMN author varchar(255); SQL command so the table contains more data:

```
sqlite> SELECT * FROM articles;
```

id	title	author
1	ActiveRecord Basics	Jeffrey Hardy
2	Advanced ActiveRecord	Cloves Carneiro Jr.
3	Setting up Subversion	Cloves Carneiro Jr.
4	Databases 101	Jeffrey Hardy

There's quite a bit of duplication in the author field. This can potentially create problems. Although you could search for all articles by a particular author using a standard SELECT query, what would happen if someone's name were misspelled? Any articles by the misspelled author wouldn't show up in the query. And if there were such a typo, you'd need to update a lot of records in order to fix it. Moreover, searching on a text field like author is both unreliable and rather slow when compared to searching using an integer type.

You can improve this design significantly by putting authors in their own table and referencing each author's unique id (primary key) in the articles table instead of the name. Let's do that now. Create a new table called authors, and change the author field in the articles table so it can store an integer instead of text. The new authors table looks like this:

```
sqlite> CREATE TABLE "authors" ("id" INTEGER PRIMARY KEY AUTOINCREMENT NOT NULL,
"name" varchar(255));
sqlite> ALTER TABLE articles ADD COLUMN author_id integer;
```

Note how instead of a text field called author, you now have a numeric field called author_id that *references* the author's primary key from the authors table. This field holds a *foreign key*, which is a reference to the primary key of the table it relates to: in this case, the author who wrote the article. For each author in the articles table, you use INSERT to create a record in the authors table. You can then update the value of the author_id field using an UPDATE statement for the data set you're working with. If you now look at the data from both tables, you see that you've eliminated the duplication:

```
sqlite> SELECT id, author_id, title FROM articles;1|1|ActiveRecord Basics
```

```
2|2|Advanced ActiveRecord
```

```
3|2|Setting up Git
```

```
4|1|Databases 101
```

```
sqlite> SELECT * FROM authors;
```

```
1|Cloves Carneiro Jr.
```

```
2|Jeffrey Hardy
```

You can now use this relationship in your SELECT queries by joining the two tables together using their association. In this association, the author_id in the articles table is equal to the id column in the authors table. Adding the JOIN directive requires only a slight change to the SQL:

```
sqlite> SELECT articles.id, title, name FROM articles
JOIN authors ON articles.author_id = authors.id;
```

```
1|ActiveRecord Basics|Cloves Carneiro Jr.
```

```
2|Advanced ActiveRecord|Jeffrey Hardy
```

```
3|Setting up Git|Jeffrey Hardy
```

```
4|Databases 101|Cloves Carneiro Jr.
```

Now you get the author names returned with the query, which effectively spans two tables. This is the crux of relational databases. Updating an author's name is now easy because there is only one instance of a given author. Updating that author affects all of their associated articles:

```
sqlite> UPDATE authors SET name = 'Packagethief' WHERE id = 2;
```

This changes the name of the author with the id of 2 to Packagethief. When you run the JOIN query again, you see that all instances of the author's name have been updated:

```
sqlite> SELECT articles.id, title, name FROM articles
JOIN authors ON articles.author_id = authors.id;
```

```
1|ActiveRecord Basics|Cloves Carneiro Jr.
```

```
2|Advanced ActiveRecord|Packagethief
```

```
3|Setting up Git|Packagethief

4|Databases 101|Cloves Carneiro Jr.
```

SQL and Active Record

This brings your database crash course to a close. This was by no means a complete reference, nor was it intended to be. Its purpose was to illustrate the basics of how databases work and to introduce you to their native language: SQL. Now that you have a taste, you can safely enter the world of Active Record, where most of this tedious work is handled for you.

Why did we bother showing you this if Active Record takes care of most of it for you? Because it's important to know what Active Record is doing behind the scenes. Although you can effectively use Active Record like a black box, you'll eventually need to debug your programs and figure out why something isn't working the way you expect. Having a basic understanding of SQL helps. Moreover, every bit of SQL that Active Record generates is logged by Rails. You can find the logs in the log/ directory of your application. Now, when you see these SQL commands in the logs, you'll have a good idea what they mean.

■■■

The Rails Community

Rails development is driven by a vibrant and passionate community of open source developers. The Rails community encourages its members to participate actively in Rails development. You can start by asking questions and discussing new features. As your knowledge increases, you can help others by writing about your own experiences in a personal blog, answering questions on the mailing list, contributing to the wiki, and fixing bugs and writing patches to make Rails even better. Whatever your intention, be assured that participating in the community will help you get the most out of Rails.

Beginning Rails 3 Channels

As a companion to this book, we're opening a few communication channels with you. Feel free to contact us and other readers using the medium you feel most comfortable with:

- *Web site:* A resource to update you about changes in Rails 3 and later versions that may affect some of the code in the book, and to direct you to more information in the Ruby and Rails worlds. You can check our web site at http://beginningrails.com.

- *Mailing list:* A mailing list for those interested in exchanging ideas or asking questions to the authors and/or other Rails developers. You can discuss changes in the Rails framework; or, if you find a bug in the framework, you can discuss proposed solutions. You can subscribe to this list at http://groups.google.com/group/beginning-rails.

- *Twitter:* The Twitter account is used to notify users about changes in Rails 3 and allows direct conversation between the authors and you. You can follow us at http://twitter.com/beginningrails.

Rails Mailing Lists

You can subscribe to several Rails-related mailing lists:

- *Talk mailing list:* A high-volume list where users can seek help, announce open source or commercial Rails projects, and discuss any miscellaneous matters about the Rails framework. You can subscribe to this list at http://groups.google.com/group/rubyonrails-talk.

- *Core mailing list:* A low-volume list for those interested in Rails development. This list is for developers interested in discussing changes in the Rails framework itself. You can expect to find technical threads about Active Record, Action Mailer, Action Pack, and Rails performance. You can subscribe to this list at `http://groups.google.com/group/rubyonrails-core`.

- *Security mailing list:* A list for those who want to keep abreast of Rails security concerns. You can subscribe to this read-only mailing list at `http://groups.google.com/group/rubyonrails-security`.

Rails IRC Channel

If you want to interact with other Rails developers live, you can try the Rails IRC channel. Open your favorite IRC client, and connect to the Freenode IRC network at `irc.freenode.net`. Enter the `#rubyonrails` channel, and you'll find hundreds of Rails developers at any time of the day (or night) willing to help you and chat about their favorite web framework. If you want to be seen as a caring community participant, make sure you follow some basic etiquette on how to ask appropriate questions; look at `www.slash7.com/pages/vampires` for some guidelines.

■ **NOTE** Internet Relay Chat (IRC) is a type of real-time Internet chat, where users talk about their interests in topic-specific areas called *channels*. All you need to connect to IRC is IRC client software. The most commonly used IRC clients are the shareware mIRC (`http://mirc.com`) for Windows and the open source Colloquy (`http://colloquy.info`) for the Mac.

Rails Blogs and Podcasts

The number of blogs dedicated to Rails information is growing very fast, and most of the new Rails features are covered here even before they're released to the public. You can subscribe to the blogs of your choice to keep up with news in the Rails world.

The following are some of the more rewarding Rails-related blogs you can visit, including the official Rails podcast:

- `http://weblog.rubyonrails.org`: The official Rails blog. You'll find information about upcoming releases, new functionality in Rails, and news that's considered important (such as documentation updates and Rails adoption worldwide).

- `http://rubyinside.com`, `http://rubyflow.com`, and `http://railsinside.com`: Blogs by Peter Cooper, author of *Beginning Ruby* (Apress, 2007). They contain a lot of Ruby and Rails information that will help keep you updated and will likely be very helpful in your development adventures.

- `http://railscasts.com`: A great web site by Ryan Bates with a series of informative screencasts that teach a wide range of Rails tricks, covering all aspects of the Rails framework.

- `http://5by5.tv/rubyshow`: The weekly Ruby Show podcast by Dan Benjamin and Jason Seifer. This fun and informative podcast contains lots of Ruby and Rails updates you may be interested in following to learn about new libraries, blog posts, and announcements.

- `http://ruby5.envylabs.com`: The Ruby5 podcast. In 5 minutes or less—or a bitmore—you can listen to Ruby and Rails news.

Rails Guides

The Rails community has started a documentation effort called Rails Guides, which you can find at `http://guides.rubyonrails.org`. It's a great effort to document various parts of the frameworks, from the basic beginner-oriented documentation to more advanced material.

Rails Wiki

The Rails wiki (`http://wiki.rubyonrails.org`) is a collaborative effort to enhance the amount of documentation about Rails. It includes information about everything related to Rails; feel free to visit when you have some spare time, and make sure you explore as much as you can. Along with a lot of source code, it contains information about open source and commercial products, job posts, Rails training, tools, screencasts, tutorials, and much more. You can also easily contribute to the wiki.

Rails APIs

It's close to impossible to remember the names, methods, and possible parameters of all the functions and classes in Ruby and Rails. To help you with your coding tasks, we recommend that you keep the Ruby and Rails application programming interface (API) documentation open, or at least that you put them in your favorites. The API documentation contains all the information about specific functions you're trying to use, including the function source code.

You can find the Rails API documentation at `http://api.rubyonrails.org`. The Ruby API is at `www.ruby-doc.org/core`. For more user-friendly and searchable API documentation, head over to `http://gotapi.com` and select the Ruby/Rails option, or go to `http://apidock.com/rails`.

Rails Source and Issue Tracking

You can find the Rails source code at `http://github.com/rails/rails`. It's powered by the GitHub application, a hosting service for projects using the Git revision-control system. GitHub allows you to download the Rails source code using a web interface. You can subscribe to the Git change log using RSS, to be notified about changes to the Rails source code.

You can also participate in the development of Rails by submitting bug reports and patches to the Lighthouse account at `https://rails.lighthouseapp.com/projects/8994-ruby-on-rails` (don't forget to read the submission guidelines) or by looking at the existing tickets and trying to fix them.

Working with Rails Directory

Now that you're a Rails developer, you can add your name to the Working with Rails directory at www.workingwithrails.com. In this directory, you can find Rails developers by country, company, and popularity, as measured by the directory's recommendation and ranking system. Feel free to recommend us if the information you found in this book was valuable:

- *Cloves Carneiro Jr:* http://workingwithrails.com/person/4725-cloves-carneiro-jr

- *Rida Al Barazi:* http://workingwithrails.com/person/5114-rida-al-barazi

■ ■ ■

Git

Developers normally work in teams. You write plenty of code, sometimes you test some and decide to delete it, and other times you decide to stick to it. Managing this can be a painful process, which is why you can use Source Control Management software: to help you focus on what you do best—writing beautiful code. That way, you can forget about managing changes to the SCM software.

What Is Source Control Management?

Source Control Management (SCM) software helps you keep track of code changes and gives you the ability to easily collaborate on that code with your teammates. The two main features of any SCM are as follows:

- *Versioning:* When you're using SCM for your project, files and directories in the project are tracked. Every time you make changes to your files, you can save those changes as a new version. Your project then has several versions—one for every change set—giving you the ability to browse those changes and revert to any one at any time.

- *File merging:* Let's say you worked on a file, and your colleague John worked on the same file, and you both committed (submitted) your files to the SCM system. Both files are merged by SCM your involvement; if SCM can't handle the merge for any reason, it lets you know and gives you some useful information about how to manually merge conflicting changes yourself.

How Does It Work?

Generally, when you add your code base to a SCM system, a *repository* is created, which is the store of all the versions of your code base. Then, you can take a copy of that repository and work on it; this is normally called your *working copy*. You can add files, change or delete some, and then *commit* those changes and send them back to the repository as a new revision. If your colleague John is working with you on the same code base, he can check out or pull those changes from the repository to update his working copy, letting the SCM take care of any necessary file merging.

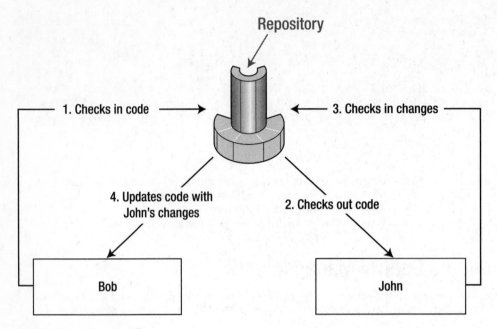

Figure D-1. *SCM workflow*

Git

The Git SCM was developed by Linus Torvalds for managing the Linux Kernel source code. It's also been used for several open source projects recently, including Rails.

Git is different from other SCMs because it's a *distributed* source control system. This means that instead of having a single repository on your server that all your teammates use to check out working copies (*client-server* or *centralized* SCM), each team member has their own repository along with a working copy, and you all *push* a copy of that repository to a remote repository.

This approach has some great benefits, such as the ability to work and commit your code even if you're offline, and to be able to operate on your repository more quickly.

Now that you have a good understanding of what an SCM is and how it works, let's install Git and try it.

Installing Git

Installing Git is relatively easy. Thanks to open source contributions, several Git installation packages are available to facilitate a quick installation for most platforms.

Installing on Windows

If you're on Windows, you can install Git on your system using Git on Windows, also knows as msysGit, which is an open source project available at http://code.google.com/p/msysgit/.

Download the Git installation executable from the download section of the project web site. The current version of the time of this writing is Git 1.7.0.2, and it's available to download from this URL:

`http://msysgit.googlecode.com/files/Git-1.7.0.2-preview20100309.exe`

Start the installation following the default options. You end up with Git installed on your system. The package also adds some interesting tools: Git GUI, which gives you a nice graphical interface to use Git; Git Bash, which you use to execute Git commands; and three context menu items integrated with Windows Explorer—Git Init Here, Git Bash, and Git GUI—to start the tools from the folder you're calling them from.

Use the Git Bash tool to execute the commands mentioned in this appendix.

Installing on Mac OS X

To install Git on Mac OS X – Leopard, you can either compile it from source using Macports or use Git OS X Installer, which you can find at `http://code.google.com/p/git-osx-installer/`.

Download the Git OS X Installer from the project's web site. The current version at the time of this writing is Git 1.7.0.3, available to download from this URL:

`http://git-osx-installer.googlecode.com/files/git-1.7.0.3-intel-leopard.dmg`

The file you download is a disk image; it has a package installer named `git-1.7.0.3-intel-leopard.pkg`. Run the package installer, selecting the default options. When the installation is complete, Git is available from the Terminal.

Installing on Linux

Most Linux distributions ship with a package manager. The most common one is the Debian package manager apt, and Git is part of its library.

To install Git using apt, run the following apt-get command from the Terminal:

`sudo apt-get install git-core`

Accept if the package manager asks your permission to use additional disk space for this installation. When the installation is complete, Git is ready to use.

Setting Global Parameters

Every commit you make in your repository has flags for the user who did the commit; those flags are the user's name and e-mail. Now that you have Git installed on your system, it's important to set a global username and e-mail address for Git to use for any new repository you work on.

To set global parameters, you use the `git config` command with the `--global` option, followed by the parameters you want to set. Listing D-1 shows the command to set up both the `user.name` and `user.email` parameters.

Listing D-1. Setting the Global Git Username and E-mail

```
git config --global user.name "dude"
git config --global user.email my.email@address.com
```

These parameters can be set on a repository level as well; you can do that by using the same commands but without the `--global` option in your repository's working directory.

Initializing a Repository

The first thing you want to do is to start a new repository for your application. Begin by creating a test application:

```
$ rails testapp
```

```
create

create  README

create  .gitignore

create  Rakefile

.

.

.

create  tmp/cache

create  tmp/pids

create  vendor/plugins

create  vendor/plugins/.gitkeep
```

Now, initialize a local repository for that application by calling `git init` in the application directory:

```
$ cd testapp
$ git init
```

```
Initialized empty Git repository in /tmp/testapp/.git/
```

The git init command initializes an empty local repository for the application, but it doesn't add any files to the repository. To determine which files you can add to the repository, you call the git status command:

```
$ git status
```

```
# On branch master

#

# Initial commit

#

# Untracked files:

#   (use "git add <file>..." to include in what will be committed)

#

#       .gitignore

#       Gemfile

#       README

#       Rakefile

#       app/

#       config.ru

#       config/

#       db/

#       doc/

#       lib/

#       public/

#       script/

#       test/

#       vendor/
```

```
nothing added to commit but untracked files present (use "git add" to track)
```

As you can see, all the folders and files of the Rails application are in the untracked files list, which means they're still untracked. To start tracking those files, you need to *add* them to the track list; as the last line says, you can do so using the `git add` command.

Ignoring Files

Before you add those files, let's think a little: do you want all your files to be tracked? Are there any files that you don't want to track? Normally, those would be configuration files that contain passwords, such as `database.yml`, the `tmp` folder, log files, and SQLite databases. If you add those files, your teammates will have this information, and it may even conflict with theirs.

To skip those files in any `git add all` and `git status` commands, and to tell Git to never bother you about them again, you must configure Git to ignore them. You do that by declaring those files in a hidden configuration file called `.gitignore`, which is normally stored at the root of your working copy (in this case, at the root of the `testapp` directory). The `.gitignore` file is a regular text file, it is generated by Rails in all new projects; edit it using your text editor of choice, so it looks like Listing D-2.

Listing D-2. .gitignore File Content in testapp/.gitignore: http://gist.github.com/287051

```
.bundle
config/database.yml
log/*.log
db/*.sqlite3
tmp/**/*
```

As you can see, the files and folders listed in the `.gitignore` file weren't listed in the `git status` command you issued earlier.

Adding and Committing

You can add the untracked files to your repository by using the `git add` command and passing a dot to it, which refers to the current directory and all its content:

```
$ git add .
```

Try the `git status` command again:

```
$ git status
```

```
# On branch master
#
# Initial commit
```

```
#
# Changes to be committed:
#   (use "git rm --cached <file>..." to unstage)
#
#   new file:    .gitignore
#   new file:    Gemfile
#   new file:    README
#   new file:    Rakefile
.
.
.
#   new file:    script/rails
#   new file:    test/performance/browsing_test.rb
#   new file:    test/test_helper.rb
#   new file:    vendor/plugins/.gitkeep
#
```

The git status command still shows all the files, because the git add command just added those files to be committed, but they aren't committed yet.

In order to commit the changes you added to the commit list, you have to call the git commit command. Use the -m argument to include a message describing the purpose of and the changes in this commit:

```
$ git commit -m "Empty Rails application"
```

```
[master (root-commit) 046116c] Empty Rails application

 41 files changed, 8434 insertions(+), 0 deletions(-)

 create mode 100644 .gitignore
```

```
create mode 100644 Gemfile

create mode 100644 README

.

.

.

create mode 100755 script/rails

create mode 100644 test/performance/browsing_test.rb

create mode 100644 test/test_helper.rb

create mode 100644 vendor/plugins/.gitkeep
```

Congratulations—you've completed your first commit to your local repository. If you check the git status command now, you see that there are no changes to be added or committed:

```
$ git status
```

```
# On branch master

nothing to commit (working directory clean)
```

Starting from this point, if you edit any file in your working copy, rename it, move it, or delete it, it will show in your git status output, allowing you to pick which of those changes you would like to add to your commit list and then commit them to your repository.

Branching and Merging

Let's say you decide to work on a new feature for your project that you know will take you some time to finish. Meanwhile, you want to be able to keep working on the main project without changes from the new feature breaking your application. To implement this new feature in a separate copy of your project, you need to create a *branch*. A branch is a duplicate of your project that you can work on in parallel to the master copy of the same project.

When you called the git init command earlier, Git initialized a new repository for your application with a default branch called master. To create a new branch in the repository, use the git branch command followed by the name of the new branch you want to create:

```
$ git branch articles
```

This command creates a new branch named articles as a duplicate of the current branch master. To see a list of the branches in your project, you use the git branch command again but without any parameters:

```
$ git branch
```

```
  articles

* master
```

You have two branches, articles and master. The asterisk next to master indicates that it's the *current* branch you're working on. To switch branches, use the git checkout command followed by the name of the branch you want to switch to:

```
$ git checkout articles
```

```
Switched to branch 'articles'
```

The articles branch is the current branch now. You can confirm this by listing the branches again:

```
$ git branch
```

```
* articles

  master
```

Now, let's implement a new feature—an articles scaffold:

```
$ rails generate scaffold Article title:string body:text
```

```
      invoke    active_record
      create    db/migrate/20100420235045_create_articles.rb
      create    app/models/article.rb
      invoke    test_unit
      create    test/unit/article_test.rb
      create    test/fixtures/articles.yml
```

```
    route      resources :articles

    invoke     scaffold_controller

    create     app/controllers/articles_controller.rb

    invoke     erb

    create     app/views/articles

    create     app/views/articles/index.html.erb

    create     app/views/articles/edit.html.erb

    create     app/views/articles/show.html.erb

    create     app/views/articles/new.html.erb

    create     app/views/articles/_form.html.erb

    invoke     test_unit

    create     test/functional/articles_controller_test.rb

    invoke     helper

    create     app/helpers/articles_helper.rb

    invoke     test_unit

    create     test/unit/helpers/articles_helper_test.rb

    invoke     stylesheets

    create     public/stylesheets/scaffold.css
```

You're done with the new feature changes. It's time to add the changes and commit them to the articles branch:

```
$ git add .
$ git commit -m "Adding Article scaffold"
```

```
[articles 33a538e] Adding Article scaffold

 15 files changed, 308 insertions(+), 0 deletions(-)
```

```
create mode 100644 app/controllers/articles_controller.rb

create mode 100644 app/helpers/articles_helper.rb

create mode 100644 app/models/article.rb

create mode 100644 app/views/articles/_form.html.erb

create mode 100644 app/views/articles/edit.html.erb

create mode 100644 app/views/articles/index.html.erb

create mode 100644 app/views/articles/new.html.erb

create mode 100644 app/views/articles/show.html.erb

create mode 100644 db/migrate/20100420235045_create_articles.rb

create mode 100644 public/stylesheets/scaffold.css

create mode 100644 test/fixtures/articles.yml

create mode 100644 test/functional/articles_controller_test.rb

create mode 100644 test/unit/article_test.rb

create mode 100644 test/unit/helpers/articles_helper_test.rb
```

When you check the git status command now, you see that you have nothing to commit in the articles branch:

```
$ git status
```

```
# On branch articles

nothing to commit (working directory clean)
```

The articles branch now has an article scaffold, and the master branch doesn't. If you switch back to the master branch, notice that none of the article scaffold files exist there:

```
$ git checkout master
```

Switched to branch 'master'

You can modify the project in the master branch completely in isolation from the articles branch if you want to, but for now let's *merge* the articles branch into the master branch. You do that using the git merge command followed by the branch name you want to merge into the current branch main:

```
$ git merge articles
```

Updating 88c63c5..33a538e

Fast forward

```
app/controllers/articles_controller.rb         | 83 +++++++++++++++++++++++++++
 app/helpers/articles_helper.rb                 |  2 +
 app/models/article.rb                          |  2 +
 app/views/articles/_form.html.erb              | 24 ++++++++
 app/views/articles/edit.html.erb               |  6 ++
 app/views/articles/index.html.erb              | 25 ++++++++
 app/views/articles/new.html.erb                |  5 ++
 app/views/articles/show.html.erb               | 15 +++++
 config/routes.rb                               |  2 +
 db/migrate/20100420235045_create_articles.rb   | 14 ++++
 public/stylesheets/scaffold.css                | 60 ++++++++++++++++++
 test/fixtures/articles.yml                     |  9 +++
 test/functional/articles_controller_test.rb    | 49 +++++++++++++++
 test/unit/article_test.rb                      |  8 +++
 test/unit/helpers/articles_helper_test.rb      |  4 +
 15 files changed, 308 insertions(+), 0 deletions(-)
```

```
create mode 100644 app/controllers/articles_controller.rb

create mode 100644 app/helpers/articles_helper.rb

create mode 100644 app/models/article.rb

create mode 100644 app/views/articles/_form.html.erb

create mode 100644 app/views/articles/edit.html.erb

create mode 100644 app/views/articles/index.html.erb

create mode 100644 app/views/articles/new.html.erb

create mode 100644 app/views/articles/show.html.erb

create mode 100644 db/migrate/20100420235045_create_articles.rb

create mode 100644 public/stylesheets/scaffold.css

create mode 100644 test/fixtures/articles.yml

create mode 100644 test/functional/articles_controller_test.rb

create mode 100644 test/unit/article_test.rb

create mode 100644 test/unit/helpers/articles_helper_test.rb
```

The task is complete: you developed a new feature in a separate branch without affecting the master branch; and when you finished, you merged those changes back into master.

Remote Repositories and Cloning

As we said before, Git is a distributed SCM; therefore, your repository is hosted locally on your machine, hidden inside your working copy directory. No one else has access to it.

If you want to set up a repository that you and your team can work on, you first have to create a *remote* repository that all of you can access and clone from. Your remote repository can be hosted on any machine that is available to all developers who need access to the repository and that has Git installed. It can be hosted on your local network; online; or with a third-party Git hosting provider like the famous GitHub (http://github.com), which hosts Rails and many Rails plug-ins and gems.

We used Git for this book's blog application, and we hosted the repository on GitHub. It's publicly available for you at http://github.com/ccjr/blog/. This means you can clone a copy of the blog repository to your machine and browse the code locally. To do that, you need the Public Clone URL, which is git://github.com/ccjr/blog.git. Let's clone the blog application repository using the git clone command:

```
$git clone git://github.com/ccjr/blog.git
```

```
Initialized empty Git repository in /tmp/blog/.git/

remote: Counting objects: 1085, done.

remote: Compressing objects: 100% (575/575), done.

remote: Total 1085 (delta 539), reused 898 (delta 436)

Receiving objects: 100% (1085/1085), 222.28 KiB | 362 KiB/s, done.

Resolving deltas: 100% (539/539), done.
```

Now you have a local copy of the blog application repository cloned to your machine. You can change files and even commit them to your own local repository, but what you *cannot* do is share those commits with others. In order to *push* your changes, you need write access to the remote repository, which you don't have.

If you want to try that, sign up for a free account on GitHub and create a repository of your own there. You then have two URLs: a *public* one that everyone can see, and your clone URL, which gives you full access to this remote repository.

The concept is simple: after you clone your own repository using your own URL, you can work normally in your working copy, commit changes, and add and remove files. Whenever you want to share those commits with the rest of the world, you push them to the remote repository on GitHub using the git push command. If you have teammates pushing changes to the same repository, you can retrieve those changes by using the git pull command.

To sum up, you create a remote repository to allow more than one developer to work on the same repository. Although all developers on the team have their own copies, they still need to push their copies to the remote repository to allow the rest to pull from it and stay in synch.

When you sign up for a free account on GitHub, the repositories you create are publicly available for everyone to clone from. If you want your repositories to be private, so only you and your teammates can access them, you can either upgrade your account with GitHub or host them on your own server with your own setup.

Learning More

Git is a great tool and has a lot of commands; however, this appendix has covered only the basic features and commands. We highly encourage you to read more. You can see a list of the most-used Git commands using the git help command:

```
$ git help
```

```
usage: git [--version] [--exec-path[=GIT_EXEC_PATH]] [--html-path]

[-p|--paginate|--no-pager] [--bare] [--git-dir=GIT_DIR]

[--work-tree=GIT_WORK_TREE] [--help] COMMAND [ARGS]

The most commonly used git commands are:
```

add	Add file contents to the index
bisect	Find by binary search the change that introduced a bug
branch	List, create, or delete branches
checkout	Checkout a branch or paths to the working tree
clone	Clone a repository into a new directory
commit	Record changes to the repository
diff	Show changes between commits, commit and working tree, etc
fetch	Download objects and refs from another repository
grep	Print lines matching a pattern
init	Create an empty git repository or reinitialize an existing one
log	Show commit logs
merge	Join two or more development histories together
mv	Move or rename a file, a directory, or a symlink
pull	Fetch from and merge with another repository or a local branch
push	Update remote refs along with associated objects
rebase	Forward-port local commits to the updated upstream head
reset	Reset current HEAD to the specified state
rm	Remove files from the working tree and from the index
show	Show various types of objects
status	Show the working tree status
tag	Create, list, delete or verify a tag object signed with GPG

See 'git help COMMAND' for more information on a specific command.

To learn more about a specific command, you can use git help *COMMAND*, which shows that command's documentation and how to use the command.

Other SCM Systems

Although Git is the most talked about SCM nowadays, you may either be required to use a different SCM, or may want to investigate the alternatives. Here's a list of other SCMs you may choose.

- *Mercurial:* Just like Git, Mercurial is a distributed SCM. Mercurial is often compared to Git due to their similarities; feel free to try it if you want to explore another option. You can find out more about Mercurial from its official web site: `http://mercurial.selenic.com/`.

- *SVN (Subversion):* Considered the most dominant source control system at the moment. Well known for being used by many open source projects, including Apache, FreeBSD, KDE, Python, and Ruby. Even Rails was hosted in a Subversion repository until it recently moved to Git. You can find out more about Subversion from its official web site: `http://subversion.tigris.org/`.

- *CVS (Concurrent Versions System):* One of the earliest SCM systems (initial release in 1990). It's still popular, although due to some limitations like sparse Unicode support and expensive branching operations, developers have begun moving toward other version control systems like Subversion and Git. You can find out more about CVS from its official web site: `www.nongnu.org/cvs/`.

Online Resources

After the beta launch of GitHub, Git received huge interest from developers, including the Rails core team—they decided to switch from Subversion to Git and host the official Rails repository on GitHub. This attention to Git encouraged more developers to try it, and a number of tutorials and blog posts began to appear in the community.

The following are some resources you can visit to dig deeper and learn more about Git:

- `http://book.git-scm.com/`: The Git Community Book. As the name implies, this book is written by the Git community to the Git community. It's a cumulative resource to help newcomers to Git get started and quickly find what they're looking for.

- `www.ricroberts.com/articles/2009/06/01/getting-to-grips-with-git`: A tutorial series written by Ric Robert on his personal blog, explaining some of the core features of Git and why and when to use them.

- `http://peepcode.com/products/git`: A 60-minute screencast by PeepCode, available with an in-depth PDF explanation on how Git works under the hood.

Index

■ E

■ F

■ G

You Need the Companion eBook

Your purchase of this book entitles you to buy the companion PDF-version eBook for only $10. Take the weightless companion with you anywhere.

We believe this Apress title will prove so indispensable that you'll want to carry it with you everywhere, which is why we are offering the companion eBook (in PDF format) for $10 to customers who purchase this book now. Convenient and fully searchable, the PDF version of any content-rich, page-heavy Apress book makes a valuable addition to your programming library. You can easily find and copy code—or perform examples by quickly toggling between instructions and the application. Even simultaneously tackling a donut, diet soda, and complex code becomes simplified with hands-free eBooks!

Once you purchase your book, getting the $10 companion eBook is simple:

❶ Visit **www.apress.com/promo/tendollars/**.

❷ Complete a basic registration form to receive a randomly generated question about this title.

❸ Answer the question correctly in 60 seconds, and you will receive a promotional code to redeem for the $10.00 eBook.

THE EXPERT'S VOICE™

233 Spring Street, New York, NY 10013

Offer valid through 11/10.